INSURANCE AND CRIME:
A Consideration of Effects Upon Society

INSURANCE AND CRIME:
A Consideration of Effects Upon Society

S.S. Banwait

CYBER TECH PUBLICATIONS
4264/3, Ansari Road, Daryaganj, New Delhi-110002 (India)
Ph.: 011-23244078. Fax: 011-23280028
E-Mail: cyberpublicationsdelhi@yahoo.com

INSURANCE AND CRIME: A CONSIDERATION OF EFFECTS UPON SOCIETY

S.S. Banwait

First Edition 2009

Published by :

G.S. Rawat for **Cyber Tech Publications**
4264/3, Ansari Road, Daryaganj, New Delhi-110002 (India)
Ph.: 011-23244078. Fax: 011-23280028
E-Mail: cyberpublicationsdelhi@yahoo.com

Printed at . Asian Offset Printers

Preface

Insurance for lenders is an emerging market segment, with new products, possibilities and concerns for all who participate. It represents a significant step forward in the evolution of meeting and transferring environmental risks from the participants in a transaction to an insurer. Obtaining the maximum benefits from this form of risk transfer requires an understanding of what is involved, how the policies operate, and where more traditional forms of risk assessment and analysis still have a role to play.

The purpose of this book is to provide the reader with a fundamental guide to these issues and how this area evolved, how the policies operate, and what role they can play in lending transactions. It is a basic guidance and educational document, rather than a comprehensive treatise or a legal treatise, addressed to an audience in the lending industry.

Necessarily it must be something of a snapshot, because even during the period of its preparation, the market for insurance and crime addressed in this book evolved significantly. This process will continue, and this area promises to remain exciting for a long time to come.

—Author

CONTENTS

1

Introduction

Human beings can never be totally sure of the outcome of their decisions. Ergo, all decisions are risky decisions. You have already taken a risky decision by opening this book and reading the first few lines, and having done so, you are now facing another: to read on or to put it back on the shelf.

And what do I do as the author of this book? It goes without saying that I would like you to read all of it, just as I wrote all of it. If you choose to read on, there is a chance, however slight, that you may afterwards feel that you could have put your time to better use. If, right now, you put it back on the shelf, you may later be nagged by the feeling that you missed out on an opportunity to learn something of importance to your own life expectancy, to that of your loved ones or to people in general. So, which of the two risky decisions do you take?

I chose a writing style and presentation of content that will, I hope, encourage you to read on. But, contrary to my intentions, you may judge my style too popular or too academic, the content too wide or too limited. By trying to reach large numbers of diverse readers, many a writer has in fact pleased very few, despite the vital importance of the topic to all.

So, both reader and writer engage in risk taking, although the possible consequences in this case may be relatively trivial. But there are more serious risks: those of accidents, injuries, substantial property damage, of death, disease and physical disability. It is these serious risks that form the main topic in the pages to follow.

A large number of these mishaps are the consequence of our daily actions, habits and lifestyles. We add to the probability of these mishaps every time we drive our car, board a plane, climb a ladder, have another cigarette or alcoholic beverage, cross the street, lift a heavy object, have sex with somebody we hardly know, light a fire, go swimming or jogging, handle work tools, and so on.

When mishaps occur, they usually involve comparatively few people, but as they are so common, these 'minor' disasters add up to large numbers in a nation's statistics. Millions of people engage routinely, if not daily or even several times per day, in dangerous activities, and it is with their actions that this book is concerned. The focus will not be on the more infrequent decisions made by few people with potentially disastrous consequences for many, like deciding to go to war, to install and operate a nuclear plant, or to move dangerous cargo through a populous area.

In discussing statistics and research information on the more serious risks taken by large numbers of people, we will encounter many findings that may surprise at first. For instance, we all know that smoking cigarettes is associated with various diseases of heart and lungs, and thus with early death. And we know that stopping smoking reduces the likelihood of contracting these diseases. So you might expect a lower incidence of lung and heart disease amongst people who were told by their physician to quit smoking and who did quit. And your expectation would be right. These illnesses did, in fact, develop less often in this group.

However, if you also expected a lower mortality rate for this group, the facts prove you wrong. In one comparison between a group of quitters and a control group, the life-span of the quitters was found to be a little *shorter!* The difference in mortality rates between the quitters and the control group was not statistically significant, meaning that the probability of its occurrence on the basis of mere chance was greater than one in twenty. But, surely, these findings do not confirm common popular or common scientific expectation.

We all know that drivers who wear seatbelts are, on average, more likely to survive a crash than those who don't. So you might be inclined to expect that laws compelling drivers to buckle up, and that increase the seatbelt-wearing rate, will reduce a nation's traffic fatality rate per head of population.

You would probably expect similarly beneficial results from the construction of more crashworthy cars and the building of more forgiving highways. But again, this is not what has been found in fact. To err is human. Our perceptions and reasonings are susceptible to mistakes. When looking at Figure 1.1, you will probably judge the line between the first and the second arrow (line **a**) to be longer than between the second and the third (line **b**). Measuring the two lengths with a ruler will soon convince you that your perception was wrong. If your ruler is precise enough, you will discover that line b is actually a little *longer*, by almost 1%.

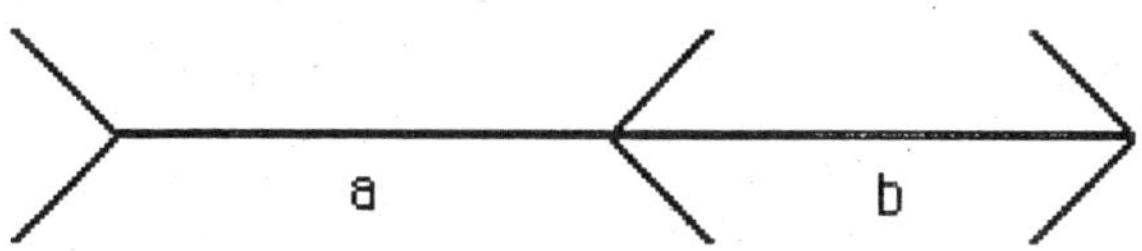

Figure : Which line is longer, a or b?

You probably are familiar with syllogistic arguments such as:

All human beings are mortal.

Socrates is a human being.

Thus, Socrates is mortal.

The conclusion follows from the first two statements. Now consider the two arguments below:

In many accidents cars skid before they collide. Anti-lock brakes reduce the likelihood of skidding. Thus, installing such brakes will reduce the number of accidents.

Many intersection accidents involve cars colliding at right angles. Traffic lights reduce the frequency of right-angle collisions. Thus, installing lights will reduce the number of intersection accidents.

Because of the apparent similarity with the Socrates case, it may be tempting to assume that the conclusions in the two arguments are valid. The similarity, however, is deceptive and the conclusions are wrong. While Socrates himself—were he alive today—would be unlikely to fall victim to this trap, people often do. And people are more likely to agree with an erroneous conclusion when this fits their social attitudes and preconceptions. This is especially true for people who are not inclined to be analytical in the way they look at the world around them, the 'fuzzy set' so to speak.

To err is human, but human, also, is awareness of that very fact. To the extent that this awareness helps to correct the error, further insight is gained and progress can be made. It has been said that popular wisdoms contradict each other, but then this observation itself is popular wisdom, too.

In some parts of the world, deaths due to floods in low-lying areas are a problem. The building of levees reduces the likelihood of floods. It might be expected that such constructions would reduce the number of flood victims. Once again, this is not what has been found in fact. It may also come as a surprise that, in most developed countries, the mortality rates associated with violent death—mostly due to accidents—have remained virtually unchanged in the first three quarters of the current century, with the exception of war periods.

These rates include fatal accidents of all types per head of population, and are corrected for historical variations in the gender and age composition of the populations concerned. They show no clear downward trend, in spite of the massive technological, legislative, educational and medical advances made during the same period.

These observations seem difficult to believe. It also seems hard to comprehend why these rates are not much influenced by the visible progress in safety engineering, by prescriptive or prohibitive laws and their enforcement, by informing the public about risks, or by more successful medical treatment of accident victims who do not die instantly. What could possibly account for these and many other similar findings?

I suggest that all of the observations above may be explained by a relatively simple theory of human conduct in the face of risk, and that theory is the central theme of this book. The theory can be roughly outlined as follows:

Risk Homeostasis Theory maintains that, in any activity, people accept a certain level of subjectively estimated risk to their health, safety, and other things they value, in exchange for the benefits they hope to receive from that activity (transportation, work, eating, drinking, drug use, recreation, romance, sports or whatever).

In any ongoing activity, people continuously check the amount of risk they feel they are exposed to. They compare this with the amount of risk they are willing to accept, and try to reduce any difference between the two to zero. Thus, if the level of subjectively experienced risk is lower than is acceptable, people tend to engage in actions that increase their exposure to risk. If, however, the level of subjectively experienced risk is higher than is acceptable, they make an attempt to exercise greater caution.

Consequently, they will choose their next action so that its subjectively expected amount of risk matches the level of risk accepted. During that next action, perceived and accepted risk are again compared and the subsequent adjustment action is chosen in order to minimize the difference, and so on.

Each particular adjustment action carries an objective probability of risk of accident or illness. Thus, the sum total of all adjustment actions across all members of the population over an extended period of time (one, or several years, perhaps) determines the temporal rate of accidents and of lifestyle-dependent disease in the population.

These rates, as well as more direct and frequent personal experiences of danger, in turn influence the amount of risk people expect to be associated with various activities, and with particular actions in these activities, over the *next* period of time. They will decide on their future actions accordingly, and these actions will produce the subsequent rate of human-made mishaps. Thus, a 'closed loop' is formed between past and present, and between the present and the future. And, in the long run, the human-made mishap rate essentially depends on the amount of risk people are willing to accept.

In short, the theory of risk homeostasis proposes that a nation's temporal loss due to accidents and lifestyle-dependent disease is the output of a closed-loop regulating process in which the accepted level of risk operates as the unique controlling variable. Consequently, if we wish to make an attempt at reducing this misery, that attempt should be aimed at reducing the level of risk accepted by the population.

With this theory as a key, you now have the means to unravel the puzzling findings that have been mentioned so far. As you may have guessed, the key to understanding proposed in this book is the following notion:

People alter their behaviour in response to the implementation of health and safety measures, but the riskiness of the way they behave will not change, unless those measures are capable of motivating people to alter the amount of risk they are willing to incur.

We now have a plausible explanation for the fact that the technological efforts toward flood control in the USA failed to reduce the number of flood victims. Improved impoundment and levee construction did make certain areas less prone to flooding. But, as a consequence, more people settled in the fertile plains, because these now appeared 'safe enough'. The end result was that subsequent floods, although fewer in number, caused more human loss and more property damage. If one wishes to reduce the problem of excessive flow of water, it would seem more sensible to seek a solution *upstream*—for instance in the form of reforestation or the careful maintenance of wetlands—so that more-than-normal precipitation is contained and does not run downhill.

We now have a possible explanation for the fact that a random selection of cigarette smokers who were advised to quit by their physician, did indeed reduce their cigarette consumption to a much greater extent than a comparison group. They did develop a lower frequency of smoking-related disease, but they did not live longer. In fact, their lives were a little shorter.

We now also have a possible explanation for the fact that the construction of modern multi-lane highways has contributed to a reduction in the number of road deaths per unit distance driven, while the number of traffic deaths per head of population remained the same or even increased. Consider the following argument:

A river empties into the sea through a delta.

The delta has three channels, all of equal size.

Therefore, damming two of the channels will reduce the flow of water to the sea by two-thirds.

In all likelihood, you will not accept this argument. This isn't surprising, because it is so obviously wrong. One cannot stem the flow as long as there remain alternative routes to the destination. One cannot reduce mortality due to accidents and lifestyle-dependent disease unless *all* opportunity for premature death were eliminated by law or made impossible through technological intervention. And that, of course, can never be fully achieved. In the case above, the river would simply develop a fourth channel.

What is perhaps more surprising, then, is that safety and health authorities have traditionally told people what they should or should not do to avoid injury or lifestyle-dependent disease, without offering them motivation to reduce risk, without offering them a reason to live longer. And what may be more surprising still is that the wisdom and effectiveness of this prevention practice is so rarely questioned. The 'delta illusion' is a very powerful illusion indeed.

It is obvious that a sure way to reduce the accident rate on a particular road to zero is to simply close that road to all traffic. It is almost as obvious that road users will move to other roads and that the accidents will migrate with them to other locations. Road closure is no effective remedy. Obvious, isn't it? So why should prohibiting drinking and driving, or closing the borders to the illicit drug trade, be effective remedies? To believe so is to fall victim to the delta fallacy.

The chapters following call the traditional prevention practice into question. Specifically, it is argued that the traditional reliance on enforcement of laws, on informing the public of certain dangers, and on engineering the physical features of the human-made environment is not very productive towards greater health and safety insofar as these are dependent on human conduct. An effort is made to explain why this is so.

At first, this may appear to be a pessimistic exercise, but nothing could be further from the truth. The theoretical ideas, developed for the purpose of explaining the limited success of the traditional approach, also point the way to the design of effective safety interventions. Not surprisingly, these alternative interventions are aimed at increasing people's desire to be safe and to live a healthy style of life. Thus, as an alternative to the enforcement, educational, and engineering approaches of the past, a *motivational* approach to prevention is presented. This is an approach that offers people a reason to live longer and, therefore, to adopt safer and healthier ways of life. The documented experience obtained with this strategy to date strengthens confidence that it is considerably more effective than the traditional approaches. And because the motivational approach seems to cause fewer negative side-effects than the traditional countermeasures and to be cheaper to implement, it also offers hope for a happier society throughout.

TOWARD A COMPACT THEORY OF RISK TAKING

The idea that accident rates might be understood as the output of a self-regulating feedback process originally occurred to me (in a loose form at first) some 25 years ago. I had just read a puzzling and exciting article about some work by British psychologist Donald H. Taylor, and that article proved to be very seminal to my subsequent thinking about risk homeostasis.

At the time, with the assistance of a doctoral student, I was preparing a literature review of psychological factors in accident causation for the Canadian federal government. This was an interesting exercise.

We knew, of course, that "Traffic, like God, Football and Politics, belongs to that select group of subjects on which everyone, when the spirit seizes him, instinctively feels that he can speak with overriding authority and conviction". What we didn't know, since we were novices in the scientific study of the field, was that the available literature was, and still is, extremely disconnected, fragmented and beset with a multitude of narrow views and pet solutions to the problem. Accidents have been associated with everything from mud flaps to poor eyesight, low barometric pressure, anti-social tendencies, narrow roads, driving too fast, driving too slow, alcohol use, abstinence, being young, being old, bad weather, good weather, being left-handed or in the process of getting a divorce.

Many of these factors are blessed with empirical evidence for their support, but that this blessing is rather mixed becomes apparent if one considers that the resources for the development of accident countermeasures and research are limited. If it is agreed that nothing is as practical as a good theory, one must regret the sparsity of comprehensive theories relative to the available body of findings. How can governments, social agencies and citizen groups decide where to focus their efforts in research and countermeasure development when so many divergent directions for action appear to present themselves? And what can you, as an individual, do to reduce your risk of accident? What is needed is a theory which compresses a lot of experience in a format that is concise enough to guide remedial action.

Having to write a global and coherent review forced us to seek the nature of the forest rather than the identity of the individual trees. Entering a new field while having to scan its full expanse can provide useful preventative medicine against developing that peculiar disease of experts—knowing progressively more and more about less and less, until one eventually knows everything about nothing.

So, we were looking for the big waves, not the minor ripples. The biggest wave, we discovered, was the one described below, and it has ever since been one of the strong influences in directing my thoughts on safety and lifestyle-dependent health.

Taylor's Study

A British psychologist, Donald H. Taylor, instructed a sample of 20 drivers to follow a preselected route that included Windsor and the western boundary of London. This route went across a great variety of road environments: urban shopping streets, suburban residential areas, winding country roads and a four-lane highway. The drivers were hooked up to a piece of equipment that measured changes in the electrical resistance of their skin.

As we all know, anxiety increases perspiration. Fortunately for those of us who are concerned about social composure, most perspiration is not visible to the naked eye, but perspiration also increases the electrical conductivity of the skin, and even minor variations in perspiration alter this resistance and are "no sweat" to be picked up by sensitive equipment that is specially designed for its measurement.

Galvanic Skin Response (GSR) is the term psychologists and physiologists use to describe this phenomenon, which is named after its discoverer, Luigi Galvani. For anybody interested in the history of science, it is a truly galvanizing experience to see his sculpture at the entrance of the University of Bologna in Italy. This is the oldest university in the western world and was established in the 11th century. By the 13th century it had some 10,000 students.

The Galvanic Skin Response can be expressed as a percentage change in skin conductance and offers a quantitative measure of the degree of fear or risk—or other arousal—experienced by a person in reaction to some event.

A driver approaching a traffic light and seeing it change from green to amber may show a small GSR, but the sudden discovery of another car approaching in the same traffic lane is likely to produce a major GSR. In Taylor's study, three important variables were measured for each of forty different road sections:

(a) The Accident Rate per Vehicle-Mile. This is calculated by dividing the record of accidents over the past two years (as documented by the police) by the number of passing vehicles, and then dividing this ratio by the length of the section measured in miles. This variable represents the *spatial* and *objective* accident risk per vehicle per mile of movement through specific road sections.

(b) The GSR Rate per Mile. Total GSR activity (the combination of the number and the size of responses) is divided by the length of the section. This gives a variable which represents the *spatial* and *subjective* accident risk per driver per mile of movement through specific road sections.

(c) Average Speed. The average moving speed, in each separate section, for all drivers in the study.

The degree of association between these three variables was expressed in terms of correlation coefficients. Whenever two variables are perfectly and positively related, the correlation coefficient equals +1; when the association is negative and perfect, the correlation coefficient equals-1, and it will be zero when there is no association at all. For example, the correlation between body height and body weight is typically in the order of r = + 0.7. Taylor found the following correlation coefficients (abbreviated as **r**):

Between Accident Rate per Vehicle-Mile and Average GSR Rate per Mile. r = + 0.61

Between Accident Rate per Vehicle-Mileand Average Speed. r =-0.67

Between Average GSR Rate per Mile andAverage Speed. r =-0.75

So, what is the significance of these findings (apart from the fact that their likelihood of having occurred by chance was less than one in a thousand)? The positive association between Accident Rate per Vehicle-Mile and the GSR Rate per Mile can be interpreted to indicate that the drivers experienced more subjective risk in road sections that were also marked by high rates of accidents in the historical records. Apparently, then, drivers on average are sensitive to conditions in which many accidents happen, and react with increased fear.

And what did they do in these conditions? The observed negative correlation between the Accident Rate per Vehicle-Mile and Average Speed indicates that in these conditions they slowed down, while they moved faster in road sections with a low accident rate per vehicle-mile.

Finally, and most interestingly, the negative correlation between Average Speed and GSR Rate per Mile in the forty road sections indicate that the drivers kept the amount of risk they experienced relatively stable over time as they drove through the various road sections. In those road sections where they experienced a lot of risk, they slowed down and thus spent more time in these locations, thereby spreading the GSR activity out over a longer period of time. In contrast, where the GSR Rate per mile was low, they moved at higher speeds, so whatever GSR activity there was occurred in a shorter time frame. The end result was that GSR activity, or subjective risk experienced per time unit of travel, appeared to be relatively stable and independent of the particular road sections in which the driving was done, and thus independent of the accident rates per vehicle-mile of these road sections. To quote Taylor:

> *With subjective and objective risk thus defined [i.e., not per mile or km, but per time unit of exposure to risk], the conclusion from the present data is that they are both independent of what we normally mean by*

variations in road conditions. A possible reason why the subjective risk should be distributed thus may be found in the driver's ability to vary his performance. To some extent at least, he can voluntarily influence the risks taken (for example, by accepting or not accepting opportunities to overtake, or simply by going slowly or fast). Provided that he has this control, there would usually be no reason why he should wish to engage in more risk on one part of the road than on another, and in fact he could be said to be performing a self-paced task. When it is considered that the major restriction on his speed is due to other vehicles, the drivers of which may be expected to be behaving in much the same way, driving could be called a "collectively self-paced task".

Some Possible Consequences

Thus, *spatial* accident risk, objective as well as subjective, showed a heterogeneous density distribution with major variations from one road section to another. That is not surprising. But what is surprising in these observations by Taylor is that *temporal* experience of subjective risk was homogeneous from one time period to another and thus *independent* of the road section and its past accident record per vehicle/km. Apparently, the drivers managed to respond to the objective variations in spatial risk in such a manner that temporal objective risk was independent of variations in spatial objective risk.

Allow yourself a moment to go beyond Taylor's article, as I did at the time, and imagine what far-reaching implications this interpretation might have. Engineering improvements of motor vehicles and the road environment can reduce the objective spatial risk, but what happens to objective temporal risk? If drivers adjust their behaviour in response to these improvements, it is no longer logical to presume that the accident risk per time unit of driving will also be reduced. In fact, if the total amount of time people spend on the roads is not affected, the accident rate per head of population would not change at all. And if the engineering improvements make driving more attractive so that people spend more time on the roads, the accident rate per head of population will even increase. All this is possible despite, or rather because of, engineering improvements that led to a reduction in the accident rate per km driven.

Accordingly, the prospect for greater public safety is unlikely to be found in a "technological fix" because of the way people respond to such fixes. Instead, the prospect for safety is inside the human being, not in the human-made machine or human-made physical environment. Where it is located in the human being and how it may be influenced will be proposed in the chapters that follow.

Replicating Taylor's Findings

There can be no question that these ideas occurred to me because of the literature I had read some ten years earlier, when still a student at the University of Amsterdam and receiving a generalist type of education in psychology. I had the fortune of having been exposed to the writings of Norbert Wiener and others on cybernetics and the essentials of control theory, and on their potential implications for understanding the human condition.

Excited and bewildered as I was by these rather unconventional but potentially very significant speculations, I grabbed the first possible opportunity to visit the author of the study that had triggered them. In this day and age of academic pressure to publish or perish, and the consequent threats to the quality and dependability of what appears in the scientific press, one wishes to check that one is relying on a serious person, and I myself have many times been subjected to inspection for that very purpose. Years earlier, a professor of surgery at the University of Amsterdam had told me that he went to scientific conferences, not primarily for the purpose of receiving the latest bit of information, but to get a personal impression of the reliability of authors whose publications he had read.

The second thing one of my students and I did was to see if we could replicate Taylor's findings while using a somewhat different method of data collection on drivers in locations as far afield as Windsor in England and Kingston in Ontario. We asked our sample of drivers to give a continuous indication of the amount of risk they perceived on a rating scale from one to ten. The results of these verbal ratings were the same as the earlier findings regarding GSR: the reported amount of risk per time unit of driving was essentially independent of where the driving was done and, just as Taylor had found, less experienced drivers gave higher risk ratings than old hands at the task of driving. This corresponds neatly with the fact that inexperienced drivers are more likely to have accidents.

Years later, another student produced another replication and extension of the preceding studies and found the following correlation coefficients:

Between Accident rate per vehicle-km and Average Risk Rating per km	**r** = + 0.89
Between Accident Rate per Vehicle-Kmand Average Speed	**r** =-0.74
Between Average Risk Rating per Kmand Average Speed	**r** =-0.92

Compare these findings with those in Section 3.1 above and you will see that they amply support the earlier ones. Moreover, the eleven individual drivers in this study showed considerable agreement with one another regarding the average perceived riskiness per km of the ten different road sections that were included in the study. The inter-rater reliability amounted to **r** = + 0.83. So, drivers are not only sensitive to conditions of different accident histories, but also show marked similarity in their risk perceptions. We return to this issue in Section 10.4.

The French Connection

So far, what we have seen is that drivers are apparently quite capable of controlling their vehicles in such a manner that they keep their subjective accident risk at a more or less stable and above-zero level when their momentary perceptions are averaged over the time they take to negotiate diverse road sections.

The formulation of what would eventually become Risk Homeostasis Theory (RHT) has taken a long time. A major step forward was made in the early seventies during a sabbatical leave, that leisure of the theory class, at the then National Institute of Road Safety in Montlhéry near Paris. It was then that I had an opportunity to try to accommodate the many factors known to be associated with accident likelihood in a single comprehensive model. For that purpose, I had written the elements I felt had to be entered in such a model on separate filing cards and arranged them in various different flow diagrams in hopes that one of these diagrams might be a reasonable representation of reality. One morning, while organizing the cards, I was suddenly hit by a two-pronged idea. The first prong was the notion of a closed-loop control process between accident occurrence and driver adjustment action. Thus was born the idea that changes in driver behaviour influence the accident rate (which is obvious) *and* that changes in the accident rate influence driver behaviour (which may be less obvious). The second prong was the concept of a target level of risk, which ultimately controls the accident rate, as the *only* important causal factor.

Eureka, everything on the filing cards seemed to fall into place. But the next moment I was filled with doubt. The notion of homeostasis appeared too much of an "idealization" to account for the complexities of human behaviour and "too rational", so to speak, to hold in a world where people only have incomplete information. Could the multitude of factors that play a part in accident occurrence really be grasped in such a comparatively simple model? Weren't there numerous ways in which such a theory could go wrong? People being so different from each other in skill and motivation, each having faulty perceptions of risk, and nobody—not even the experts—really knowing the precise dimensions of the accident toll, there seemed to be plenty of reasons to question the idea. On the one hand, it seemed to me that it had to be true and on the other, that it couldn't.

Wasn't it heresy to propose a theory that might suggest that obvious advances in engineering, education, legislation and medicine have failed to reduce the rate at which people die as a result of accidents?

Making a first attempt at finding supporting evidence, I discovered some World Health Organization statistics that seemed to indicate that, although the per capita rate of traffic fatalities increased over this century, the total mortality rate due to all violent death remained very much the same. As it turns out, later studies would shore this up more firmly.

For a long, long time I have swayed between the feeling of jubilation and the fear of making a fool of myself. In fact, there have been several critics who felt that I had been quite successful in doing the latter. While some made congratulatory remarks, the idea of risk homeostasis has been mocked as a Freudian and pseudo-scientific belief held by a morally and religiously prejudiced Dutch-Calvinist preacher (bien étonnés de se trouver ensemble!) who is blazing the notion of a perverse death wish. Other colourful reactions referred to the theory as "Wilde's law of the conservation of misery", "the devil's idea to some in the safety community", or wondered if it is as difficult to prove as the existence of God (which it isn't, thank God) or wrote in the process of quoting RHT that it wasn't worth quoting!

In another statement, the theory was rejected because "...the claim that risk per unit time is a constant is no more a theory than the claim that all people are the same height, or think they are the same height". This criticism reveals a lack of understanding of homeostasis and attacks RHT on a position that is not even held by that theory. Homeostasis does not mean constancy. Another comment in the literature says: "In my view, a sufficient argument against the validity of risk homeostasis is provided by the incoherance [sic] of its "theoretical formulation"; unfortunately, this critic does not explain his reasons for the "incoherance" allegation.

Others have blamed RHT for being "negative" or "pessimistic" with respect to the potential for accident prevention. Neither accusation seems to make much sense: there is nothing negative in saying that the sun does not revolve around the earth, as people have believed for centuries and some authorities even longer. How could being negative, in the sense of saying that something isn't true or doesn't work, ever be a scientific vice?

There is nothing pessimistic in RHT with respect to the potential for accident prevention. In the first place, it does acknowledge that the accident rate per kilometre of travel can be brought down. Secondly, it states that some accident countermeasures are unable to reduce the per capita accident rate, but also spells out how the accident rate per person in the population can be reduced by accident countermeasures of a different nature. Thus, proponents of RHT are no more pessimistic than physicians who tell their patients that a strep throat cannot be cured with bloodletting, while at the same time handing over a prescription for antibiotics.

Apart from a not-so-subtle pressure on journal editors to refrain from any further publication of the theory or even a bibliographical reference to it, perhaps the most extraordinary, and indeed bizarre reaction, was that of an editor who had invited me to write a chapter for a study guide. He did not like a large part of what I had written and replaced it with his own views. And then, unbeknownst to me, he published the text under my name. Plagiarism in reverse! Evidently, even within the academic world there are forces that would like to see the ivory tower lean in their preferred direction, the ivory becoming tainted in the process of their pushing. In case you, reader, are experiencing similar objections from your peers, here is my consolation: if your ideas are immediately acceptable to most of your colleagues, they are unlikely to be of much interest. Stanislav Lec offers another word of comfort: "People's understanding may be slow to kindle, but it will catch on by the next generation."

But these unfavourable reactions to RHT were not to occur until several years later. I return to the time when I was still in sweet and wonderful France and comfortably close to the perfectly straight Eiffel tower. In addition to Taylor's work and my much earlier exposure to cybernetics, there was another publication that I had read within weeks, if not days, of that morning in the hills of Montlhéry, and it would give me a measure of confidence in my feedback model that tries to explain the accident rate.

That publication was the Report of the Club of Rome, which was widely discussed at the time and has added a major momentum to concerns about world-wide environmental degradation and pollution. It had just appeared as a book entitled *The Limits to Growth* and it contained many examples of rather surprising feedback effects of technological innovations upon social and economic variables. One of these innovations, the so-called Green Revolution—a "technological fix" combining new seed varieties, fertilizers and pesticides—is a telling example of unforeseen and undesirable side-effects. This "revolution" produced greater rural prosperity in some countries but greater poverty in others, because of feedback mechanisms that are easily understood after the fact, but were apparently more difficult to predict in advance.

In areas of the world where an equitable system of land distribution was in existence, the number of agricultural jobs grew faster than the population and real income rose. But in other areas, where most people worked very small lots and the vast majority of the land was owned by very few land-owners, the inequality was accentuated by the Green Revolution. The big-scale farmers adopted the innovation first, made profits and bought the landholdings of the small farmers. Increased unemployment among the latter, poverty, and migration to the cities was the result.

The Green Revolution produced a greater harvest yield per unit of arable soil, but not necessarily a greater prosperity per head of population. The effect of the technological innovation depended upon the nature of the human condition that adopted it. Because of the powerful impact that *Limits to Growth* had on me, and the obvious parallel between that book and the theory I am describing here, I have been tempted to call this book of mine *The Limits to Safety*.

At any rate, my mind was made ready to conceive and even to advance, albeit at first with hesitation, the idea that safety measures that reduce the accident rate per km driven do not necessarily enhance safety per head of population and may even diminish it.

The hesitation originated not only from the fear of being plainly wrong or the threat of ridicule, but also from my strong allegiance to the applied mission of ergonomics, that is, the notion that by "fitting the task to the operator", gains can be made in productivity, safety, health, comfort and satisfaction with the task, and all this by altering the physical features of the task environment rather than by interventions that try to change the operator. At first it seemed to me, as it must have to others, that by proposing the new views, I was guilty of disloyalty to the professed goals and methods of ergonomics. There is no need for such misgivings, because, depending upon societal goals, it can indeed make good sense to modify roads and cars in ways that reduce the accident rate per km driven, even if such interventions do not reduce the accident rate per time unit of road use.

The theory that resulted from this turmoil of conflicting considerations and inclinations I originally labeled "risk compensation theory." And in choosing that label I clearly made a mistake. The term "risk compensation" is, strictly speaking, incorrect because, according to the theory, road users are not expected to compensate for risk in such a way as to reduce it to zero, but instead to show some form of behavioural adjustment in response to what might be called "changes in *intrinsic* risk". These are the changes in risk that would theoretically occur under the condition that road users would not alter their behaviour in the face of interventions, for instance, if they did not decide to drive faster when cars are made more crashworthy and roads are widened.

However, risk compensation theory says that they will alter their behaviour. Thus, labels such as "conservation of risk" or "safety compensation" might have been more appropriate, but unfortunately, these do not clearly point at the mechanism of homeostasis. Quite a number of authors have referred to my work using the terms "risk compensation" or "danger compensation", and some have made a distinction between "risk compensation" and "risk homeostasis" as if compensation were a soft-pedalling or watered-down version of homeostasis. They suggest that compensation might be partial and fall short of homeostasis, that is, complete compensation. That is not what I meant. Despite the relative unfamiliarity of the word "homeostasis", the term "risk homeostasis" seems to be preferable to "risk compensation", "risk conservation" or "safety compensation". Another possible label would be "the theory of behavioural compensation in response to changes introduced in intrinsic risk". But, although correct, this title is rather awkward. At any rate, all four labels are merely different names for the same fare.

INDIVIDUAL DIFFERENCES

Several studies have tried to identify the relationship between individual differences in driver behaviour and the risk-taking measures derived from the Brinkmanship and

Guessmanship tasks described in the preceding chapter. Such relationships were found to exist, but they are weak. Sometimes no statistically reliable relationship was found, but when it was, this went in the expected direction, meaning that people with the larger risk-seeking deviations from the optimum had incurred more demerit points in the past. They reported more moving violations, and took more economic and social risks. The experimental measures of risk taking, however, showed no clear and convincing relationship to accident records.

Personality, Attitude and Lifestyle

In general, it has been found that correlations between personal characteristics and accident record, when they exist at all, are weak and often statistically unreliable. In other words, the likelihood that the observed association could have been due to mere chance was greater than 5 in 100. The weakness of association should not come as a surprise, for a variety of reasons that will be discussed below.

To begin with, consider the special case of relating the experimental risk-taking measures to accident records. The most salient feature of traffic accident risk is the risk of physical injury. In our games the participants did incur a risk, but the risk usually consisted of not making any financial gain or losing out on an opportunity for acquiring social recognition. The expected strength of the relationship between the experimental outcomes and accident record would thus depend on the degree of consistency in people's risk-taking tendencies from one type of risk to another.

Some researchers have distinguished four types of risk: physical, financial, social and ethical. Social risk is the risk of incurring social disapproval as a consequence of one's actions, and ethical risk refers to doing something one may feel guilty about afterwards. Positive association between the four types of risk has been observed, but the association is weak. People who take more-than-average risk of one type do take more risk of another type, but only slightly more so. No salient personality trait of all-pervasive risk seeking or risk avoidance has been identified. In other words, no *general* risk-taking personality trait emerges from the research studies. This is not surprising, for two reasons. First, if people's deviations from optimal risk taking were quite similar in all four types of risk taking, that would have been so obvious that we would have known it all along and it would no longer be a subject for research. Second, a general risk-taking trait would also be highly counterproductive to success in life, since it would mean that people who are less likely to be successful in obtaining satisfaction in one area would also be less likely to obtain satisfaction in another, other things being equal (including skill).

If there is one particular habit that is often believed to be associated with risk-taking personality traits, it must be gambling, especially pathological or compulsive gambling. In everyday language, "to gamble" is almost synonymous with "to take a risk". Yet, the many studies undertaken in order to identify the personality traits that might characterize these people have failed to indicate that gamblers are more-than-average risk takers in other aspects of life as well, and they do not systematically differ from non-gamblers in their personality traits. Even the trait of stimulation seeking—called "sensation seeking" by some—shows no consistent pattern. Some studies find gamblers higher than average on this trait, others lower. The same holds for extraversion.

Just as gambling is the proverbial form of risk taking, the sensation-seeking questionnaire has become a frequently-used instrument for the assessment of individual differences in risk-taking tendency. Maybe this is because the author of this questionnaire defines sensation seeking with specific reference to risk: "the need for varied, novel, and complex sensations and experiences and the willingness to take physical and social risks for the sake of such experiences". Maybe, too, the questionnaire does not quite measure up to the author's definition, because recent research evidence—including his own—seems to indicate that people who get high scores on this questionnaire feel that the personal risks involved in the risky activities they like are less severe than is true for the people who dislike those risky activities and obtain low scores.

Similarly, Dutch drivers with high sensation-seeking scores were found to follow more closely to the car in front of them than drivers scoring low on the questionnaire. Their self-reports and physiological measures of arousal, however, indicated that the sensation seekers experienced about the same sensation of risk as those with low scores. Thus, "the seeking of sensation" is largely reduced to "estimating that the risk is low". Although sensation seekers have been reported to be more inclined to engage in apparently risky driving habits like speeding, drinking and driving, and to run up a record of moving violations, various studies found no relation between sensation-seeking scores and traffic accident history. Skiers with high sensation-seeking scores have been found to have significantly *fewer* skiing accidents than sensation avoiders.

A comprehensive review of the literature on the relationship between the habit of gambling and any personality traits of habitual gamblers has this to say: "What little agreement exists suggests a difference in locus of control, with high-frequency gamblers being more external than low-frequency gamblers. However, if such a relationship is a reality, then it is just as likely that the gambling causes the trait as that the trait causes the gambling." For the meaning of "locus of control", see Section 10.3 below. If a habit as risk-riddled as gambling has not been found to be strongly related to personality traits that one associates with a positive inclination toward risk taking, there would seem little hope for finding any marked relationships between accident involvement and personality.

Yet, numerous studies have been conducted in hopes of identifying individual characteristics that are related to accident history. Some have met with a degree of success, although it is not uncommon for significant findings in one study to find either no support or even contradictory results in another. Greater accident involvement has sometimes been found for introverts and, in other investigations, for extraverts. Similarly, sensation seekers were sometimes found to have had more accidents, and sometimes sensation avoiders were found to have more. Greater accident involvement has been found for people who tend to attribute the occurrence of important events in their lives to fate or chance rather than to their own doing. The same holds for impulsivity, easy-goingness and low self-control.

Some studies find more accident involvement in people with what is called a "field-dependent perceptual style". But a larger number of investigations found no relationship. This is also true of reaction time, or quick reflexes, and accidents. Field dependence characterizes people who do not have an analytical style in the way they look at the world that surrounds them, and are more likely to fall victim to erroneous syllogisms. Perhaps not surprisingly, differences in intelligence have not been found to be related to accident history.

Individual differences in attitudes, however, *have* been found to be related to involvement in past as well as future accidents: drivers with less aggressive, less macho, less authoritarian and more socially-oriented values show safer driver careers. The same holds for people with a history of better school marks for citizenship (diligence and proper behaviour as rated by their school teachers) and stable employment histories. Some of these studies found biographical characteristics, including increased incidence of criminal records, more strongly associated with accidents than personality variables were.

Contrary to what may seem to be suggested here, crash rate has not invariably been found to be associated with traits that are generally considered to be socially undesirable by mainstream society. For instance, accident-involved bus drivers in the USA and in India were found to more frequently display a Type-A personality. This label refers to people marked by a patent display of energy, competitiveness, alertness, ambition and a view that action is urgent because time is short. However, a subsequent study of the same kind of drivers, conducted in Britain, did not find them to be more often involved in accidents, although they more often reported fast driving. To sum up this paragraph: weak, inconsistent and contradictory findings galore!

THE UNRELIABILITY OF ACCIDENT LIABILITY

Even if there were such a thing as a general risk-taking trait, there is a further reason for the weakness of association between a personality trait such as this, or any other personality trait, and accidents. This is because the tendency to have accidents is not a stable human characteristic. Test-retest reliability is very low. No variable can correlate better with some criterion than the reliability of that criterion, that is, the correlation of that criterion with itself.

The facts contradict the notion that most accidents are due to a small minority of people with dangerous, anti-social personalities. To think so, however, seems very tempting. After all, about one-half of all whisky is being drunk by no more than some 5% of all consumers, 100% of all murders are committed by a very small number of people, 100% of all venereal disease is carried by a small proportion of people. Almost 100% of all pianos in a country are found in a small percentage of homes. Moreover, there is evidence that 100% of all automobile accidents in a given year are incurred by less than 10% of all drivers. So, why should the bulk of accidents not be due to a small minority of people?

However, the evidence is clear that this is *not the same minority* every year. Consider some findings of a study conducted in North Carolina in the USA. Of all drivers who had two accidents in two consecutive years, 87% did not have a traffic accident in the third year. The 13% who did accounted for 1.6% of all accidents in the third year. Although it is true that their accident rate in the third year was about twice that of the average driver, an action even as drastic as deporting drivers with accidents in two consecutive years (or any other action that effectively eliminates them from the roads) would reduce the total accident rate in the third year by no more than 1.6%. Obviously, this offers no justification for the assumption that the accident rate can be reduced substantially by preventing those who have had accidents from further driving.

In passing, we may note that there is also precious little in these North Carolina data to support the beliefs of those who think that cracking down on violators of traffic laws might bring about a major reduction in the accident rate: "If you took all drivers with three or more violations in the past two years [that is, about 1.3% of all drivers] off the highway and kept them off effectively for two whole years, North Carolina would still experience 96.2 per cent of the accidents it would have had anyway. Moreover, of the drivers removed from the highway, 71% would not have been involved in an accident anyway."

The ability, though very limited, to predict future accidents from past accidents or violations might still be useful to insurance companies in their effort to select low-risk customers from among the large numbers of all those who seek insurance, or to set fees in accordance with the level of risk. It would be nearly useless, however, to attempt to predict the accident career of specific individuals and restrict their legal rights accordingly. This fact has long—though not universally—been recognized: "It is not to be expected that within a democracy, the authorities could impose selective treatment on any class of operators, the majority of whom show no need for it."

A very similar pattern of results has been obtained in several other studies. There is, indeed, a difference in the accident rate between drivers with previous accidents or previous violations, but the difference is so small that it accounts for only a minor fraction of all accidents that happen. From data collected in California, it can be calculated that only about 2% of all accidents in a given year were due to drivers who had experienced accidents in both of the two preceding years. About 87% of these drivers were accident-free in the third year. Not surprisingly, the researchers concluded: "Consequently, it is unrealistic to expect that programs toward reducing accidents by focusing on the accident repeater can effect a large reduction in the total accident picture." Accident countermeasures aimed at accident repeaters and violation repeaters cannot diminish the accident rate by a substantial amount, even if they were 100% effective in reducing to zero the accidents of these individuals in the near future. If complete elimination of their accidents is viewed as unrealistically high, and the accident rate of accident and violation repeaters were reduced to average levels in the population, the reduction in the future accident rate of course, would be even smaller.

That the removal of accident-involved drivers from the road can reduce the future accident rate only by a few measly percentage points was already established some time before the Second World War—at least as far as the USA is concerned—in a publication aptly called "The normal automobile driver as a traffic problem". Yet, cracking down on accident-involved drivers continues to have some political appeal, and this is probably why such action is being proposed from time to time by individuals or advocacy groups in one country or another. But from a public health promotion point of view, this approach is virtually useless. Human history is replete with cases in which an identifiable minority of people is blamed for society's ills. They are made to suffer injustices as a consequence, while the ills are not remedied. The fact is that the accident problem is not located at the far side of society's bell curve. Therefore, accident countermeasures, if they are to have a significant effect upon a nation's accident rate per inhabitant, have to be directed at the driver population as a whole, that is, basically all of us, or at least at large subgroups in the population.

It is evident that risk taking is not a personality trait that is consistent from one situation to another. Similarly, the tendency to have accidents is not consistent from one time period to another. To believe otherwise may well be an example of the "fundamental attribution error". This expression is used by social psychologists to refer to the fact that people typically attribute another person's behaviour to that person's lasting character and not often enough to that person's passing state or the prevailing environmental condition. Steal once and be forever called a thief—hence the use of the term "error", and the error is called "fundamental" because the first and natural impulse of people (psychologists not excepted!) is to make an attribution of this kind. The development of a more considered and controlled opinion does not occur unless a more deliberate and conscious effort is made.

Nevertheless, in a fashion reminiscent of the delta fallacy, there seems to be a persistent urge to search for stable personality features that might predict accidents. The dogged search may be due to the occasional success in identifying a relevant factor, however small its influence. Many researchers, this author not excepted, seem to have been thinking (but yours truly no longer so) that a clearer relationship would emerge if only we had more valid tests of attitude and personality and if we had more trustworthy measures of accident involvement. The notion that current measures of accident involvement are not trustworthy is justified, since a considerable proportion of all accidents remains unreported. Maybe this problem could be overcome by looking at professional drivers. Not only do these drivers cover a much greater annual kilometrage under comparable circumstances (which would give personality traits a greater opportunity to become apparent in the safety record), but it is also rather difficult, in the environment in which these people operate, to hide any accidents from the record keepers.

And indeed, a somewhat greater stability in the tendency to incur accidents from one period to another has been observed in professional drivers. These are people (such as taxi drivers and long-haul truckers) who drive very large distances per year under relatively comparable conditions from one year to another. Bus drivers and streetcar drivers in Helsinki, Northern Ireland, Belgrade, Israel and England have been found to show greater-than-zero correlation between the number of accidents they had in one period and in a subsequent period of one or more years. Still, earlier crash involvement correlated no more than about **r** = +0.30 with accident involvement in the next period.

Translated into everyday arithmetic, this means the following. Suppose you have a sample of 1000 drivers who were accident-free in one period, and a sample of 1000 drivers who were not. Suppose, too, that you predict that all the accident-involved drivers will have accidents again in the second period, and those who were free of accidents would remain so. A correlation **r** = +0.30 implies that your prediction would turn out to be correct for a little less than 60% of all drivers and wrong for just over 40%. So, you are doing better than chance; 60-40 is better than 50-50, but not by a whole lot.

The authors of the studies mentioned above, in reviewing the evidence, concluded: "This implies that *transient* factors must play by far the most important role in crash causation" —emphasis added. As they are saying this, one hears the echo of a conclusion, drawn some twenty years earlier, that "certain people are accident-prone, but sometimes only for short periods of time, and that there are others who are accident-prone over extended periods of time, perhaps for several years or most of their remaining lifetime. Furthermore, different persons are accident-prone for different reasons, and the same person may move in and out of a state of accident-proneness each time because of different circumstances." Among those different circumstances that have been identified in the literature are interpersonal problems, loss of a loved one, job and financial problems, episodes of suicidal thoughts and gestures. One study found that female and male drivers with marital difficulties were more often involved in accidents in the period surrounding the date at which they filed for divorce.

Another factor causing the lack of stability in drivers' accident records is that people may learn from past accidents, other people's as well as their own. Once bitten, twice shy, in other words. A recent accident may be followed by a period of increased caution.

This is what we saw in the laboratory and what was also observed in a German study. Drivers who had been injured in accidents rated the risk of road accidents significantly higher and adopted more safety-compatible attitudes and driving behaviours. On the other hand, having had no accident may dull people's alertness and make them more daring, at least until an accident follows. As a result, the accident likelihood of an individual would fluctuate from one time period to another, rather than be stable. The search for personality traits in accident causation appears even less rewarding than the proverbial search for a needle in a haystack. Even if you find one, by the time you do, the haystack will likely no longer be the same.

And then there is the rambling role of chance. Whether a driver error results in a reportable accident or not depends largely on factors unforeseen, if not unforeseeable. These are factors that we usually call chance, or good or bad luck. Drivers losing control of the vehicle or driving through a red light, for instance, may crash or go scot-free, depending on whether there are other vehicles in their path. Even if there are other vehicles, their drivers may perceive the danger and take evasive action so that no accident occurs. This is why even consistent poor driving does not lead to consistent accident careers. We are, in fact, so used to the environment being forgiving in one way or another that, when a crash does occur, this is called "an accident" in everyday language.

PROSPECT AND RETROSPECT

Some studies may actually lead to overestimation of the relationship between personality and what little stability there is in accident involvement. This can happen when current scores on personality tests are investigated on their association with past accident record. Take the case of "external locus of control".

This term refers to persons who attribute the occurrence of important events, such as accidents, to external factors, rather than to their own doing. The latter is called *internal* locus of control. When applied to driving, external locus of control is measured in terms of the respondents' agreement with statements like: "driving with no accidents is merely a matter of luck" and "most accidents happen because of bad roads, lack of appropriate signs, and so on". Internals typically endorse statements such as "accidents happen because drivers have not learned to drive carefully enough".

We have already noticed that far more than 50% of drivers feel that they are better than average drivers. People like to present themselves in a favourable light, not only to others, but also to themselves. Thus, it is to be expected that the very human eagerness to justify oneself will lead people to attribute any accident they had to factors other than their own incompetence, carelessness, inattention, hurry, or what-have-you. So, *after* an accident they may become more inclined to agree with external-type statements, while before the accident they were actually more internal. Bus and streetcar drivers in Helsinki, with accidents in the past, attributed the occurrence of traffic accidents more often to their tight schedules, fatigue and duration of work shifts than did accident-free drivers.

Performance on tests of skill may, of course, also be influenced when people know or suspect that they are being tested because of their accident history. It has been said that "drivers tend to explain their traffic accidents by reporting circumstances of lowest culpability compatible with credibility". In this effort they may be more or less successful. Witness some excerpts of supposedly true-to-life letters from Canadian drivers to their automobile insurance firms:

- I knocked over a man. He admitted it was his fault, as he had been run over before.
- The guy was all over the road; I had to swerve a number of times before I hit him.
- The pedestrian had no idea which way to go, so I ran over him.
- An invisible car came out of nowhere, struck my vehicle and vanished.
- I bumped into a lamp-post that was obscured by a pedestrian.
- I pulled away from the side of the road, glanced at my mother-in-law, and headed over the embankment.

- I was on the way to the doctor with rear end trouble when my universal joint gave way, causing me to have an accident.

Most studies in the current information base are of a retrospective nature: a sample of individuals with valid driver's licences is drawn from the population, or happens to be conveniently available. They are given tests of personality, and other personal characteristics are ascertained, with the inclusion of their *past* accident career.

It is worth noting that the correlations calculated from this information do not include the very people who, in a sense, are the most interesting from the point of view of accident prediction and accident prevention. These are the people who have had a fatal accident or were so severely injured that they cannot participate in investigations, as well as those whose driving behaviour was so deviant that their driving licences have been withdrawn. These people are not included in the samples. Thus, the most dramatic (and possibly the most telling) extreme of the distribution of accidents or violations is missing. This, in turn, may have the effect that the correlations obtained between personal characteristics and accidents underestimate the true strength of association.

One remedy for this problem is to conduct *prospective* studies: a sample of drivers is drawn from the general population, for instance, at the moment of licensing or even before. This is a point in time at which no accident, or at least no culpable accident, has yet occurred. Demographic data (age, gender, occupational status and so forth) and personality information are obtained from these people, who are then followed up over a multi-year period. At various points in time after the starting date, information on whether they had an accident or not is gathered and checked for any association with the personal data collected earlier.

Prospective investigations are expensive, in part because they demand large samples. This is because no more than 10 in a hundred drivers can be expected to get involved in an accident in any one year. Thus, if you wish to have a sub-sample of 100 accident-involved drivers at a point in time one year into the study, you have to start with an initial sample size of 1,000. In fact, you need even more, because a general problem of prospective studies is attrition of participants. People move, change names, or they themselves or their accident careers cannot be traced for other reasons.

Another potential problem of prospective studies is that people may change their behaviour as a consequence of participating in an investigation. Jocular minds have called opinion surveys the art of asking people about the opinions they don't have. They may then form an opinion as a consequence of being asked for one. Physicians may question their patients at annual check-ups on their eating, exercising, drinking and smoking habits. Having been asked, people may start thinking about these matters and possibly change their behaviour.

Researchers in Ottawa, Canada, obtained a sample of 1273 Grade 9 and 10 high-school students in an effort to determine whether future traffic accidents could be predicted from information collected from these youngsters, most of whom (more than 86%) did not have a driver's licence at the outset of the investigation although, three years later, 96% did. Participation attrition amounted to 20% in the second year, despite repeated attempts by the investigators to make contact. In the third year, the loss amounted to 30%, and reached 66% in the fourth year, meaning that follow-up data in the fourth year could be collected on only 34% of the original sample.

Nevertheless, significant relationships between several personal characteristics and future accident involvement were reported, including that greater accident likelihood was found among those with lesser adherence to traditional social values regarding school and religious worship, as well as greater tolerance for deviance.

The individuals with accidents had more liberal attitudes towards alcohol use, drank more regularly, and drank larger quantities per occasion. As well, they indicated more risky driving behaviour, including driving after the use of alcohol or street drugs, and failure to use seatbelts. Among them there were more cigarette smokers, and they reported fewer behaviours conducive to health such as having dental check-ups, a balanced diet, and regular exercise. They also reported a greater frequency of unhealthy behaviours such as eating junk food and not allowing themselves enough sleep. As regards their personality traits, they scored higher on "thrill and adventure seeking" and "experience seeking", which are two of the subscales in the sensation-seeking questionnaire mentioned above.

The researchers reported that combined consideration of all these personal characteristics allowed correct identification of 78% of the study participants as either accident-involved or not accident-involved during the follow-up period.

This finding, however interesting it may seem at first sight, does not detract in any way from our general observation that individual differences in personality characteristics only have a limited bearing on individual differences in accident involvement.

This is because it can be calculated from the researchers' report that the percentage of participants who remained accident-free during the follow-up period was 77.6. In other words, if one had predicted that all participants would have been accident-free in the subsequent period of time under study, this prediction would have been correct in 77.6% of the cases. The percentage of correctly predicted cases on the basis of knowing something about the individuals should, of course, be compared with the percentage of correct prediction on the basis of not knowing something about the individuals, that is, on the basis of mere chance. In this study, there was no clear evidence that prediction based on knowledge of individual characteristics was better than prediction ignorant of individual differences.

And even if it had been better, such a finding might give an unrealistically optimistic impression of the true predictive power of the personality and lifestyle characteristics just mentioned. This is because the number of predictor variables that were found to be related to the accident criterion was appreciably smaller than the number that was tested. The implication is that some of the supposedly significant findings may have been due to chance.

The larger the number of correlations calculated, the greater the likelihood that the "significant" ones are due to chance. If you find this notion of "significance by chance" a little puzzling, think of tossing a coin. Throwing heads five times in a row has a small chance likelihood, namely 0.5 x 0.5 x 0.5 x 0.5 x 0.5, which is about 3%. If you stopped tossing at that point, you would have a "significant" finding and might suspect that the coin is not balanced. But toss each of 100 perfectly balanced coins five times and you may expect five heads to turn up in about three of the 100 coins; that is three cases of "significance by chance". Now toss each of the coins five times again. Once more, you will expect to see the five-heads pattern in about three of the coins, but not in the same three. Hence, when one personality characteristic among several tested emerges as "significantly" related to accidents, one should not consider this a reliable finding until the same characteristic does so again in further investigations.

Consider a recent prospective study that was carried out on male Finnish army conscripts.

Two personality traits—boldness and the tendency to be trusting—among the sixteen traits measured when they were enlisted, showed significant relation to accident occurrence during their military service. Do these results justify any confidence in the notion that individual differences in accident involvement can be predicted on the basis of personality? You would probably wish to suspend judgement until you know how these traits stand up in subsequent validation studies, especially since the study found no significant correlation for any of the six other traits which, in various earlier studies, had been reported to be associated with traffic accidents. Your confidence would probably be further reduced by the fact that individual differences in the accident rate of the soldiers before induction into the armed forces bore no relation to their accident involvement while in military service. This reflects zero-order reliability of individual differences in the accident rate from one period to another. There was no relationship between the number of traffic fines obtained before and during military service, or between the number of traffic fines incurred by the men before they entered the service and while they were in the army, and their pre-army violation rate was not related to accidents while in the service. In short, there was no connection between violations and accidents, and both were unstable over time.

On the other hand, the men who had more than the average of 64,000 km of driving experience before being enlisted were found to be less likely to have an accident during their military service. This is a finding that deserves more general credence.

DEMOGRAPHIC CHARACTERISTICS

In contrast to personality traits, there are other characteristics that have *repeatedly* been shown to be related to accidents. These are gender, age and driving experience, although, even here, the association is not strong enough to produce individual differences in accident likelihood that are stable from one time period to another.

In the last several years, in Ontario, about 16% of all licensed drivers were between 16 and 24 years of age, yet they accounted for about 30% of all fatalities. They were thus 1.9 times more likely to be killed in road accidents than drivers on average.

This overrepresentation, although it varies in size from country to country and from time to time, is an international phenomenon. It holds true both per km driven as well as per person. There is also some indication that elderly drivers have more accidents per km driven than those of middle age, but not necessarily more per person-year. This is because they tend to drive much less, thus reducing their exposure to accident risk. Furthermore, males are more often involved in accidents as compared to female drivers, both per km driven and per person-year.

It takes novice drivers some five to seven years for their accident rate to drop to the average accident rate of the driver population as a whole, and the younger the driver at the time of licensing, the longer this period. This implies that the overrepresentation of novice drivers in the accident statistics is due to two different factors, immaturity and inexperience. In Ontario data, for instance, the overrepresentation of 16-year-old males during their first year of driving is about twice as great as the overrepresentation of male drivers aged 30 or older during their first year of driving.

In their fourth year of driving, male drivers who obtained their licence when they were 30 years or older had about the same accident rate per 1000 drivers as the average of all male drivers in the population. In contrast, males who had acquired their licence when they were 16 incurred accidents at a rate about 40% higher during their fourth year of driving than was true for all males drivers in the population.

This raises two questions: what is it about being a late teen, or a sprouting adult, that makes young people more likely to have accidents, and why is inexperience related to greater danger? Before attempting to answer these questions, let us first consider what requirements a driver must fulfil to prevent a potential accident from occurring.

Obviously, (1) the driver must be awake. But to be awake is not enough. The driver may be fully awake, but inattentive to the driving task and paying attention to other things, for instance, the cellular telephone, the radio or conversation with a passenger. Thus, (2) the driver must be attentive to the traffic situation. But paying attention to the traffic situation is not enough, because the driver may not have the sensory abilities (vision and hearing, among other things) to clearly perceive the danger-relevant aspects of the traffic situation. Thus, (3) the driver must have the necessary sensory abilities. But having the necessary sensory acuity is not enough, because the driver may fail to be aware of the amount of risk that is contained in the traffic situation he or she perceives. Risk perception, like the perception of beauty, is a product of experience and reasoning, however rudimentary, intuitive or subconscious these may be. Thus, (4) the driver has to be able to infer the amount of accident risk that is contained in the traffic situation. But risk recognition is not enough, because for the driver to be motivated to take action to reduce the accident risk, the amount of risk acknowledged must be greater than the level of risk the driver is willing to accept. So, (5) the risk must be greater than the driver is willing to tolerate. But the wish to reduce the risk is not enough, because the driver may or may not have the ability to decide what should be done in order to reduce the risk. Therefore, (6) the driver has to have the necessary decision-making skill for risk reduction. But to have the decision-making skill is not enough, because even the driver who knows what ought to be done may not have the vehicle-handling skill to carry out the necessary manoeuvre. Hence, (7) the driver has to have the necessary vehicle-control skill. Moreover, all these conditions must be fulfilled at a point in time at which an imminent accident can still be averted. This simple logic might suggest that there are as many as seven different factors involved in accident avoidance, but this is a misconception since these factors do not operate independently of one another. If a person's decision-making or vehicle-handling skills are poor, that person's level of perceived risk should be high, and if it is not, this reflects overconfidence in one's skills.

The same holds for sensory abilities. To be colour-blind or hard of hearing does not imply a significant increase in accident liability, provided the driver considers these handicaps in the estimation of risk. Poor night vision will not increase a person's accident risk unless the person is unaware of it or is willing to accept high levels of accident risk.

Deficiencies in skills and sensory functioning, other things being equal, can increase a person's accident likelihood only to the extent that these deficiencies are being underestimated by the person in question, and thus lead to an inappropriately low level of perceived risk.

Poor skill will not enhance a person's accident risk if that person is fully aware of his or her poor skill, because—risk acceptance level being the same—that person is less likely to engage in manoeuvres he or she cannot handle very well.

It is not surprising, therefore, that sensory abilities and other driving skills have generally been found to show no association, or weak association, with accident involvement. In Section 6.3 we noticed that better-than-average driving skill—presumably both on the level of decision making and vehicle handling—may sometimes be associated with *greater* accident likelihood, because the driver is being lulled into an illusion of safety.

Inattentiveness to the driving task implies either that the driver estimated the risk of accident as very low and permitted paying more attention to other things, or that the driver considered other things to be at least temporarily more important than safety, thereby accepting a higher level of accident risk.

Finally, lapses in wakefulness during driving will not occur unless the driver underestimated the chances of falling asleep behind the wheel or accepted them. Here again, the underlying cause is either risk underestimation or increased risk acceptance.

It may thus be concluded that the seven factors in our original analysis shrink to only two that are truly relevant to increased accident likelihood. It may further be argued that individuals with a very low risk acceptance will be motivated to ensure that they do not underestimate risk and that, therefore, only one dominant factor remains: risk acceptance.

We now will attempt to explain why inexperienced drivers have more accidents than experienced drivers. Obviously this is not because of their lower level of skill per se. *In principle*, unskilled people can reduce accident risk by choosing manoeuvres that match their level of skill in driving, and by reducing their exposure.

However, *in practice*, this is not so. They cannot fully adjust their driving manners to their driving skill, because they operate as a minority in a road system in which most drivers are experienced. There are strong forces at work that compel inexperienced drivers to drive at a certain speed and at a certain following distance, and to do other things similar to what the more experienced majority does.

Thus, in order to acquire experience, they have to drive above their own level of competence and comfort, and that is why they experience more risk when driving. Their elevated experience of risk corresponds with the increased risk they incur.

The point made here is neatly illustrated by the case of "Mrs. Cautious Driver". This is the name we will give to a lady whose problems were presented at the Grand Rounds in Psychiatry in the Kingston General Hospital in Ontario in the mid-'70s. She suffered a serious nervous breakdown and an acute case of driving phobia. This is her story.

In the course of four years she experienced four traffic accidents. This is a rare occurrence, with a frequency of less than one in 10,000 drivers. In none of these accidents was she at fault. That makes her predicament a much rarer occurrence still. In all cases she was driven into at an intersection by another car. She was an extremely cautious driver in the sense that she drove her station wagon well below the speed limit on four-lane highways and she always buckled her seatbelt in a period before this was compulsory by law. At stop and yield signs, she was in the habit of waiting very long before she would accept a gap wide enough to her liking and go ahead. In such circumstances she would sometimes brake and stop again. Three times she was rear-ended in this situation, the third time by a police patrol car.

Mrs. Cautious Driver presents an interesting paradox. She was very careful indeed, in fact, so careful that her behaviour was rather unpredictable to other drivers. This made her liable to having accidents. On the other hand, if everybody were to behave as cautiously as she, there would be fewer crashes.

Greater risk, and acceptance thereof, is inevitable if one wishes to become experienced. Experience must be bought; accidents are part of the price. Nobody can expect to be able to learn to play the violin and perform a piece at the required tempo without making many mistakes in the learning process. There is no royal road to learning.

The number of mistakes made by the novice violinist and the inexperienced driver could be reduced if they were allowed to perform at a reduced pace, solo, and in concert with other inexperienced persons. In other words, there are reasons for assuming that the accident rates of novice drivers would have been lower if there were only novice drivers making use of the roads. It is not their inexperience per se, but the *experience mix* in the collective of road users that makes the inexperienced driver more prone to having accidents.

This view is supported in findings obtained by the method of verbal risk ratings. Drivers of different levels of experience orally express, on a numerical rating scale, the level of risk they perceive while driving. An observer sitting in the front passenger seat, who may be either experienced or inexperienced as a driver, makes observations using the same scale. The experimenter does not allow any communication between driver and observer and keeps a record of their independent risk estimates.

It is found that inexperienced drivers' danger ratings tend to agree more with other inexperienced drivers' ratings than with those of experienced drivers. Similarly, ratings by experienced drivers do not agree with those by inexperienced observers as much as with experienced ones. In simpler words: drivers of similar levels of experience show greater similarity in the amount of risk they perceive. In a situation of traffic conflict, an experienced driver will, therefore, be better able to predict what another experienced driver will do to avoid a collision. Similarly, inexperienced drivers will predict the reactions of other inexperienced drivers more accurately than they will predict those of experienced ones.

The implication is that the overrepresentation of novice drivers in accident statistics—insofar as it is due to lack of experience—might be reduced by techniques that speed up the process of learning to perceive the risks of the road in the same manner as experienced drivers do. The current research interest in risk-perception skills may thus lead to the development of new didactic methods.

In order to explain the overrepresentation of novice drivers—especially male—in relation to their youthfulness, a variety of factors may be surmised. Young people have higher stimulation-seeking scores, and we know that such scores are associated with a tendency to view the risk in "risky" activities as rather low. Moreover, young people tend to have fewer responsibilities to others; they are less likely to be married and have children. and they have fewer accomplishments.

Thus, apart from the potential loss of a few more years of life, they have less to lose by taking risks. These are factors that may be assumed to have an increasing effect on the level of risk they are willing to accept. At the same time, they have more to gain from risky behaviour. For example, by showing bravado they may gain prestige among their peers. Furthermore, the general culture expects them to be daring and venturesome: young colts will canter. They often drive cars that are not their own. Thus, they would seem to lose less and gain more from risky conduct. Similar factors may well explain why men have more traffic accidents, per person-year as well as per km driven, than women.

Returning, finally, to the motto at the heading of this chapter, should we conclude that people drive as they live? The original study which affirmed this "has serious methodological shortcomings". For one thing, the drivers were questioned by interviewers who knew their accident history and thus could keep asking questions until they received answers which satisfied their need to explain the interviewee's accident record. This has led to a gross overestimation of personality and lifestyle factors in the causation of accidents. In other words, an association does exist, but it is so tenuous that it would seem unwise to focus upon it in prevention efforts that wish to achieve more than accident reduction by just a few percentage points. It may be more promising to attempt to alter the driving style of the population as a whole, or a demographic subgroup, and to do this by focusing on the level of risk people are willing to accept.

2

Motivating for Safety and Health

The demonstrating data, however, were collected in the laboratory and, as has been noted in that same chapter, "variables always change when they are brought into the laboratory". Risk homeostasis theory is primarily concerned with health and safety, not with risk taking in the pursuit of money or social recognition, or other risk taking that may be fit for laboratory experimentation. There is, however, no fundamental reason why the same principles should not hold in these domains as well. In fact, since risk is ubiquitous, it may be argued that RHT is a general theory of human behaviour.

At any rate, it is in this chapter that we will demonstrate that it is possible to motivate people to adopt a safer behaviour repertoire under real-life conditions, and that accident rates per person can be greatly reduced. The target level of risk—in other words, the level of risk at which people prefer to operate—can be reduced by interventions in four categories of tactics. Thus, the safety measure may aim to:

Increase the perceived benefit of cautious behaviour.......... Tactic A.

Decrease the perceived cost of cautious behaviour............. Tactic B.

Increase the perceived cost of risky behaviour........ Tactic C.

Decrease the perceived benefit of risky behaviour............ Tactic D.

As examples of Tactic A, one might think of instituting administrative rewards for accident-free and violation-free driving through discounts in insurance premiums, free licence renewal, discounts in vehicle permits and medical insurance premiums, rewards for being healthy, discounts for people with appropriate health habits. Examples of Tactic B might be the institution of flexitime so that the need to rush to work will be reduced, subsidies for public transportation, enhancing the efficiency and comfort of public transit, tax exemptions on safety equipment, making safety equipment more pleasant to use.

Using Tactic C, the perceived cost of risky behaviours may be enhanced by actions such as increased taxes on tobacco, increased penalties for traffic violations, building vehicles that become uncomfortable (noisy and vibrating) when driven at high speeds, manufacturing vehicles with frail exteriors and crashworthy interiors which would increase repair costs but reduce the severity of injury, reduction of the right to restitution for damages incurred by individuals who don't wear a seatbelt, reduced sick pay for employees who were not complying with safety rules and regulations at the time of their accidents. Finally, Tactic D might be the rationale for measures such as paying taxi drivers per time unit instead of per kilometre, making it mandatory that all employees involved in risky work be paid by the hour and not per unit of productivity.

A word of warning! The above examples are meant to illustrate and are not necessarily recommended. Many of them would likely fail to produce lasting reductions in the rate of accidents or lifestyle-dependent poor health. This is because they are directed at particular behaviours, such as speeding, drinking and driving, or smoking tobacco. They do not, in themselves, stimulate the desire to be safe and in good health. If you tax alcohol beyond people's financial reach, they may try making the stuff themselves, with the potential for much greater damage to health due to poisoning. To increase the likelihood of being stopped for a traffic violation is to increase surrogate risk. This may motivate drivers to avoid a penalty, but does not heighten the desire to be safe; neither does it reduce the accident rate.

Countermeasures that are oriented towards specific behaviours instead of towards the outcome—having, or not having, an accident—do not prevent behavioural adaptation from occurring. Those who fail to realize this suffer from the delta illusion. Reduction in the frequency of one particular immediate accident cause may simply make room for other immediate causes to become more prominent.

Years ago, this phenomenon was referred to as *equifinality*. The same final outcome, for instance, the accident rate per person-hour, may emerge although the pathways are different. Sobriety is no guarantee of safety; neither is driving at the average speed. Abstinence is no guarantee of health; neither is jogging. Similarly, accidents may be avoided and safety achieved through a variety of different behaviours.

Punishing unsafe Acts

The notion that safety may be enhanced by acting upon motivation has a long history, as is clear from the universal presence of punitive law. Although enforcement of punitive law is one of society's traditional attempts at motivating people towards safety, the evidence for its effectiveness has not been forthcoming. We found that even if selective enforcement and increased police surveillance of some aspect of road-user behaviour were to reduce the prevalence of a particular circumstance in accident occurrence (the presence of alcohol, for instance) this does not imply a reduction in the overall accident rate, since the rate of sober accidents may increase.

Instead of increasing police surveillance and thereby the likelihood of detection, one might consider increasing the penalty for the offence. Such action, however, may take insufficient account of the social context in which the law has to operate. Drinking and driving is folk crime; large segments of the population admit to it. Of nearly 10,000 Canadian drivers surveyed, 72% reported they had been driving after drinking at least once during the 12 months preceding the interview, while 22% said they had been driving while "high" on alcohol during that period. Analogous American statistics indicated 60% and 29%, respectively. Canadian roadside surveys found as many as 6% of all passing drivers to have BACs over the legal limit. And prior to the introduction of the statutory BAC limit in the Netherlands, the percentage of night-time drivers exceeding this limit varied between 13% and 17%. Between two and four o'clock in the morning, these percentages were no less than between 31% and 36%. Roadside surveys are conducted over a few hours only, during a few days. One wonders what percentage of drivers exceed the legal limit at least once a year.

It is one thing to declare a frequently committed act a crime, but quite another to treat it as such on the level of police enforcement and court action. Can it be surprising that police officers are hesitant to charge, that defence lawyers find many grounds for clemency, that juries are reticent in passing a guilty verdict, and that judges, very serious cases excepted, tend to refrain from severe sentences?

In what is known as the "Chicago Crackdown" on drunk driving, judges in that city agreed to impose a seven-day jail sentence on all persons deemed guilty of the offence, but in a period of six months, only 6% of over 6,000 drivers arrested for driving under the influence had actually received such a sentence. In New York State it was found that about 27% of all individuals arrested for violations including driving under the influence were never prosecuted.

It would seem that a law cannot be enforced if its strictness exceeds popular opinion about the immorality or deviancy of the act concerned. The approach that takes the form of punishing people for specific unsafe acts suffers from several other problems as well, some of which have been identified in the context of organizational psychology.

First, there is the self-fulfilling effect of attribution: labelling people with undesirable characteristics, and expecting that they will show them unless kept in check by the threat of punishment, may cause individuals to behave as if they had these characteristics. To illustrate this by its classic example: suppose you pretend that a perfectly solvent bank is about to go bankrupt (your attribution), and that you spread that rumour. The rumour you spread may cause depositors to withdraw their funds, with the end effect that the bank develops solvency problems and ends up by going bankrupt. Similarly, the very imposition of a speed limit may provoke some people to drive faster than they otherwise would. It is well known that some drivers find pleasure in activating the electronic devices installed along highways that tell the speeding driver: "You are going too fast".

Second, the emphasis is on "process controls", or specific behaviours (such as using a piece of safety equipment or obeying the speed limit), instead of focusing on the outcome of safety. Process controls are cumbersome to design and implement. Prohibitive process controls do not clearly communicate what course of action should be taken instead. Research on traffic signs has clearly indicated that prohibitive signs such as "no left turn" have less of a guiding effect upon drivers' decision making than signs that tell them what turns *are* allowed, i.e., permissive signs. In passing, we may note that, although they are not more conducive to safety, the near-universal use of prohibitive signs may be due to the fact that they make it easier to establish blame when they are not heeded.

Moreover, process controls cannot effectively cover all undesirable specific behaviours in any situation. Roadside observation of driving speeds on an urban expressway in Montréal, for example, has shown that the ratio of incidences of drivers speeding by at least 10 km/hr over the posted limit relative to the number of charges laid for speeding was in the order of 7,000-to-one. Similar and even higher ratios have been found elsewhere. And, in Canada, it has been estimated that about 25,000 km of driving with blood alcohol levels over the legal limit are accumulated for every charge that is laid for this offence. During the same time period in which this study was done, the impaired kilometrage per charge was about 136,000 kms in the Netherlands and 150,000 kms in France.

Punishment brings negative side effects; one of these is a dysfunctional social climate, a climate of resentment, uncooperativeness, antagonism, sabotage. As a result, the very behaviour that was to be prevented may in fact be stimulated. Punishment may increase the inclination to beat the system. It has been estimated that between 40% and 70% of drivers whose licences have been suspended or revoked continue to drive. American, Dutch and Swedish studies found that the longer the period of disqualification, the more likely that the driver will continue to drive without a licence.

A Swedish investigator compared drivers who had obtained a relatively severe sentence for driving while under the influence, with another group who had received relatively light punishment. The heavily punished drivers were found to be *more* likely to repeat the offence! This is not so surprising if one realizes that the likelihood of being caught for the offence is very small. The ones unlucky enough to get caught know that, too, and feel unfairly treated by a system of arbitrariness. Their resentment may be further fed by factors such as long time delays between the traffic incident and the announcement of suspension. Thus, they become even more antagonistic towards authority and the law of the land. These hostile feelings may not only overshadow any feelings of guilt and shame, but create a state of mind that is incompatible with effective re-education and rehabilitation. Some convicted Swedish drivers went as far as complaining that the state had committed a crime against their person.

EXTENDING INCENTIVES FOR

In contrast, incentive programmes for safety have both the effect for which they are intended—greater safety—and usually the positive side effect of creating a more favourable social climate.

In the mid-1970s an innovative and relatively large-scale experiment was conducted in California. The Division of Highways in that state contacted 9,971 drivers who had caused collisions or committed violations in the previous year and, thus, had incurred recent demerit points. These drivers were informed by letter that they would receive a free 12-month extension to their driver's licence on the condition that they achieve a clean record during the coming year. Apart from the financial incentive, amounting to a few dollars per year, this offer also implied deferral of the obligation to submit oneself again to the written part of the driver's examination, which, in California, is administered repeatedly throughout a driver's career.

A control sample of another 9,976 drivers was not approached in this manner, but they too were followed up, along with the experimental group, over a period of several years. The findings include the following: In the first follow-up year, there were significantly fewer accident-involved drivers in the experimental group, particularly among the younger drivers and among those drivers whose licence renewal was to come up within one year after receipt of the letter. In this latter group, the accident rate was 22% lower than in the appropriate controls. The drivers who actually earned the bonus after one year showed 33% fewer accidents in the second follow-up year than did the controls.

More recently, a report was published about a long-lived incentive project in Germany that has not, as yet, received the amount of attention that it deserves from the road safety community. Professional drivers employed by the German branch of Kraft Foods Corporation, with a fleet of about 600 trucks and vans, were told in 1957 that they would receive a bonus of 350 Deutschmark for every half year of driving without culpable accidents, that is, without accidents in which they were judged to be at fault.

In the first year after the initiation of this incentive scheme, the frequency of culpable accidents per 100,000 km driven fell abruptly by about one-third, and subsequently continued to drop more smoothly; in 1981, the accident rate per km amounted to about 14% of what it had been in 1956, prior to the programme. The rate of all accidents, culpable or not, fell to 25% of what it had been in 1956. The direct financial accident costs per km driven showed a steeper decline than the accident frequency per km driven. This indicates that the incentive programme was particularly effective in reducing the occurrence of more serious accidents. The total implementation costs of the programme were estimated at some $ 35,000 U.S. per annum, but these costs are reported to be far outweighed by the reduction in insurance fees resulting from the much-improved safety record. This programme has been in force for over three decades without showing signs of waning effectiveness. An American team-based incentive programme addressed at transit bus operators yielded a 25-35% reduction in accident rates as compared to randomly selected controls within the same company. The ratio between programme costs and benefits was estimated at almost seven-to-one. After the programme was withdrawn, the safety records of the incentive group dropped to a level that was still better than that of the no-treatment employees, but no longer significantly so.

The effectiveness of incentives programmes in enhancing safety has been very clearly established. In a recent review of over 120 published evaluations of different types of occupational accident prevention, incentives were generally found to be more effective in enhancing safety than were engineering improvements, personnel selection and other types of intervention (including disciplinary action, special licensing, and exercise and stress reduction programmes). Reductions in accidents per person-hour of between 50% and 80% of the base rate are not uncommon in manufacturing, construction and other industries.

The degree of cost-effectiveness of any accident countermeasure is naturally of great interest to those who are responsible for such programmes. These are often expressed as benefit/cost ratios: the amount of money saved through the programme divided by the money needed to run it. This can be calculated and constitutes a benefit over and above the reduction in human pain and suffering, which are more difficult to quantify in monetary terms. The ratios are usually greater than two-to-one, while any ratio greater than one means that the company is making money on the accident prevention effort. The economic attractiveness of incentive plans is largely due to discounts in fees payable to workers' compensation boards and other insurance; companies with favourable safety ratings pay lower insurance premiums.

These favourable effects continue to last over time. Incentive plans in two American mines were studied over periods of 11 and 12 years, respectively. In one mine the number of days lost due to accidents was reduced to about 11% of baseline, and in the other to about 2%. From year to year, benefit/cost ratios varied between 18 and 28 at one mine and between 13 and 21 at the other. There was no sign that the effectiveness of the incentive plans diminished over time at either mine. A benefit/cost ratio as high as about 23-to-one has been observed for incentives for safety in the resort hotel business.

Incentive programmes generally meet with approval from the people to whom they are addressed, and in this respect they compare favourably with the much less popular action of the law and of the police. To put it popularly: a small carrot is not only much better liked than a big stick, it is also much more effective. Only one negative side effect that has been noticed so far, and that is the tendency of people to under-report accidents when incentive programmes are in effect. Fortunately, however, in a review of some 25 published reports on incentive programmes, such under-reporting has been found to occur with respect to minor accidents only.

Disincentives

A well-controlled field trial, in which the expected cost of being at fault in an accident was increased, resulted in a marked reduction in the accident rate of the driver population involved. Military personnel at a U.S. air force base in Texas were informed that their ranks were in jeopardy, and that they even ran the risk of dishonourable discharge from the service, if they were found to be at fault in an accident. Referral to a psychiatrist was another unpleasant possible consequence. These measures were put into effect for one year and the results were compared with the accident rate before the measures were instituted, as well as with the accident rates of military personnel at other bases without the programme and with general trends. The authors concluded that the number of accidents of personnel at the experimental base diminished by 50%, the total frequency of personal injuries by 54% and of personal injury to the driver by 60%.

Merely engaging in the risky act of driving was economically discouraged in another case. As a consequence of the elimination of Connecticut state subsidies for driver education in high schools, nine school boards decided to drop the courses from the curriculum, while others continued to offer them. Obtaining a driver's licence thus became more expensive. Subsequently, the total number of licensed years of 16-and 17-year-olds diminished by 18% in the communities that eliminated high-school driver education, as compared with 7% in communities where this education was retained. The former communities showed a 27% decrease in the traffic accident rate of 16-and 17-year-olds, in comparison with 7% in the other communities. These figures may be calculated from graphs in a report on the Connecticut experience. In passing, you may notice that the reduction in crash rate was considerably greater than the reduction in the number of young drivers who obtained high-school driver education. Once again, one wonders if this type of "education" lulls its graduates into an illusion of safety and thus leads them to behave more dangerously.

REQUIREMENTS FOR EFFECTIVE INCENTIVE PROGRAMMING

The recorded experience with incentive programmes shows that some programmes have had much greater effect than others. For instance, the German incentive plan, which promised professional truck and van drivers a financial bonus for each half-year of driving without being at fault in an accident, reduced direct accident cost to less than one-third in the first year of application, and remained at that level for over three decades. In the California "good driver" experiment, in which drivers in the general population were offered free extension of their driver's licence by one year in return for each year of accident-free driving, the accident rate dropped by 22% in the first year of the programme.

It may be of interest to note that the reduction in accidents was greatest for drivers under 25 years of age. Reductions in accident rates to between 2% and 11% of the pre-incentive base rates were seen in the two American mines. Thus, the question arises as to what are the distinctive features of the more successful incentive schemes.

An effort has been made to cull the ingredients of the most effective incentive plans from the various published reports. This has, by necessity, been an effort largely based on inference, because to date there are no well-controlled experiments in which one particular incentive characteristic is being varied and all other factors are kept constant. For obvious reasons, such experiments are not likely to be forthcoming either; industry is not in the business of running such experiments. Yet, the items that appear in the checklist below would seem to make very good sense.

Managerial Vigour. The introduction and long-term maintenance of incentive programmes should be conducted with managerial vigour, commitment and coherence. Workers or drivers should not only be informed of the programme in existence, but they should also frequently be reminded of it in attention-catching ways. In order to motivate and to inform the relevant audience, those in charge of incentive programmes should provide clear and frequent knowledge of results to the audience.

Rewarding the Bottom Line. Incentive programs should reward the outcome variable (the fact of not having caused an accident), not some process variable like wearing the seatbelt, driving when sober, obeying the speed limit. This is because rewarding specific behaviours does not necessarily strengthen motivation towards safety, and a potential safety benefit due to an increased frequency of one specific form of "safe" behaviour may simply be offset by road users less frequently displaying other forms of "safe" acting. "The risk is there that while the rewarded behavior may improve, other related safe behaviors may deteriorate."

Attractiveness of the Reward. Incentive programmes can be expected to be the more successful the more they widen the utility difference between the perceived benefit of not having an accident and the perceived disadvantage of having an accident. Rewards for accident-free operation in industry have taken many different forms, ranging from cash to public commendation. They include trading stamps, lottery tickets, gift certificates, shares of company stock, extra holidays and other privileges. While the flexible uses of money prevents satiation from occurring, merchandise, especially customized merchandise, may have the advantage of constituting a lasting reminder of the value of safety. Merchandise items also have a value-added component in the sense that they can be obtained at a lower price than the recipients would likely have to pay if they bought the items at retail. Not surprisingly, in the United States a substantial industry has sprung up to provide companies with merchandise for safety prizes. Gift certificates hold a middle ground between cash and merchandise; they can be put to flexible use and yet be personalized and imprinted with a commemorative message. As noted above, drivers have also been rewarded with cash, free licence renewal, and automobile insurance rebates.

Awards do not have to be very large to be effective. In fact, a case can be made for relatively small awards being preferable. Small awards make it possible to hand out awards more frequently, they are probably less conducive to under-reporting of accidents, and they may foster the internalization of pro-safety attitudes through the process of cognitive dissonance reduction. When a small reward changes a person's behaviour, that person may justify that change by reasoning that the change was for safety's sake rather than due to the insignificant inducement. No such internalization of pro-safety attitudes is necessary when the external inducement is large, because in that case, it fully justifies the behaviour change.

It should be noted, however, that the attitude-shaping effect of modest awards can only take place *after* the operators have changed their behaviour for some minor external inducement. So, the award should be big enough to achieve some behaviour change to begin with. In some cases, a small material reward might imply a major social reward because of its symbolic function. Safe behaviour may thus become "the right thing to do". This might help explain why a modest incentive such as free licence renewal for one year produced a major reduction in the accident rate of California drivers.

Moreover, earlier studies that found that wage increments for dangerous work were exponentially related to increases in the accident rate (to the third power), suggest that small increments in wages as a reward for not having an accident should reduce the accident rate by a comparatively large amount. This is exactly what seems to have been the case in the German company mentioned above.

Progressive Safety Credits. The amount of the incentive should continue to grow progressively as the individual operator accumulates a larger number of uninterrupted accident-free periods. It is more difficult to achieve 10 consecutive accident-free years than to simply accumulate 10 years that were accident-free. Proper motivational stimulation demands that the bonus for 10 uninterrupted years of accident-free driving should be greater than 10 times the bonus for one year of accident-free driving.

Simple Rules. The operational rules of the programme should be kept simple so that they are easily understood by all persons to whom the programme applies.

Perceived Equity. The incentive programme should be perceived as equitable by those to whom it is addressed. The bonus should be such that it is viewed as a just reward for not causing an accident in a given time period. Similarly, incentive systems should be designed in such a way that those workers who are not eligible for an award do not resent this, and those rewarded will be seen by others as justly receiving the award. Since chance plays a part in whether any behaviour is followed by an accident, the actual receipt of the award may be made to depend upon the additional requirement that the accident-free worker in question also maintains cleanliness and safety in his or her workstation. In the event that disincentives are used as well, it is necessary that the public view the imposed penalty as justified.

Perceived Attainability. Programmes should be designed in such a way that the bonus is viewed as attainable. This is of particular importance if the bonus is awarded in a lottery system. Lotteries make it possible to hand out greater awards, and this may enhance the attention-getting appeal of an incentive programme. But fewer of the people who have accumulated the safety credit will receive the bonus, and this may discourage some people from making an active attempt to accumulate the safety credit to begin with.

Short Incubation Period. The specified time period in which the individual has to remain accident-free in order to be eligible for the bonus should be relatively short. Delayed rewards and penalties tend to be discounted, and are thus less effective in shaping behaviour than more immediate consequences. Periods as short as one month have been used in industry. In the cited California experiment, those drivers whose licences were coming up for renewal within one year after being informed of the incentive programme showed a greater reduction in accident rate than did people whose licences were not to be renewed until two or three years later.

Rewarding Group as well as Individual Performance. Incentive programmes should be designed in such a way that they strengthen peer pressure towards the objective of having no accident. Thus, the plan should not only stimulate individual operators' concern for their own safety, but also motivate them to influence peers, so that their accident likelihood is also reduced. In industrial settings this is achieved by offering a bonus for accident-free performance to the work team as well as to the individual. The team bonus has been found to increase competitive motivation towards winning the team award. A dual bonus plan—individual *and* team—for drivers in the same age bracket and living in the same city has been suggested and is known as the "Saskatchewan plan". Social pressure towards safe conduct can also be enhanced by informing families about the safety award programme, its safety goals, and potential rewards. Team awards add a material incentive to act as "one's brother's keeper", and they have also been found effective in isolation, that is, in the absence of awards for individual performance.

Operator Participation in Programme Design. Any incentive scheme should be developed in cooperation and consultation with those people to whom it will be applied. People are more likely to achieve goals they themselves have helped define. An "incentive" can be an incentive only to the extent it is considered to be an incentive by the audience to whom it is addressed. A programme that fails to have the endorsement of the target audience may be resented and lead to unwanted consequences similar to those observed when unsafe acts are being punished.

Prevention of Accident Under-reporting. Thought should be given to the question of how to counteract operators' tendency not to report their accidents. The stimulation of such tendencies seems to be the only, currently identified, negative side effect of incentive programmes, although, occasionally, moral objections have been raised against rewarding people for obtaining a goal they should aspire to on their own, without being "bribed into safety". Some incentive programmes have clauses providing for deduction of safety credits if accidents are not reported. Fortunately, only minor accidents tend to go unreported, but the greater the safety bonus, the more frequent this phenomenon (as well as hit-and-run accidents) may become.

Reward all Levels of the Organization. Supervisors and middle management, as well as shop-floor workers, should be rewarded for safe performance. This creates a more cohesive and pervasive safety orientation within a company.

Whether or not to Supplement Rewards with Safety Training. Although educating towards safety is different from motivating towards safety, and a person's ability to be safe should be clearly distinguished from that person's willingness to be safe, some authors in the field of incentives in industrial settings feel that it may be helpful to safety if workers are told what specific behaviours will help avoid accidents.

Maximizing net Savings versus Maximizing Benefit/cost. In the planning of an incentive programme, thought should be given to the question of what actually constitutes its primary goal: the greatest possible cost-effective accident reduction or a maximal benefit/cost ratio. Some programmes may reduce the accident frequency only slightly, but achieve this at a very low cost. The benefit/cost ratio may thus be higher than is true for another programme where the ratio between benefits and costs is lower, but the capability to reduce accident rates is much greater. As distinct from the issue of the size of the benefit/cost ratio, the total amount of money saved may well be much greater in the latter case.

Consider the following example. Safety programme *A* can save $700,000 at an implementation cost of $200,000. Programme *B* can save $900,000 at a cost of $300,000. In terms of benefit/cost, *A*'s ratio is 3.5, while *B*'s ratio equals 3.0. Thus, against the benefit/cost criterion, *A* is superior, but if net savings are considered, the picture is different. While programme *A* saves $700,000 minus $200,000, or $500,000, programme *B* saves $900,000 minus $300,000, or $600,000. In terms of net savings, programme *B* is to be preferred.

Research Component. Like any other accident countermeasure, an incentive plan should not be introduced without prior research into its short-term and long-term feasibility and its best possible form. Nor should it be introduced without provision for scientifically adequate evaluation of its implementation costs and its observed effectiveness in reducing the accident rate. The knowledge base of the safety research and application community is unlikely to grow without proper evaluation and ready access to publications. Without such research, the surprising effect of one particular reward programme would never have come to light. There seems little chance for safety incentives to have a negative effect, but one variation of a series of California reward/incentive programmes for the general driving public produced *worse* driving records. In this programme, a benefit was given to drivers with no accidents on their records, without their prior knowledge of that benefit. It took the form of an unexpected reward rather than an incentive, and this highlights the importance of the distinction between incentive and reward for effective motivational safety programming. The term "incentive" refers to a pre-announced gratification or bonus extended to workers or drivers on the specific condition that they do not have an accident that is their own fault within a specified time period.

COMPARING WORKERS WITH DRIVERS

Although incentives for accident-free performance have been shown to be effective in making industrial workers safer, as well as drivers in the general population, there are differences between these two types of operation that have implications for programme design and application. For one thing, workers usually operate in relatively small teams of people who know each other. Drivers in the general population operate in a situation of near-anonymity. Workers in industry occupy positions within a clear line of command, while there is no formal hierarchy amongst drivers beyond the content of the highway code. Thus, it is more difficult, though not impossible, to design an incentive system that enhances peer pressure towards safe conduct on the road. In industry it is relatively easy to keep the incubation period of the award quite short, for instance, as short as a month, like the pay cheque; for drivers in the general population, this would be unmanageable for administrative reasons. More importantly, perhaps, it is obviously advantageous to companies to institute incentive systems, because the savings (including discounts in insurance fees) are usually very much greater than the implementation costs. The most attractive incentives to drivers in the general population are likely to be those that could, in principle, be offered by automobile insurance companies, and that might take the form of tangible discounts or rebates for claim-free driving.

On the other hand, the very fact that one can purchase insurance against certain hazards diminishes the threat of the consequences of these hazards. Insurance, therefore, may be expected to increase people's willingness to expose themselves to these hazards, with an increase in the number of casualties as a consequence. Similarly, it is not surprising that increases in workers' compensation payments for injuries may increase the rate of workplace accidents.

WHAT A GOVERNMENT CAN DO?

Suppose a government wishes to develop an incentive programme. What potential incentives does it have available? In industry many different incentives have been used: merchandise; tokens (coupons, stamps) that can be saved up by the recipients and then exchanged for merchandise; cash awards; extra holidays or other privileges and symbols of social recognition.

It is obvious that not all of these would be relevant. Moreover, since cultures, social climates, nations and their governments differ, some incentives may be more useful in one case than another. For one thing, it would make a great deal of difference whether the government in question rules over a jurisdiction where automobile insurance is placed under public or under private control. At this point we will assume that it is in private hands.

Following the California example mentioned above, a government might offer a one-year free driver's licence extension for each year drivers are accident-free. In addition, and as a disincentive, the validity of a driver's licence might be shortened by one year as a penalty for each year in which the driver had one or more culpable accidents. Another way of using driver's licence renewal as a source of incentives/ disincentives could consist of discounts and surcharges in the renewal fee.

Following the Connecticut example, a government might abolish any existing subsidies for the provision of driver training. Such subsidies effectively stimulate driving. When they are discontinued, fewer young people obtain a driver's licence and expose themselves to the risk of an accident while driving a car. This, naturally, would be a one-time intervention, rather than an ongoing one.

Another opportunity for incentives is offered by reducing the charge for the annual validation sticker of vehicle permits (the annual road tax). This incentive could be based on the "culpable accident experience of the vehicle", that is, regardless of the identity of the driver(s) of the vehicle, but depending upon whether the driver was at fault. The incentive would be extended to the owner. Surcharges in annual permit fees might be used as an analogous disincentive.

Discounts and surcharges on income taxes paid by holders of driver's licences might be considered, and this would be justified if a government's expenditures for medical treatment of people injured in accidents exceeds revenue from contributions to medical insurance. Similarly, discounts and/or surcharges related to drivers' culpable accident experience might be applied to their medical insurance fees.

Finally, a government might attempt to exert pressure on private automobile insurance companies to install incentive and disincentive schemes of their own. Other companies, like the ones that sell gasoline and tires, might be requested to provide free merchandise or discounts to drivers who are accident-free over a specified period of time. The companies in question might well find this an appealing proposition in their attempt to attract loyal and creditable customers.

Obviously, some of these bonus and penalty systems would be more cumbersome to implement and administer than others. Part of the administrative difficulty arises from the need for verification of driver and vehicle record accuracy and recency.

We will refrain from elaborating here on the procedural details of the above suggestions, for two reasons. First, each of the suggestions offered is in need of an in-depth feasibility study by officials in administrative domains, and in countries in which the present author cannot claim to have expertise. Secondly, although there is reason to believe that the potential accident-reducing effect of the above suggestions is sizable enough to warrant serious consideration, this effect is likely to be relatively modest in comparison with what may be achieved in terms of accident prevention through discounts and surcharges in automobile insurance.

THE ROLE OF AUTOMOBILE INSURANCE

What *can* insurance companies do to improve traffic safety? The ability to widen a driver's utility gap between having or not having an accident, and thus to lower the target level of risk, would seem considerably greater for automobile insurance companies than is true for any other social agency. This is simply due to the fact that automobile insurance fees in most jurisdictions are much larger than the annual cost of a driver's licence or a vehicle permit, so insurance fees offer much more room for differential incentives and disincentives. Consequently, insurance fee discounts and surcharges, with the inclusion of deductibles, are the best available source for incentives and disincentives.

But what are insurance companies *likely* to do? This is a highly interesting question for a number of reasons, and the striking diversity in points of view is just one of them. Consider, for instance, the following quotations:

> *"...it is obviously of great interest for the insurance companies [...] to reduce the number of traffic accidents and consequently their cost."*

> *"...insurance...is essentially neutral and indifferent with regard to the occurrence of the events that society defines as accidents... Hence, one can rightfully ask if the very mention of 'preventive action by insurance' is not stupid, though well-intentioned".*

In a similar vein, an insurance commentator writing in Lloyd's List while commenting on inventors and their safety gadgetry:

> *"All it needs is the insurance industry to require such equipment to be mandatory, suggest these hopeful people—once again falling into the age-old trap of assuming that the purpose of insurance is in some way to increase safety, or alter human nature, or dramatically to affect statistics. It is an argument which apparently has right and justice on its side, until the truth dawns that insurers are not philanthropists or safety agencies, but merely takers of commercial risks—nothing more, nothing less. Consider the conflict of sentiment which would flash through an underwriter's mind if a wild-eyed inventor burst into his office, waving plans for some equipment that would make ships virtually unsinkable".*

According to the first view, the insurance industry has a positive interest in accident reduction. The second holds the view that the insurance industry is not interested in this objective and that it is nice but naive to suggest that preventive action be undertaken by the insurance industry. A third view—expressed by the present author—states that the interests of the insurance industry would actually be served if the accident rate remained at a high level.

> *"Substantial reductions in the per-driver accident rate may not be welcomed by the automobile manufacturing, retail, repair and insurance industries, as such reductions would likely decrease the demand for new cars and car parts, as well as people's willingness to pay current insurance fees against a level of risk that would no longer exist. Profits and employment opportunities in these sectors would thus go down."*

> *"This is another way of saying that the higher the accident rate, the greater the insurance industry's opportunity for absolute profit. Apart from a sudden and short-term drop in accidents, the insurance companies cannot rationally be expected to show a positive concern for the reduction of the accident rate."*

The insurance industry is in a peculiar situation. It offers a much-wanted, even compulsory, service in providing protection against the more serious financial consequences of accidents that happen to their customers. On the other hand, the very fact that insurance can be bought against certain hazards diminishes the threat of the consequences of these hazards and, therefore, may be expected to increase people's willingness to expose themselves to these hazards, with an increase in the number of casualties as a consequence. This has also been noticed by several analysts, just as others have reported that increases in workers' compensation payments for injuries may increase the rate of workplace accidents. Phrased in simple terms: to offer people protection against the consequences of risky behaviour encourages risky behaviour; to offer people better protection against the consequences of risky behaviour encourages riskier behaviour still. A Dutch automobile insurance company advertised its services, quite honestly, by showing a picture of a collision of two cars in front of their office, with the slogan:

> *"Our own driving isn't always all that fantastic either. That's why our insurance coverage is so complete."*

Automobile insurance sells peace of mind, which is nice, but it is also a problem for that very reason. Not surprisingly, automobile insurance was, at one time, forbidden by law in some parts of the world. It was seen as encouraging imprudence. In short, "l'assurance pousse au crime"—insurance stimulates crime.

Another example of the nefarious effect of "better protection" upon safety is the institution of no-fault insurance for drivers. No-fault insurance means that drivers who collide with one another are entitled to compensation for the damages incurred, regardless of who was responsible for the collision. Thus, the cost for being responsible for an accident is reduced. A law to this effect came into force in Québec in 1978, along with some other minor regulations. An economist working in that part of the world, and interested in establishing the effect of the law, calculated that accidents with property damage only increased by 11%, accidents with personal injury by 26%, and fatalities by 7%. The economist noted that, while the "centralized compensation system [...] generally increased the speed, frequency, and size of compensations, it also probably led to a condition that would lower the incentive to drive safely", and that "lowered the average quality and motivation to safety of the stock of drivers because of the sudden subsidy given to relatively risky drivers and the suppression of the notion of fault for all drivers".

So, the very existence of automobile insurance, as well as its specific operational rules, may have the effect of increasing the size of the problem it sells protection against. The opportunity for profit to the insurance industry also increases in this process.

Therefore, for the sake of safety, it is desirable that insurance practices are structured in a manner such that risk-taking tendencies of customers are being counteracted. One attempt in this direction is to offer premium discounts to young drivers who have had a particular type of driver training. Another is premium discounts for periods of accident-free driving.

In North America it is not uncommon for insurance companies to offer discounts for newly licensed drivers, provided they have taken a driver education course offered by high schools. There is no evidence whatsoever that such a course has a beneficial effect upon the accident rate of graduates. The fact that, they are, nonetheless, offered an insurance discount, could either be explained by the insurers suffering a mistaken belief in the accident-reducing effectiveness of such courses, or their expectation that the discount will effectively subsidize driving by young people and thus enlarge the market of potential insurees and thus the potential for profit. The marked sensitivity of young people to subsidies that help them obtain a driver's licence and, thus, the ability to drive, has been clearly established. Where such subsidies were eliminated, there was a sharp decline in road accidents among the relevant age groups.

In the province of Ontario, Canada, it is common practice for insurance companies to give fee discounts that are greater as the number of claim-free years increases. But this is only true for up to five years of accident-free driving, as if such discounts would have no accident-reducing effect beyond that period. In passing, we note that Icelandic drivers receive free automobile insurance during the 10th year, if they are claim-free during the preceding nine years. And what may be worse from the point of view of accident prevention in Ontario, is that a driver with five or more fault-free years, who has an accident in which he or she is at fault, is not likely to incur an increase in insurance fees. The reason the insurance companies have this "forgiveness clause" would seem to be that the driver in question is seen as a relatively good risk whose business would be badly missed if it went to the competition. This practice, however, fails to bring the accident rate down to a level as low as it perhaps could have been otherwise. The same may be true for insurance that is offered in some countries, Great Britain, for instance, against losing one's driver's licence as the consequence of some behaviour such as driving while under the influence of alcohol.

One thing that's clear from these considerations is that the optimal accident rate is different for different people. Years ago this was emphasized by an author who, for reasons of social equity, proposed the notion of an "accident tax" to be levied on companies in order to compensate for the fact that only part of accidents costs are carried by the company in question, and the other part by society in general. This accident tax would be expected to stimulate companies to make an additional effort at accident reduction. Because different social factions are interested in different levels of safety, and interested in different means for attaining it, safety is a bone of contention, a political issue. Safety is not as sweet and innocent as motherhood and apple pie. Rather, it is an apple of discord and it would be wise to be cognizant of this fact.

While, as individual persons or as corporate citizens, people in the private insurance industry may have a genuine interest in promoting safety, one cannot expect a business to act against its direct commercial interests. However, it is no less relevant to note that the absence of a strong concern for reducing the accident rate may also be reflected by many of the countermeasures taken by those governments that have no direct financial or political stake in actual accident reduction. This is because politicians may be tempted, for public relations reasons, to take measures whose main or exclusive merit consists of showing the electorate that something is being done about the safety problem. Surely, political expedience demands that safety is seen to be promoted; whether it actually *is* promoted is another matter.

Unfortunately, when the recent history of road safety management in various countries or smaller jurisdictions is compared with other government concerns such as health care, it will be obvious that many governments have failed to develop coherent and vigorous strategies for traffic accident prevention. In part, this may be due to the fact that responsibility for safety is usually divided across various ministries, such as health, education, justice, transportation and internal affairs. This very division of responsibility may reflect lack of governmental concern for the issue.

In this context it should be noted that general public pressure for greater safety is also lacking. Apart from occasional outcries by some citizen groups in some jurisdictions against the omnipresent infestation of automobiles, against the safety threat posed by heavy trucks or by the young or drunk drivers, there seems to be no strong and persistent demand for greater safety throughout the general population.

If, in fact, such a demand existed, people would not wait for government action, but simply resort to their own capabilities to reduce the accident rate by voluntarily changing their amount and manner of road use. In other words, people in any jurisdiction have the accident rate they are collectively willing to accept, in return for the amount and manner of mobility they enjoy. Unless the desire for safety is somehow stimulated, people will exert only a little pressure on their government to reduce the accident rate, and in turn, the government is not likely to develop the political will that is necessary to take more than symbolic measures towards accident reduction. It would seem fair to conclude that there is little ongoing governmental, corporate or public interest in reducing the traffic accident rate. Whether this is irrational or not is another matter. So far in this book, we have made the tacit assumption that the accident rate should be reduced, but against the criterion of *net* social benefit maximization, this may not be so. Even if it were true that reduced speed limits save lives on the road, the increased travel time may produce greater costs to society than the benefits in casualties saved.

We will return to this issue in the next chapter, but it's worth noting that enforcement of speed limits may merely have the effect of "accident migration". A German study reports a 21% reduction on an expressway following the introduction of a speed limit where no limit had existed. A stretch of expressway running parallel to the one with the new speed limit experienced a 29% increase in accidents, apparently as the result of the fact that drivers who did not want to forgo speedy progress simply took an alternative route.

In order to break this vicious circle (vicious from the safety promotion point of view) between people's complacency and a lack of political will on the part of their elected representatives to reduce the accident rate, what can a government do?

Suppose we are dealing with a government that is fully aware of the tremendous costs of traffic accidents to its jurisdiction. Suppose, too, that we are dealing with a government that wishes to play a leadership role in reducing the traffic accident rate per head of population, rather than to remain a mere follower of existing public attitude and conduct. In that case, the answer to what a government could do in order to reduce the traffic accident rate is very simple: (a) assume public responsibility for automobile insurance, and (b) impose insurance fees that take account of each individual driver's past accident record and of the requirements for effective incentive programming described above. In doing so, a government would be able to achieve two things: it would pull itself up by its own bootstraps in becoming more concerned about safety promotion than before, and it would enhance the general public's desire for safety and strengthen public support for government action toward that goal.

In addition, there is reason to expect that a government's commitment to road safety promotion will increase with time if it assumes responsibility for accident insurance. When claim costs rise from year to year as a consequence of continued inflation, there would seem to be three options for a government to cope with this:

- Impose higher insurance fees upon the electorate.
- Absorb the increased costs through other revenues, including taxes.
- Attempt to reduce the accident rate.

Since the first two alternatives are unlikely to be attractive to a government that wishes to stay in power, it will be more inclined to develop a stronger thrust in the pursuit of accident reduction.

RECAPITULATION

The argument developed in this chapter may be summarized as follows. Of all accident countermeasures that are currently available, those that affect people's motivation towards safety seem to be the most promising. Of all countermeasures that affect people's motivation towards safety, those that reward people for accident-free performance seem to be the most promising. Of all possible incentive schemes that reward people for accident-free performance, some promise to be more effective than others because they contain the elements that appear to enhance motivation towards safety.

Of the two major social establishments that can offer incentives—governments and automobile insurance--automobile insurance institutions would seem to be able to offer the most effective ones. Automobile insurance companies, however, when run by private enterprise, cannot be expected to implement incentive programmes with vigour and persistence, because a very low accident rate in the jurisdiction in which they operate is not in their business interest.

Governments, on the other hand, often are more interested in being seen by the citizenry to be doing something about the road safety problem, rather than actually doing something about it, while citizens seem to accept the road accident toll in return for the benefit of the amount and style of road use they enjoy. Citizens, however, can be made more interested in displaying self-protective behaviour if they are better rewarded for safety. Then they will put greater pressure on governments to pursue the goal of safety more vigorously.

Ergo, the merits of public, as opposed to private, ownership of automobile insurance deserve to be seriously debated.

Besides having the possible negative side-effect of accident under-reporting, incentives also have *positive* side effects. For one thing, they are a money-making proposition in industry: savings in terms of accident reduction usually exceed by far the costs of implementing a programme of this kind. For another, they lead to better company morale. As is true for successful productivity gainsharing programmes, safety incentive programmes can help improve the general organizational climate and, therefore, make a positive contribution to productivity over and above the gain due to accident reduction. Safety incentives give workers a common cause with each other as well as with management. Reinforcing safe acts "removes the unwanted side effects with discipline and the use of penalties; it increases employees' job satisfaction; it enhances the relationship between supervisors and employees...." Is it unreasonable to expect that incentives for safety and health, applied to the general population, would not only promote safety and health, but also have the favourable side effect of improving the general social climate including people's respect for the authorities and the law of the land?

A leading literature review contains the following statement: "The major finding was that every study, without exception, concluded that incentives or feedback enhanced safety, and/or reduced accidents in the work place, at least in the short term. Few literature reviews find such consistent results." So, if incentive programmes are found to be the most powerful tools for safety on the job and on the road, why are they not implemented much more frequently than is presently the case? One factor may be plain ignorance of their very existence, or lack of knowledge as to how they are best implemented. Another factor may be the fear that accident under-reporting will be the result. While there is some justification for this, it is also valid to say that, in industry, it may be possible to conceal a minor injury, but one cannot hide a corpse. There may be resistance because of the attitudes of unions, of management or, more generally, because of company climate.

Particular incentives that appeal to operators in one cultural context may be viewed as mere "hoopla" in another. In addition to ignorance and opposition, there may be indifference to the notion of accident reduction because it would have little consequence for the company concerned. This may be the case if the company has proper insurance against accident consequences and if the insurance premium to be paid does not depend upon the safety record of the company in question. An official in one such company told me that there was more interest in having a good estimate of *how many* accidents were likely to happen in the future, rather than in having *fewer* accidents, because having that estimate would help in planning for equipment and personnel that would have to be replaced.

FURTHER PERSPECTIVES

The preceding chapter contains ample evidence to show that the accident rate per person-hour, at work or on the road, can be greatly and durably reduced. This can be achieved by interventions that are specifically aimed at bringing down the level of risk people are willing to accept. The evidence supports the main tenet of this book—that the temporal accident rate depends on the level of risk of death, disease and damage that people accept in return for the expected benefits of risk taking. When the benefits of risk taking are reduced and the advantages of cautious action are enhanced, people will be *motivated* to take less risk. They will react accordingly and consequently society's accident losses will be reduced.

It also seems fair to conclude that major reductions in the traffic accident loss per person-hour or person-year, and thus per head of population, have *not* been achieved by interventions in the form of training, engineering or enforcement. This has been clearly documented in other chapters, notably Chapters 5 through 8. Although some of the interventions of this kind may have been capable of reducing the traffic accident rate per unit distance driven, or the number of accidents at a particular location, these interventions do not seem able to achieve a reduction in the accident rate per time-unit of participation in traffic, or per person-year in the population. Such measures may be useful in allowing people to drive more accident-free kilometres per hour of road use and per year of life, but they fail to add years to their lives. This failure, too, can be understood as being a consequence of the mechanisms postulated by Risk Homeostasis Theory.

The theory says that a nation's accident rate per head of population is the outcome of a closed-loop control process. In this process, fluctuations in the accident rate determine fluctuations in the degree of caution people subsequently apply in their behaviour. And fluctuations in the degree of caution are the cause of the ups and downs in the nation's per capita accident rate. We have also seen that potentially occurring fluctuations in the accident rate are greatly reduced by people's ability to anticipate the potential consequences of health and safety interventions of the technological—read "non-motivating"—kind. Feedback, together with anticipation, leads to adaptive behaviour which has a stabilizing (not a reducing) effect on accident risk. The homeostatic nature of the "accident-production" process implies that a jurisdiction's ability to reduce the accident rate per head of population depends upon that jurisdiction's ability to reduce the amount of risk people choose, accept, prefer, tolerate—their target level of risk, in short.

3

Effective Treatment of the Problem

As we have seen from the previous chapter, incentives for safe performance are able to reduce the accident rate per person-hour of participation in the risky activity. Effective treatment of the problem is directed at its cause, not at its symptoms, while treatment of symptoms provokes symptom substitution. It is not difficult to conceive of effective measures for safety and health insofar as these are dependent on human behaviour, once we have liberated our reasoning from the tyranny of the delta fallacy. By obstructing the channels, one cannot prevent the water that flows through a river delta from reaching the ocean. The solution has to be found upstream. One cannot reduce the accident rate and the lifestyle-dependent damage to health by piecemeal measures that fail to affect the superordinate cause.

Sometimes the delta fallacy is obvious and displayed in simple terms, for instance, in the belief that clearer edge-markings will reduce the highway accident rate in a population. At other times, the fallacy is shrouded in a more complicated argument that has at least the appearance of sophistication.

As an example, consider the type of reasoning that has been put forward to demonstrate the life-saving benefit of seatbelt legislation. Accident analysis in the USA has shown that, in years prior to mandatory seatbelt use, about half as many front-seat passenger-vehicle occupants, who had their seatbelts buckled, were killed in their collisions as compared with front-seat occupants, involved in collisions of similar impact, but who were not wearing their seatbelt. Thus, assume that seatbelts, when worn, are about 50% effective in preventing a fatality. Now compare the numbers of front-seat occupants killed in collisions before and after seatbelt wearing became compulsory. On the basis of the numbers killed who had their seatbelt on, an estimate is made of how many front-seat occupants must have survived their collisions due to using their belts (i.e., about the same number). Finally, show that there has been an increase in seatbelt wearing as a result of the legislation, and the number of people "saved by the seatbelt legislation" can be calculated.

In one study, this type of reasoning led to an estimate of some 7,000 lives saved in the USA during the five-year period between 1983 and 1987. Here, the delta fallacy is reflected in the tacit, but faulty, *assumption* that seatbelt legislation only influences the seatbelt-wearing rate, while no other aspect of driver behaviour is affected. On the basis of *factual* data, it may be further noted that the number of fatally injured seatbelt-wearing front-seat occupants in passenger vehicles increased more than six-fold, from 714 in 1983 to 4,709 in 1987. The percentage of fatally injured front-seat occupants of passenger vehicles relative to all traffic fatalities rose slightly, from 63.7 to 65.1%. In the same period, the total number of traffic deaths per annum rose from 41,609 to 45,406, which is equivalent to an increase of about 9%, or about 2% per year (and about twice as fast as the population growth). Note that the data are presented in the very same US government report that claims that thousands of lives were saved!

So, where is the evidence for the thousands of lives that were supposedly saved by the seatbelt legislation? When we rid ourselves of the delta illusion, what we see instead is an *increase in lives lost*. This increase may be related to the drop in the unemployment rate that occurred in that period. Another possible explanation is that we are dealing here with yet another case of seatbelt legislation leading to an increase in accident frequency. This is what seems to have taken place in various other countries. Evidence has been presented in Section 8.2 which also suggests why this may be so.

The traffic safety issue described above has its analogue in the area of health. In discussions of deaths in relation to unhealthy habits and lifestyles, it is not uncommon to read statements to the effect that, in a given country, so many thousands of people per year die as a consequence of being overweight, or sexually contracted disease, or cigarette smoking. Obviously, if we take an estimate that 10,000 people per year die as the result of smoking-related illness, it cannot logically be inferred that the country would count 10,000 more citizens at the end of the year if these 10,000 people had never smoked.

Although risk homeostasis theory is not only concerned with accidents, but lifestyle-dependent disease and death as well, this book has included rather little evidence for its validity in that area. This is because of a dearth of definitive data. The number of people who die in accidents can be assessed with a relatively high degree of accuracy. It is, however, much more difficult to determine with a similar degree of certainty how many people die prematurely as a result of smoking, sunbathing, consuming too much alcohol, being overweight or underweight, being sexually promiscuous, having too little or too much physical exercise, and so on. There are simply too many other factors at work at the same time, factors of unknown degrees of importance and over which the individual has no direct control. These factors include genetic predisposition, environmental conditions (including pollution as well as threats posed by nature itself), and bacteria and viruses.

EXPECTATIONISM

In connection with incentives for safe performance, it is of interest to note that they may be viewed as *just one example* of a wider class of interventions that hold the promise of reducing much more than the fatal accident rate per capita. They also hold promise for reducing lifestyle-dependent disease and death rates, as well as diminishing the level of violence in society.

Offering a person a reward for not having an accident in the future implies offering that person a reason for looking forward to the future with increased expectations. Therefore, it also amounts to motivating that person to be more careful with life and limb and to take the measures necessary to be alive and well when that future comes.

As an alternative to the traditional "Triple E" (Engineering, Education and Enforcement) ideology for increasing safety—an ideology that we have seen to be rather ineffective in reducing the accident rate per head of population—a "Single E" approach is being suggested for the purpose of reducing the accident rate per head of population: "Expectationism". Expectationism is the name of the preventative strategy for reducing the accident rate and lifestyle-dependent disease and death rate per head of population by enhancing people's perceived value of the future. It comes in two varieties, and these may be called "specific" and "general". A *specific* expectationist strategy demands that a person fulfill a particular requirement at some future point in time, such as not having been at fault in a road accident or not suffering from alcohol-related cirrhosis of the liver, not suffering from smoking-related respiratory disease, or some other specific criterion of health. The "general" variety sets no detailed criteria; all a person has to do to receive the reward is to be alive at that future date at which the incentive has been promised to materialize.

Consider, as a very simple example of general expectationism, a society in which every citizen is promised that upon reaching the age of retirement, a sum of money that equals five or ten times the average annual wage, in addition to current pensions and old-age benefits. It would seem reasonable to expect that this prize would stimulate people to use and develop their survival skills in such a way that more people than presently is the case will reach that age and be fit enough to enjoy the bonus.

The amount of money to be paid out in this example may appear large, but the benefit may well be found to be larger still, if one considers the amount of money that could be saved. The savings would take the form of reduced costs of medical care, physical damage and disability compensation, as well as a reduction in the current economic loss due to forgone wages and a person's contribution to the gross national product. Consider, too, the savings that would accrue to a nation if governments no longer relied on safety legislation, engineering technology, enforcement practices and educational measures of various kinds. These represent large expenditures, but fail to reduce the accident rate per capita to a significant degree, as we have seen from the available evidence.

Additional benefit would come from a reduction in the social cost of *violence*. To be violent is to run a major risk to one's life or health, because of the damage that the perpetrator may incur in attacking another person. So, expectationism also holds the promise of reducing violence, not just accidents and lifestyle-dependent diseases.

With respect to accidents and violence, it is interesting to consider the statistics concerning the "violent death" rate in industrialized nations during the first three quarters of this century. The notion of violent death includes three categories: fatal accidents of all kinds (not just in traffic or in industry), homicide and suicide. Data from 31 different countries around the globe—in Europe, the Americas and around the Pacific—have been collected and may be compared. Such comparisons should be made with care because countries' populations differ from one another in their gender and age-group proportions, and these proportions may change over time within any given country. The greater the proportion of young males to the total population, the higher the violent death rate one might expect, other things being equal. Therefore, in order to insure fairness of comparisons between countries at any point in time and within the same country across different time periods, it is necessary to take account of any variations in the gender and age contingents in the populations. This is achieved by "correcting" the mortality statistics for variations in the gender-by-age distributions, and obtaining what are called *standardized mortality ratios.*

What is remarkable about these standardized mortality ratios due to violence is their pattern from roughly 1900 to 1975 (unfortunately, no comparative tabulations have been published since that time). This pattern shows that, if periods of war are disregarded, the ratios have changed remarkably little—those in the first decade of this century and in 1975 are virtually the same! The violent death rate appears to have been remarkably impervious to the improvements in medicine and the modifications in education, engineering and legislation that have been introduced in that period. Note that the human-made environment over this time period has changed dramatically, almost beyond recognition. We can look at old photographs or motion pictures for evidence of this. And note, in particular, that there were very few automobiles around in the first decade of this century while, in the 1970s, traffic deaths were responsible for about one-half of all accidental deaths.

This general pattern of findings may be surprising at first. This is not because the mortality ratios due to accidents and violence were so high in the beginning of this century, although there were very few automobiles around. According to risk homeostasis theory, the presence or absence of these vehicles has little bearing upon the per capita accident rate anyway. The massive advances made since the early 1900s in the design of roads and vehicles, in education, in safety legislation, in medicine and so forth, should not have made a difference either. According to RHT, such interventions may well influence the specific form of risk taking, but would not be expected to influence its overall level. These measures are not motivational in nature and thus fail to influence the target level of risk. In other words, they fail to enhance the desire for health, safety and a longer life.

Instead, there is the remarkable stability of the standardized violent mortality ratios, a stability which is puzzling indeed. It conflicts not only with a general belief in progress (a belief that may be cherished rather than founded in fact), but, more importantly, with a perception that the value of the future has improved over the first 75 years of this century. Pensions have improved; so has housing and health care for the elderly, the poor and the disabled; and many other forms of social legislation have been introduced in both "leftist" and "rightist" countries. These measures should have given citizens in these countries reason to look forward to the future with greater confidence and expectations, with an increased sense of control over their lives, and with more hope.

There *is* reason to believe that the perceived value of the future has increased. And the puzzle concerning standardized violent mortality ratios may possibly be resolved by considering that another factor has been at work, a factor that favours the taking of accident risk and that has become more prominent during the course of this century. This factor is the perceived value of "present time", time here and now. If present time is highly valued, that is, if every minute counts, people will be likely to speed, to cut corners and take short cuts, to jump lights, to rush to their destination. They will focus on performance and productivity, disregarding safety precautions that would slow them down or otherwise interfere with earning immediate benefit. Higher wages for greater productivity, piecework, generous overtime pay, economic booms, and so on, are all reasons for accepting greater accident risk.

The target level of accident risk in the population would thus be expected to rise with increases in the value of present time. This century has seen major increases in wages, commissions and salaries. Although the perceived value of the future may have increased, so did the perceived value of the present. If both factors increased by the same degree, no change in the violent death rate would be expected.

Therefore, from the point of view of accident prevention and the provision of health (insofar as this is dependent on lifestyle), it may be more fruitful to consider the perceived value of the future *relative* to the perceived value of the present. The greater the former in comparison to the latter, the more cautious a person would be expected to be. A study of Québec motorists that used this conceptualization found that individuals who were characterized by a comparatively high valuation of the future had more favourable attitudes to automobile safety, fewer demerit points, and fewer road accidents. American university students with a stronger future orientation have been found to refrain more often from smoking cigarettes.

These studies support the notion that habits beneficial to health and safety are more common among people who hold the future in high regard. It should also be noted, however, that the measurement procedures left something to be desired, and that the findings do not deliver proof that interventions that increase the value of the future relative to the present really do lead to a longer lifespan. All that is supported by firm evidence is that deliberate enhancement of the value of the future, through the implementation of incentives for accident-free task performance, does, in fact, reduce the accident rate per person.

Interestingly, having greater hope for the future does not only appear to stimulate people to adopt a safer and healthier way of life, but it also seems to increase people's resistance to physical diseases that may or may not be dependent on lifestyle. Numerous studies have already established that people with an optimistic view of the future also have a better-functioning immune system. Moreover, there is experimental evidence to suggest that an intervention that is capable of making people more optimistically-minded, can also improve their immune function. This leads to the striking proposition that hope helps people live longer, not just because it motivates them to make decisions that are conducive to health and safety, but also because it stimulates the effectiveness of their physiology in fending off physical disease!

Thus, it would seem worthwhile to consider what modifications could be made to our society so that citizens would have more reason to look forward to their next birthday, their next decade and their later years, than currently is the case. How can helplessness be reduced and a sense of learned hopefulness be instilled in the minds of the nation? What steps might be undertaken towards the establishment of a "safety culture" or, rather, a "health and safety culture"?

Here are some simple suggestions. For children and teens increase the weekly allowance at every birthday. Reduce tuition fees for college and university students for subsequent years of study. Increase the legal minimum wage for people as they become older. Provide longer annual holidays as employees become older. Make wages and salaries, as well as job security, more dependent on years on the job. Provide greater tax advantages and insurance discounts for people as they grow older. Offer incentives for saving money and retirement plans, so that people are stimulated to contribute to the monetary value of their future. Take measures that reduce people's fear of becoming a burden upon others, or of being neglected, abused or lonely in their sunset years. Offer older people more opportunity to live in their familiar surroundings. Make euthanasia more widely available to those who want it; for many people, its availability diminishes the dread of a dolorous and undignified death, and thus enhances confidence in the future and the desire to live. So, paradoxically, then, life may be lengthened by the prospect of a hastened yet merciful death.

Expectationism is "green". The focus is on saving, not on exploitation. With respect to life, the focus is on caution, not on daring. With respect to finance, the focus is on saving, not on spending. In short, the recurring theme of expectationism is "saving for later". One factor that contributes to the benefit of saving for later is a livable environment: a clean and green ecology and the availability of natural resources. With a sharpened focus on the future, a society is more likely to protect the environment against misuse for short-term profits.

Expectationism, however, not unlike the ideological "isms" in the political arena that range from "radical socialism" to "savage capitalism", may also bring its own problems. For instance, in an expectationist utopia, the older segments in the population will be more numerous, more prosperous, more powerful, and thus more influential. This entails the dangers of a "gerontocracy", a "rule by seniors", with increased conservatism, a stronger desire to maintain the status quo, and a weaker tendency to explore novel approaches to solving social problems. If there exists a genetic propensity towards risk taking, this will become more widespread throughout the population. This is because people with "risk-taking genes" will be more likely to survive to the age of parenthood, and thus more likely have offspring than currently is the case. The proportion of "risk-taking genes" in the human gene pool would increase as a consequence. Thus, society would become increasingly dependent upon expectationist measures for the maintenance of health and safety, just as the health and fitness of more recent generations have become increasingly dependent upon medical know-how and intervention.

EPILOGUE

According to the views presented in this book, the accident rate and the incidence of unhealthy habits essentially depend on people's orientation towards their future. The more they expect from it, the more careful they will be with life and limb. If their expectations are low, they will try to find more immediate gratification of their desires, and do so at a greater risk of jeopardizing their lives. The extent of risk taking with respect to safety and health in a given society, therefore, ultimately depends on values that prevail in that society, and not on the available technology.

As we have argued, values can be altered through change towards a social order that we have called expectationist, because of its emphasis on giving people reason to look forward to the future with a stronger sense of control, with greater confidence and more hope. Bringing about such a social order engenders benefits, but it also involves costs. The desirability of a human condition that favours cautious health and safety habits depends on human values. The willingness to take action towards the creation of such a condition depends further on the perceived effectiveness of the available means toward that end.

This book has been written in an effort to explain why traditional interventions are not effective and why some innovative ones are. Wider realization that the traditional ways do not work may stimulate willingness to innovate. Wider awareness of the effectiveness of alternative approaches to health and safety may increase willingness to debate the merits of limited or even society-wide implementation of expectationist measures against lifestyle-dependent death and disease, as well as against violence and abuse of the environment. Waiting for Godot will draw to a close. Who knows, Godot may come. And if that does not happen, let it be because we, the nation's people, have decided that Godot is not really all that welcome.

4

The Economics of Prisons

This chapter scans the English language research on prisons published since Becker's (1968) seminal paper. After first describing the economic nature of prison and parole, issues concerning comparative institutional analysis and organizational design are discussed, including the role of private prisons. Empirical evidence on production functions for prisons, recidivism and offender rehabilitation programs is reviewed. A brief overview of policy issues and suggestions for future research concludes the survey.

INTRODUCTION

From a public policy perspective, the normative theory of the economics of crime may be interpreted in terms of the following questions: (1) How many resources should be devoted to the criminal justice system? (2) How should thoseresources be allocated between the various branches of the system (police, courts, and so on)? (3) How should each branch allocate its resources amongst competinguses? Conceptually these questions are addressed by simultaneously choosing values of policy control variables to minimize the overall social cost of crime, defined as the (net) direct harm from offenses plus the cost of operating the criminal justice system, subject to the various subsystem production functions and the supply of offenses functions (Becker, 1968). This chapter highlights the third question in the efficiency hierarchy as applied to prisons (correctional institutions), with explicit consideration given to the institutional framework within which the question is posed.

Alternativesexist to the model alluded to in the previous paragraph. Ehrlich (1982) permits goals such as retribution to be reflected in the social cost function, with the degree of retribution related to the number of unpunished offenders and to the severity of their crimes (also see Miceli, 1991). Other economists (notably Shoup, 1964 and Thurow, 1970) emphasize conflicts between efficiency and equity in the provision of protection services. The optimization framework itself is inconsistent with the classical retributive justification of punishment.

Adam Smith ([1791] 1976, pp. 79, 87-91) suggestively remarks that the private demand for punishment is independent of any consideration of social advantage. In contrast to economic models, Kantian inspired retributive ('just desert') models and their cousins (for example, the 'restorative' theory of Cragg, 1992; the Rawlsian-inspired 'rectification' theory of Adler, 1991; the 'restitutive' theory of Barnett, 1977, 1998, Ch. 8, 10, 11) generally argue that punishment can and must be justified independent of the consequences as measured in a social cost function (Duff, 1986, 1996). Economic and retributive models each have difficulty rationalizingcertain policies adopted or at least acknowledged by most modern penal systems: economic prescriptions appear inconsistent with constitutional constraints on cruel and unusual punishments; classical retributive models specify punishments which may be insufficient for deterrence. Constitutional contractarian models applied to punishment can rationalize independent constraints on social cost minimization (Avio, 1993b), and will be implicitly assumed in what follows.

A seemingly natural way to organize this survey is in accordance with the individual purposes of imprisonment: incapacitation, rehabilitation, specific deterrence (the deterrent effect on released offenders of having served an imprisonmentterm), general deterrence and retribution. The problem is that the literature cannot be easily sorted in this way (consider, for example, how the topic of prison privatization might fit within such a framework). The alternative adopted here is to organize the survey in terms of the 'operational' topics treated in the literature, beginning with the economic nature of prisons and parole. Issues concerning comparative institutional analysis and organizational design are then discussed, followed by various empirical topics including production functions for correctional institutions, recidivism (a variouslydefined measure related to the criminal activity of released inmates), offender rehabilitation programs, and labor markets for former prison inmates. An overview of policy issues concludes the survey. Discussion is limited for the most part to research by economists and/or to authors taking a law and economic perspective. The reader is forewarned that general deterrence is not systematically covered here, as this would entail surveying the vast theoretical and empirical literature on offender supply functions, and undertaking that would greatly increase the lenght and scope of this chapter.

PRISONS CONCEPTUALIZED

Prisonsprovide protection services to society. In principle, these services could be replaced or supplemented by a less resource absorbing system of monetary penaltiesand/or corporal punishments, the sanctions of choice throughout most of human history. But constitutional constraints in modern democracies limit corporal punishments, and the wealth constraints of most offenders relative to thesocial value of the harm they create renders sole reliance on fines inefficient.

Moreover, Levitt (1997) notes that the authorities may not even know the wealth level of offenders, and may be unable to distinguish between individuals with different subjective disutilities of prison terms. This latter fact is important because the threat of imprisonment must ultimately lie behind any fine. Since the typical criminal has a relatively low disutility of prison term, 'the fine must be low relative to the jail sentence to be incentive compatible' (ibid., 1997, p. 181). But relatively low fines will induce other types of agents to become offenders. Nevertheless, a case can be made that fines are underutilized in Western societies, although less so in Europe than in the US. Benson (1996) favors a system of fines as restitution for victims.

He argues that the coerced supply of offender labor services may overcome the wealth constraint (at a cost), while the incentive for victims to cooperate in the prosecution of offenders increases the effectiveness of the police and courts. Conversely, convicted offenders may be induced to commit more crimes to pay off their initial fine, and the promise of fines as restitution may lead to overzealous prosecution by victims. For the remainder of this essay, the relative efficiency of incarceration as a criminal sanction is assumed. Modern prisons may be viewed as multi-product firms providing incarceration days and rehabilitation opportunities (Avio, 1973). The threat of incarceration has a putative general deterrent effect on prospective offenders (Lewis, 1986) whereas incarceration prevents inmates from committing crimes against those outside the prison walls. This incapacitation effect may be partly offset by an increased number of 'new' criminals if the returns to crime increase as incarcerated offenders are temporarily removed from the criminal market (Cook, 1977; Ehrlich, 1981). The rehabilitation effect acknowledges that a convicted offender's proclivity for crime may decrease as a result of the incarceration experience, as well as by virtue of the fact that age has an independent effect upon criminality. The school for crime syndrome, criminal stigmatization and the natural depreciation of human capital while offenders areincarcerated all pull in the opposite direction. Thus the rehabilitation effect may more properly be labelled a 'training' effect, which from a social standpoint may be either positive or negative. Insofar as this is forecasted by potential offenders, the actual discounted expected costs of engaging in current crime may increase or decrease. This result is tempered by the widely held belief that offenders as a whole tend to discount the future more heavily than non-offenders.

PAROLE

Miceli (1994) presents a model of the prison where the optimal lengths of the incarceration and parole periods for individual offenders are chosen by a central authority. The goal is to minimize the cost of a given level of deterrence, conditional upon a predetermined probability of conviction. Parole reduces social costs by prompting prison inmates to behave and by decreasing the number of person-days of incarceration supplied. On the other hand, a system utilizing parole and/or probation reduces the costs of crime to potential offenders and reduces the incapacitation effect. The efficient punishment balances these costs and benefits, and typically requires a period of imprisonment followed by supervised release, as opposed to either probation (immediate release) or unconditional release following incarceration. Miceli demonstratesthat the socially optimal policy varies across individual offenders. Garoupa (1996) generalizes these results in a model which includes the net gains to offenders in the social welfare calculation.

The information and coordination requirements in the Miceli model are substantial. This point is brought home in the recognition that the model may be understood in terms of either a determinate or an indeterminate sentencing regime. (In the latter, the trial judge sentences offenders to prison for an indefinite period; parole authorities determine when the inmate is to be released.) The behavior of all agents is invariant to the institutional framework given the rational expectations assumption: potential offenders know *prior to committingoffenses*the incarceration/parole mix they will receive if convicted, and the effort they will exert to comply with prison rules. Introducing informational imperfections in the form of a failure on the part of the authorities to correctly perceive the good behaviour efforts of confined inmates does not change the basic results of the Miceli model.

An analysis assuming a random component in the relationship between good behavior effort and subsequent proclivity to recidivate would presumably yield similar qualitative implications. Miceli concludes that a grid-style sentencing scheme such as that promulgated by the US Sentencing Commission, which leaves little room for consideration of the full range of offender-specific characteristics, increases the cost of providing a given level of deterrence. These costs are defined to exclude consideration of retribution and disparities in punishment, factors which in part motivate grid-type sentencing systems. In a somewhat different context, Garoupa's (1996) model is used to examine the effects of the UK Criminal Justice Act, 1991, which raised the upper and lower bounds for the proportion of the sentence that may be served on parole. The social welfare effects of the law are found to be ambiguous. Lewis (1979, 1983), in an attempt to provide an empirically feasible guide to parole officials, seeks to establish the optimal parole period given exogenously determined conviction rates and original sentence lengths. The maximand consists of 'the expected cost to society... during the period of the original sentence as a function of the number of months served prior to parole' (Lewis, 1979, p. 382). The model is simulated under a range of assumptions concerning the impact of time served in prison on the rate at which released offenders return to crime (the recidivism rate) while on parole.

Neither Lewis (1979, 1983), Miceli (1994) nor Garoupa (1996) account for theimpact and effects of inmate training on the rate at which released offenders return to crime. This consideration requires abandoning Becker's (1968) static framework, and including social investments in inmate training as a new choice variable (Avio, 1975). Limited progress has been made with highly stylized two-period models of punishment (Rubenstein, 1980; Davis, 1988; Polinskyand Rubinfeld, 1991; Nash, 1991; Burnovski and Safra, 1994). These papers explicitly or implicitly assume that punishment is by fine, and ignore recidivisticbehaviour. The theme of dynamic efficiency and recidivism is taken up in Flinn (1986) and Leung (1995), but in-prison investments in human capital and their impact on recidivism remain unanalyzed. A dynamic general equilibrium model has yet to be developed.

ORGANIZATIONAL DESIGN

Several commentators note that the current decentralized criminal justice system is not expected to be efficient. Insofar as the decision variables at issue (overall prison budget, sentence lengths, training opportunities, parole release) are chosen by different decision centers, each with a different mandate, it is unlikely that the resulting product mix would be efficient. With the legislature setting the overall prison budget and the courts and parole authorities determining the level of confinement days, prisons are left with zero degrees of freedom in selecting the level of support that affects post-release behavior. The product mix could be efficient if the courts and parole authorities were to select appropriate sentence lengths for the given budget.

But since the mandate of the courts is weighted more toward the provision of retribution (indeed, in some regimes judges are determined by popular vote), and the parole authorities have limited flexibility in determining the actual length of stay of prisoners, the decreed sentence lengths and consequent level of rehabilitation services would not in general be expected to be efficient for any given budget. A system of indeterminate sentences alleviates the coordination and informational problems inherent in a decentralized penal system

(Avio, 1973), while remaining consistent with the efficiency thrust of the Miceli (1994) model. The confinement and training decisions become centralized, and maximum incentives for offenders to avail themselves of rehabilitation opportunities are provided. The general rejection of such programs for all but repeat violent offenders is based upon several factors: the difficulties with protecting the civil rights of inmates under such a regime; the frustrations arising from several decades of inconclusive research on inmate rehabilitation; a perceived lack of success in predicting recidivism on an individual offender basis; and an increased emphasis on retribution as the primary goal of punishment.

Former UK Home Secretary Howard (1996) proposed a hybrid determinate/indeterminatesentencing scheme reminiscent of 'three strikes and you're out' regimes while retaining the benefits of 'marginal deterrence' (Stigler, 1970). Under this scheme, repeat violent offenders would automatically receive life sentences, while the trial judge sets a minimum period intended to satisfy the need for retribution and deterrence. Once that period is served, penal authorities would determine whether and when the inmate is released. Upon release, offenders would be subject to recall for the rest of their lives.

An earlier proposal for a two-part penalty scheme was proposed by Tabasz (1974) to alleviate the retribution-rehabilitation conflict. The first part of the sentence targets retribution. It would be determinate, independent of offender characteristics,of relatively short duration and served in an environment devoid of amenities. The offender would then pass on to a different environment to serve out the second, indeterminate stage directed to the rehabilitation goal. Again the purpose of the indeterminate sentence is to align the incentives of the offender with society's goal of minimizing the overall time-discounted social costs of crime. Tabasz suggests that the condition for release be some readily visible sign of achievement on the part of the offender such as the attainment of a definable educational or vocational training goal.

One difficulty with two-part penalty schemes is that the various penal functions(retribution, rehabilitation, deterrence) do not map separately into the determinateand indeterminate portions of the sentence. Any 'hardening' of the inmate during the first stage would presumably have to be rectified during the second, and since loss of liberty represents an important component of incarcerativepunishment, the retributive function is in play during both phases. If the first phase is thought to fulfill the offender's debt to society, then imposition of the second may be constitutionally impermissible. Of course, this latter objection may apply to any sentencing scheme that incorporates goals other than retribution, a term (like 'debt to society') of art.

Roper (1986) proposes a different solution to the decentralization-coordination problem. He conceptualizes prison output as the deliveryof a crime-free offender over the period of the court-rendered sentence. Taking this period as a constraint, Roper's prison decides whether to keep the offender in custody over the entire sentence or to release him early. As Roper puts it, 'the essence of the [prison's] role [is] to assess the risks uniquely associated with the probability of a given offender reoffending' (ibid., p. 91). The author goes on to suggest that the prison enter into contracts with prospective parolees; the prisoner agrees to desist from criminal activities for the duration of the sentence, while the authorities provide financial support, rehabilitation services, employment assistance, and so on, and release the inmate on parole.

If the released offender violates a contract term, then he or she is liable not only for the new criminal charge, if any, but also for a civil contracts suit. The argument is presented in terms of a private (for-profit) prison, but a state operated prison could function in the same manner. While Roper's proposal represents an interesting attempt to correct the principal-agent problem between the state and the offender, as well as the decentralization problem, substantial difficulties remain. First, since most prisoners are judgement proof, the contract remedy must stipulate a return to prison. This penalty would be independent of any sentence levied for the crime causing the contract violation. But it is unlikely that the courts would permit such a remedy. As an alternative, the contract could promise a financial reward subject to forfeit. This avoids the dubious remedy of confinement, but may serve toentice prospective offenders into committing crime in the first place.

Second, independent of remedy, the courts may not recognize the validity of such contracts; what economists define as a*voluntary*transaction may not fall within therange recognized by the courts, given that the offender is bargaining for his freedom and *ipso facto* is under duress.

Nardulli(1984) and Giertz and Nardulli (1985) take up the decentralization issue from the perspective of the fiscal federalism literature (also see Benson and Wollan (1989) and Benson (1990, 1994a), where the common pool/propertyrights nature of the decentralization problem is identified).

These authors view judges as rendering inefficiently severe sentences as the result of a free-rider problem emanating from a misalignment of incentives and cost-bearing. Citizens of the local government derive benefits (protection and retribution) from longer sentences, which happen to be specified by local authorities. However, the costs of providing prison services may be partly shifted from one sentencing jurisdiction onto another via prison financing by a senior level of government. Thus the local demand for confinement is not fully constrained by the cost of delivery. The tendency to prison overcrowding in the federal part of the system, and underbuilding in the local part, follows directly.

Theshort-run solution proposed by Giertz and Nardulli (1985) is to allocate total available prison space to individual sentencing jurisdictions, while continuing with the current division of cost and sentencing responsibilities. This would to an extent defuse free-riding behavior, but one could imagine disagreeable(and constitutionally questionable) inequities in sentencing arising from the constraint.

For example, suppose only shoplifters are predicted to appear before a court during some period, so that relatively harsh sentences are compatible with the given space allocation. Then if an armed robber unexpectedly appears in court, he will either receive a comparatively light sentence or else one of the previously convicted shoplifters must be released earlier than expected. Unless judges accurately forecast the distribution of upcoming cases, a shortage or surplus of prison space would develop, leading to disparities in sentences actually served for offenders committing the same crime.

This argument could apply to a senior administrative jurisdiction as well, but the greater number of cases reduces the risk of prediction errors. The *long-run* solution offered by Giertz and Nardulli is to hold local jurisdictions responsible for their full share of the cost of incarceration. An alternative is for the senior fiscal authority to impose a mandatory grid sentencing scheme upon all courts within its jurisdiction, thus to some extent negating the free-rider problem.

Gillespie (1983) proposes a market for prison space administered by a centralized correctional authority. This market would facilitate the efficient transfer of prison space from local jurisdictions with excess supply to those with excess demand. Jurisdictions comprised of citizens with relatively heavy demandfor long-term sentences backed by a willingness to pay would purchase access to penal space from other jurisdictions. Not only would the pricing mechanism overcome the short-run deficits or surpluses but the market-determined price would signal the social value of new prison space, and hence rationalize the construction of new correctional facilities. Gillespie argues that equity concerns can be addressed by altering the initial allocation accordingto whatever equity criterion is adopted. With appropriately identified prices and initial allocations, this system appears similar to one giving local authorities a portion of the state budget to be spent by them as they desire: on penal space at the state institution, on space at the local level, or on some other public expenditure (Nardulli, 1984).

Would the Gillespie proposal lead to the same results as a centralized sentencing and prison-supply agency? Probably not, simply because income distribution across the local political units would affect the demands for prison space.For given sentences, the various market-oriented systems should cost less than the standard first-come, first-served, free-rider system. But regardless of the efficiency implications, introducing a market for prison space would predictably exacerbate inequities in sentencing across jurisdictions. Other things equal, low-income sub-units would presumably impose relatively short sentences and sell their space allocations to high-income sub-units, which would impose relatively severe sentences. A general equilibrium formulation of Gillespie's model would also have to consider the possibility that offenders might change their geographical areas of operation in response to differential expected punishments.

PRIVATIZATION

Amore fundamental argument for the inefficiency of publicly-operated prisons stems directly from the theory of bureaucracy/public choice literature. Profit-maximization, and its concomitant for non-market production, cost minimization, may not be adopted as the operational goal of the public entity. Somemodels of bureaucratic behavior assume or imply cost efficiency, whereas other do not. Niskanen (1971) argues that bureaus seek to maximize bureau size, and hence overproduce; but whatever output they provide will be at least cost if the bureau is budget-constrained. Other models (for example, Williamson,1964) posit that bureau heads will optimize with respect to private objectives,and therefore cost minimization cannot be expected. The debate over private prisons typically draws on the latter genre of models, deemphasizing decentralization and informational difficulties. Privatization and the profit motive, it is argued, removes the wedge between output and returns for public employees, thus reducing agency costs.

The standard private prison contract bases remuneration for the corporate prison upon the number of person-days of confinement supplied, subject to the provision of some standard level of amenities. Thus the corporate prison has no incentive to provide rehabilitation opportunities, except insofar as the latter act to decrease the current cost of confinement. If rehabilitation activities affect post-release criminality, then regardless of market structure the standard per-diem contract is inferior to one that pays the private prison in accordance with the recidivism success of its releasees(Avio, 1993a). Appropriately designed remuneration schemes harness the power of the market to stimulate the discovery of imprisonment methods that minimize long-run social costs.

The argument has been extended to incorporate the possibility that the corporate prison operating under the traditional remuneration scheme might perversely seek to stimulate recidivism (Gentry, 1986; Avio, 1991). Under the standard contract provisions, the value of the prison corporation depends to an extent upon the continued influx of inmates, which could be enhanced by (clandestinely) providing negative training. A flow of new offenders sufficient to keep individual prisons operating at the minimum of their average cost curves, while simultaneously requiring the construction of new facilities, would maximize profit opportunities. This argument is conditional upon the exercise ofmarket power. Established prison firms would seem to be in an advantageous position to capture managerial and construction contracts for new prisons. Of course, the incentive structure embedded in the public prison system may be equally inimical to social welfare.

Whether the weak or the strong form of the argument against per-diem contracts is applied, the debate over private prisons exhibits a kind of symmetry: private prisons are socially superior to public prisons because the former seek efficiencies in the drive to maximize profits; public prisons are superior to private prisons because they are *not* driven by the profit motive. Some privatization advocates recognize the difficulty with the standard prison contract,but attempts to explain away this quasi-paradox are unsatisfactory and reveal the inconsistency: Logan (1987, p. 39) argues that rather than maximizing profits, private prisons really seek to maximize convenience subject to some minimal profit constraint; Brakel (1988, p. 34, n.92) argues that line employees of the private prison, whose actions have the greatest potential to affect post-release behavior, are too distant from profit centers to act in accordance with the profit motive. But in the same breath, adherence to the profit motive with the attendant efficiencies is given as the overarching rationale for prison privatization.

The increasing popularity of private prisons in policy circles is attributable to more than the general privatization fashion alone. The modern conceptualization of prisons as a benign warehouse has replaced the 'corrections' model in professional circles. This follows the retrenchment on treatment oriented programs in the 1980s. The prison-as-warehouse conceptualization is consistent with both the static neoclassical and the Kantian-inspired retributive models discussed earlier. In the former, prisons are simply the institutions society employs to effect the restriction of liberty necessary to attain the efficient amount of crime through deterrence and incapacitation. In

Kantian retributive models, justice requires punishment in a rights-respecting environment; the moral autonomy of the individual demands that no attempt be made to 'force' rehabilitation. The underlying function of prisons remains the same, a function that could equally well be provided by an institution operating under market incentives.

Non-economic arguments may ultimately decide the scope that private prisons are allowed to play. A feeling of unease accompanies the thought of government delegating to private individuals the authority to punish (Dilulio, 1988, 1990). Regulations such as those included in the American Bar Association's Model Code and Model Statute for Private Incarceration may be necessary to protect the civil liberties of offenders (Robbins, 1989). Benson (1990, 1994b) extends the argument. The potential for success with prison privatization in terms of technological efficiency is so great, that once bureaucratic resistance and other obstacles to private prisons are overcome, society may increasingly come to rely on incarceration as a means of social control. For example, special interest groups may press for the expanded imprisonnment of illegal aliens to control labor supply (Benson, 1994b, pp. 66-72). Prison privatization then poses a threat to both overall allocative efficiency and to individual liberty.

To date, the empirical evidence comparing private and public management of adult secure facilities has been scant and somewhat unsatisfactory. The number of surveys of these studies (McDonald, 1990; Thomas and Logan, 1993; Sellers, 1993, Ch. 4; Sichor, 1995, Ch. 9; USGAO, 1991, 1996) nearly equals the number of studies, simultaneously reflecting the youthfulness of the privateprison industry (the first modern adult secure facility went under private management in 1983), the difficulty of the research, and interest in the topic. The studies typically consist of cost and quality comparisons of matched institutions (see, for example, Edwards, 1996). Thomas (1996) notes that comparisonsof similarly designed facilities will not necessarily account for the cost-saving innovations that private prisons should bring, as design is itself a major source of efficiencies. Also, recidivism rates of the various institutions are typically ignored (see Hatry, 1989, for an exception). Econometric work on privateprisons has yet to be undertaken. Given the growth of the industry (from fewer than 3,000 [rated capacity] beds under contract in 1983 to over 84,000 in the US, UK and Australia at the end of 1996), the time is ripe for sophisticated quantitative research.

LINEAR PROGRAMMING MODELS

The empirical test of propositions relating to correctional institutions requires *a priori* modelling. Although unmodified linear programming imposes severe technology constraints, interesting questions can be addressed using this technique. In the tradition of a systems analysis of prisons (Blumstein and Larson,1969), Tabasz (1975) constructs a linear programming model of the US Federal Bureau of Prisons. The goal is to allocate different types of offenders to different types of institutions and to different sentence lengths in a manner that maximizes net social benefits subject to the capacity of the prison system and the flow of convicted offenders. In all, 2,700 decision variables are specified. Only benefits to incapacitation and rehabilitation are imputed, and the capital costs of prisons are ignored.

The results indicate that prison resources should be concentrated on relatively young and dangerous offenders: inmates over 45 years of age are assigned to 'probation' (immediate release). The model cannot directly indicate how many resources should be allocated to the prison system, but it does give an approximation to the benefit-cost ratio potentially generated by prisons (8.51 in the 'standard' version of the model applying 1973 data (ibid., p. 129)). This estimate, which at face value rationalizes the build-up in prison capacity that began in the US in the 1970s (Blumstein, 1995), should not be taken too seriously.

The relatively primitive natureof the data available to Tabasz required strong assumptions, particularly those related to the rates of crime commission, the social costs of crime, and the rehabilitative effects of incarceration. The methodology also imposes an interpretive constraint: the results do not necessarily reflect actual net benefits attained, but the potential benefits if decision variables are chosen optimally. Nonetheless, this study anticipates later attempts to evaluate the prison system as a whole.

Linear programming may also be used to identify the relative efficiency levels of individual prisons. The operations research tool known as Data Envelopment Analysis, a non-stochastic frontier methodology, is applied by Ganley and Cubbin (1992, Ch. 5) for this purpose. The underlying linear program is constructed to embody a varying returns to scale technology. Analysis of 33 UK local prisons and remand centers for the financial year 1984-85 suggests that 13 of the establishments were 'technically inefficient relative to the peer prisons on the cost frontier' (ibid., p. 66). On average the operating costs of the inefficient institutions could be reduced by about 12 percent. Prison cost studies comparing this method with the econometric methods discussed below would be helpful.

ECONOMETRIC MODELS OF PRISONS

A major policy issue illuminated by economic theory concerns the appropriate size of prisons. For example, in Canada in the 1960s new prisons were built to accommodateabout 450 inmates. In the next decade several government reports advocated even smaller institutions. Since little was known about the cost-effectiveness of prisons, this debate occurred in what was largely an empirical vacuum. Conceptualizing the prison as an economic entity leads to traditional cost and production analysis with the potential to systematically address questions such as returns to scale in the provision of prison services. Block and Ulen (1979) estimate long-and short-run prison cost functions for the state of California using elementary functional forms. The short-run results (using time-series data for each of two maximum security institutions) suggest that average costs are minimized at surprisingly large inmate populations (for example, 5,700 for San Quentin, as estimated over the years 1948-1964 (Block and Ulen, 1979, p. 200)). A 1971-1972 cross-section of jails yields a long-run cost curve indicating approximately constant returns to scale. Both the short-and long-run analyses abstract from the rehabilitative dimension of prison output; expenditures specifically earmarked for rehabilitation are eliminated from the cost data.

Schmidt and Witte (1984) (also see McGuire and Witte, 1978; Trumball and Witte, 1981-82a,1981-82b; Kritzer, 1981-82) present a comprehensive econometricanalysis of US federal and California prison systems from the mid-to late-1970s. Short- and long-run average cost functions are derived. The short-run results for each of 22 federal and 8 California prisons are derived from estimated labor demand equations corresponding to homothetic generalized Cobb-Douglas production functions. Several of the cost functions are found to be inconsistent with economic theory. The authors ascribe this result to altered operating methods within given institutions over the sample period. For those institutions conforming to economic theory, the majority are found to have short-run average costs which decrease as inmate populations increase. This finding is particularly robust for older, fortress-type institutions. While economies of scale are indicated, it would be imprudent to draw policy implications concerning the crowded conditions in many institutions today as crowding was not a widespread phenomenon during the sample period.

The impact of rehabilitation activities on costs is diverse, and 'may depend critically on the nature of the particular institution being studied' (Schmidt and Witte, 1984, p. 335). The authors summarize their results for the entire sample of federaland California institutions: 'costs generally increase until a certain level of rehabilitative activities is provided and then decline thereafter' (ibid., p. 345). Anecdotal evidence suggests that prison work experience uniquely reduces the level of violence within prisons, probably by fostering a prisoner sub-culture that rewards co-operative behavior (Fleisher, 1989, pp. 26-27; 1995, pp. 262-270). Unfortunately Schmidt and Witte lump prison work experience with educational programs and counselling services in constructing the rehabilitation activities variable (Schmidt and Witte, 1984, p. 305).

A long-run cost function is estimated using pooled quarterly data over the mid-1970s for a subset of six federal institutions found to possess similar technologies. Estimated average costs are asymmetrically U-shaped, with a higher penalty on institutions housing fewer than the efficient capacity of 1075 inmates. In this subset of prisons, rehabilitation activities are found to have no statistically significant impact on long-run average costs. This result is puzzling, especially since all but one of these institutions have short-run cost functions sensitive to this variable. Several service quality variables are found to be significant. The authors conclude that 'the minimum-cost-sized prison will probably house between 700 and 1500 inmates' (Schmidt and Witte, 1984, p. 363) and that 'providing single cells for inmates and rather substantial amounts of living space may actually decrease the cost of operating prisons' (ibid., p. 362).

Taken as a whole, these studies are indicative of the important role that econometric analysis can play in analyzing policy questions related to the management of prisons. Several extensions come easily to mind. Comparison of the costs and technologies of private and public prisons would be helpful in the ongoing privatization debate. Econometric studies of the cost-effectiveness ofprison industries should be undertaken. Linking rehabilitation*outcomes*with current costs would enhance the value of the studies. The data requirements for this latter task would be substantial but not impossible, as the next two sections suggest.

STATISTICAL MODELS OF RECIDIVISM

Serving time in prison, as well as participating in various prison and post-release programs, may have either a positive or negative effect upon the activities of released prison inmates. Nailing down the specifics of the relationships is clearly an important factor in evaluating overall social policies towards crime as well as in evaluating specific programs for incarcerated and paroled offenders. If, for example, predictions of future behavior of individual convicted offenders prove to be sufficiently reliable, then a program of 'selective incapacitation' becomes feasible, if not ethically acceptable (Greenwood and Turner, 1987). The extensive literature addressing criminal recidivism has for the most part been the preserve of criminologists, sociologists and psychologists. Here the contributions of economists Peter Schmidt and Anne Witte are noted (also see Myers, 1980a, 1983).

In a series of articles (Witte and Schmidt, 1977, 1979; Sickles, Schmidt and Witte, 1979; Schmidt and Witte, 1980, 1989) and books (Schmidt and Witte 1984, 1988), Schmidt and Witte and their associates exhaustively analyze follow-up microdata on releasees from North Carolina prisons. Since the theoretically relevant dependent variables-time devoted to criminal activity and the intensity thereof-cannot be observed, a number of proxy recidivism variables are employed. These include the traditional binary 'success-failure' measure, categories of crimes leading to reconviction, seriousness of crimes leading to reconviction, total length of prison sentences received during the follow-up period, length of time from release to first arrest leading to conviction, and length of time from release to first return to prison. Different statistical models (qualitative variable models, survival time models) are used as appropriate for the different dependent variables studied.

The polytymous logit model is used to analyze a random sample of 641 inmates in North Carolina prisons in 1969 and 1971, with follow-up periods averaging 37 months (Schmidt and Witte, 1984, Ch. 3). The seriousness of criminal activity, as measured by whether the most serious reconviction (if any) was a misdemeanour or a felony, and the type of criminal activity (crime against the person, against property, or 'other', including drug crime) are analyzed with respect to various personal characteristics and histories of individual inmates (excluding, for some unstated reason, time served for the sample sentence). The likelihood of reconviction is found to vary significantly with the number of previous convictions, age at release (older offenders have lower probabilities of reconviction), length of the follow-up period, and alcohol or hard drug use (ibid., p. 45). Surprisingly, none of these same variables are significant predictors of the type and the seriousness of offenses for which reconvictions are obtained. On the other hand, the type and the seriousness of previousoffenses are found to be related to the type and seriousness respectively of subsequent convictions, but not the overall probability of reconviction. Consistent with the criminal career syndrome, some evidence of offenders switching from property crime to personal crime is found.

A more refined indicator of the seriousness of new offenses, the total length of time sentenced for recidivist offenses, is analyzed by the same authors (Schmidt and Witte, 1984, Ch. 5) using two samples: that used in the previously reported research, and a cohort group consisting of all individuals released in North Carolina during the first six months of 1975 (25-31 month follow-up). The censored nature of the dependent variable suggests a Tobit analysis. In both samples, the dependent variable is found to vary in the predicted direction with the youthfulness of the offender, a history of alcohol abuse, the number of previous convictions, unsupervised release, and a sample incarceration for a crime against property (Schmidt and Witte, 1984, p. 73).

Theestimation sample is used to predict the dependent variable for a validation sample. Separating the samples into various race, gender and age groupings substantially improves the prediction reliability for most subgroups, as there appears to be considerable variability in the significance of different explanatoryvariables across the subgroups. The predicted total time sentenced for the entire validation sample using the best model for each subgroup is insignificantly different from the actual value of total time sentenced, suggestingan important tool for correctional planning. The overall results show the superiority of the more sophisticated models as compared with binary 'success-failure' models.

The second set of models employed by Schmidt and Witte treat survival time-the length of time from release to recidivism. Not only is this variable of interest in itself, but ignoring information on length of time to recidivism (however defined) is statistically inefficient. The authors' extensive analyses (the present discussion is limited to Schmidt and Witte, 1988) utilize various formulations found in the increasingly sophisticated criminogenic literature. Carr-Hill and Carr-Hill (1972) apparently were the first authors to apply survival models in this context, as well as innovations of their own. The data consist of two cohorts of approximately 9,500 individuals each released from all state prisons in North Carolina in separate 12 month periods, with follow-upsranging from 46 to 81 months. Data limitations, as well as the needs of the correctional authorities supplying the data, dictated the dependent variable: the length of time from release to return to prison.

Estimation using distributions with monotonic hazard ratesproved inadequate. This is unsurprising since recidivism hazard rates first rise and then rather quickly fall. The best overall results apply individual characteristics as explanatory variables to 'split population' models, thereby permitting the probability of recidivism to follow a generating process distinct from that for recidivist survival times. The best fit is found for 'a logit lognormalmodel, in which the probability of eventual recidivism follows a logit model and the timing of return follows a lognormal distribution' (Schmidt and Witte, 1988, p. 19). Those models which utilize individual characteristics as explanatory variables for each of the two recidivism outcomes yield the following results: race and gender affect the probability of eventual recidivism butnot its timing, whereas indicators of the nature of the previous offense affect thetiming of recidivism but not its probability (ibid., p. vii); age on release, the number of prior convictions and a history of alcohol abuse affect in the predicted direction both the probability of eventual recidivism and the mean time until recidivism; finally, the length of the sample incarceration increases the probability of a return to crime and shortens survival time.

These latter results appear consistent with the school for crime theory (see Myers, 1980a, for a qualitatively similar conclusion with a sample of parolee data) but selectivity bias renders this interpretation somewhat problematic.

The authors recommend the use of non-parametric methods (Cox's proportional hazards model) to first identify the appropriate explanatory variables, and then the use of parametric models to yield the best predictions. The predictions are generally superior to those elsewhere in the literature (Schmidt and Witte, 1988, p. 15), although the use of explanatory variables does not improve predictions for random samples of releasees.

Moreover, the authors emphasize that their best models (predicting false positive rates of 47 percent and false negatives of 28 percent) are unsatisfactory for implementing a policy of selective incapacitation. One can conclude that there is value in using sophisticated models in predicting recidivism for random samples of released offenders, but that the models are not yet sufficiently refined for application to individuals.

Schmidt and Witte note that further experimentation with non-linear formulations of the explanatory variables will probably lead to explaining a higher degree of the variation in the dependent variables (about 10 percent in the current study), and thus boost prediction accuracy (Schmidt and Witte, 1988, p.150). Another suggestion is to take more seriously the economic model of crime by including explanatory variables measuring the certainty and severity of punishment as well as environmental variables representing legitimateand illegitimate opportunities. Suppose, for example, that during the follow-up period there is variation across the relevant geographic jurisdictions and/or over time in police activity. Further, suppose that this leads to variation in the objective probability of arrest.

The economic model suggests that the pattern of criminal behavior of released inmates as well as that of individuals with no previous criminal record would be affected. Prediction accuracy could beimpaired (and the model mispecified) if the standard criminal justice control variables are excluded. Data limitations may intrude (ibid., p. 85). But even if the local communities in which released offenders reside are unobserved, risk and punishment variables can probably be constructed on an aggregated geographical basis for each period during the follow-up Examples of survival-time recidivism research employing environmental variables are Visher, Lattimore and Linster (1991) studying paroled California youths, and Kim et al., (1993) examining Florida drug offenders. On a more micro level, Schmidt and Witte (1988, pp. 9-11) note that the complexion of their research resultscould be attributable in part to police and prosecutors targeting offenders withcertain personal characteristics, as well as to the characteristics themselves affecting criminal activity. Sorting out the simultaneity problems remains an important part of the research agenda in the economics of prisons.

THE EVALUATION OF IN-PRISON REHABILITATION PROGRAMS

Psychologists, criminologists, sociologists and public policy commentators have contributed to the extensive literature on the rehabilitation of convicted offenders. This topic shades into a discussion of the overall causes of crime. No attempt will be made here to address the larger question, nor should the discussion be considered a survey of anything but a select subsample of the rehabilitation literature. The limited number of contributions by economists on the direct evaluation of rehabilitation programs is taken up in this section and the next.

On the important question of research design, laboratory-like experiments comparing outcomes for randomly selected program and control groups are generally not possible in the criminal justice context (some exceptions are discussed below). Researchers typically are forced to resort to quasi-experimental designs, which designate 'a group of individuals (the comparison group) that is as much like the group of program participants studied as possible' (Grizzle and Witte, 1980, p. 259). The difficulty is that subjects in the two groups may differ in some characteristic that affects post-release activities. This dictates that the researcher must have in mind an underlying model of criminal and recidivistic behavior. In this section a quasi-experimental program evaluation is contrasted with one employing a 'predicted-versus-actual' method.

Witte(1977) employs a quasi-experimental design to evaluate a program in which a non-random sample of inmates in North Carolina prisons work on day-passes with various local industries. The sample consists of men on the 'work release' program in 1969 or 1971. The experiences of the evaluation group are compared with those of a nonparticipating group who appear to be equally eligible for the program. Multiple regression techniques are used to correct for differences in personal characteristics across the two samples. The author finds no programmatic impact on the decision to return to crime, but a marked beneficial effect on the seriousness of crimes committed during the follow-up period. This latter result is confirmed by the logit and tobit analyses of Schmidt and Witte (1984, pp. 34-35, 68) utilizing work release as a binary explanatory variable.

The results here further indicate that participation in work release is significantly related to neither the type of post-release criminal activity (crime against the person or against property), nor to survival time. Schmidt and Witte (1979, 1980, 1984, Ch. 8) use a statistical model estimated from a data set consisting of information on all 4,881 inmates released from North Carolina prisons during the first six months of 1975 to evaluate a comprehensive release program for youthful offenders in North Carolina (the Sandhills Vocational Evaluation and Job/Educational Developmentprogram). The estimated model is employed to predict criminality indicators for each of the Sandhills participants (489 participants released over the period

February 21, 1975 through February 21, 1977); program evaluation proceeds from a comparison of the predicted effects with the actual criminality indicators for participants.

The advantage of this 'predicted versus actual' method is that no matched comparison group is needed. But as the authors stress, the reliability of the evaluation depends crucially on the accuracy of the model and on the implicit assumption that the relevant prison unit does not differ significantly 'from the system norm in a way not controlled for by our models' (Schmidt and Witte, 1984, p. 135). Some weak statistical evidence is found suggesting that the Sandhills program reduces the amount of recidivism during the first six months of the follow-up period. (Using a smaller sample from a different estimation, the authors also find that the program reduces the total time sentenced during the follow-up period, that is, the seriousness of follow-up criminal activity (ibid., pp. 130-133.) This study conveys what can beaccomplished by way of program evaluation with suitably specified statistical models. In their later study (Schmidt and Witte, 1988, Ch. 8), however, the view is less optimistic. Here an estimated model is again used to predict survival times for nonrepresentative subsamples, including participants in the previously discussed work-release program. The results significantly underpredict recidivism for this group (ibid., p. 138). The authors attribute this not to program effects, but rather to 'work release participants hav[ing] different characteristics than nonparticipants... our model does not adequately capture the effects of these characteristics on time until recidivism' (ibid., p. 138).

As Schmidt and Witte note, perhaps the safest and most efficient use of the predicted versus actual models is in conjunction with experiments: such models can be used to justify the initiation of costly experimental studies, as well as to indicate the factors that must be controlled. In the event that true-or quasi-experiments are impractical, the predicted versus actual approach provides a relatively low-cost but not altogether reliable alternative. Research refining and systematizing this method is called for.

Turning from methodological to substantive issues, what kinds of in-prison rehabilitative programs work, if any? The 'Nothing Works' doctrine initiated in Martinson's well-known paper (Martinson, 1974, previewing Lipton, Martinson and Wilks, 1975) ushered in an era of pessimism in penology. After reviewing the results of 231 papers (the majority dealing with programs of a therapeutic nature) published between 1945 and 1967, Martinson concluded that there was little evidence that rehabilitation programs work. This sweeping generalization was echoed by the Panel of Research on Rehabilitative Techniquesof the National Research Council (US), which restated Martinson's conclusion: 'it appears that nothing works or at least that there have not been any consistent and persuasive demonstrations of anything that works' (Sechrest, White and Brown, 1979, p. 27). This conclusion has not gone unchallenged (for example, Halleck and Witte, 1977; Gendreau and Ross, 1987; Mair, 1991), but 'Nothing Works' remains a part of penological lore.

One response follows the lead of the second report of the Panel of Research on Rehabilitative Techniques (Martin, Sechrest and Redner, 1981) in questioning whether the strength and degree of implementation of in-prison programs are sufficient for definitive tests. Lattimore and Witte (1985), responding to Englander (1983) (also see Englander, 1985), note that many vocational programs are poorly designed, rather weak in intervention (for example, a training program of short duration), and poorly and incompletely implemented (for example, inmates dropping in and out of programs).

Lattimore, Witte and Baker (1990) attempt to evaluate a vocational rehabilitation program for young property offenders in which care is taken to address these difficulties. The program consists of six integrated in-prison sub-programs (ibid., p. 120, Table 1) any or all of which may have been completed by members of the sample. The sample consists of 591 selected North Carolina male inmates aged 18-22 enrolled in the umbrella project sometime between June 1983 and May 1986. The subjects were randomly partitioned by prison officials into an experimental group and a control group. The two groups differed in their exposure to the various parts of the umbrella project and in their completion records for the various component parts of the project.

Only 16 percent of the experimental group began all of the program components, that is, the umbrella program was only weakly implemented. Nevertheless, some programmatic effects were still evident: an examination of survival times indicates that the program reduced post-release arrests by about 10 percentage points for releasees who had been out over about 600 days. Moreover, the survival history of those who completed a vocational program was significantly better than for those who did not, a result the authors could not account for in terms of their sociodemographic and criminalitymeasures. Unfortunately, doubts were recently cast on these results by one of the co-authors of the original paper: 'unpublished longer-term follow-up results show no significant differences in criminal activities between the experimental and the control groups' (Witte, 1997, p. 226).

MANPOWER PROGRAMS FOR FORMER PRISON INMATES

Perhaps partly in response to the 'Nothing Works' dialogue, the attention of economists has largely shifted from in-prison rehabilitation programs to assistanceprograms for released prisoners. Cook (1975) (also see Hardin, 1975; Marks and Vining, 1986), after reviewing various labor market studies of parolees, as well as his own study utilizing a data set (collected and analyzed by Evans, 1968) consisting of 327 male parolees from Massachusetts penitentiaries in 1959, notes that (1) 'discrimination is not an important factor in the work experience of parolees' (Cook, 1975, p. 18); (2) the quality of jobs, and not the quantity, is crucial in determining the employment record of released offenders; (3) success in the job market for released offenders leads to lower recidivism rates; and (4) in-prison therapeutic, educational and job-skills programs have little effect upon post-release success. Even though remedial education and vocational training programs 'have demonstrated success in providing prisoners and parolees with measurably increased academic and vocational skill' (ibid., pp. 47-48), they have typically not been successful in reducing recidivism rates. (Witte and Reid, 1980, obtain similarly pessimistic resultsin examining the labor market performance of a group of ex-inmates not limited to parolees.)

The survey by Long and Witte (1981, p. 128) is unequivocal: 'Evaluations of vocational training and remedial education programs in prison, parole, or probation settings have almost uniformly found thatsuch programs have insignificant effects on both labor market performance and criminality.' The hypothesis is that the programs have not improved the job-opportunities of offenders, even though they have improved their skill levels. Released offenders either are unable to find the better jobs or, if found, they cannot keep them because of inadequate preparation for the demands of such work. Cook (echoed by Witte and Reid, 1980) concludes that the evidence suggests job search and on-the-job training programs should be given priority.

Whether the prospect of improved legitimate job opportunities would act to reduce the initial deterrent effectiveness of punishment remains a concern. Cooknotes that increasing the probability of punishment may be an appropriate offset. Such a substitution would not be costless, however, and again points to an analysis stressing the dynamic and general equilibrium modelling of crime.

Borus, Hardin and Terry (1976) (also see Hardin, 1975) utilize a quasi-experimental design to evaluate a Michigan job-placement program for selected parolees. The authors find that program participants did not fair better in terms of various indicators of job-market success, and in fact 'fared worse, on the average... as to hours employed, gross earnings, and take-home pay' (Borus, Hardin and Terry, 1976, p. 394). Apparently no attempt was made to directly compare the recidivism experience of program participants with non-participants. This aspect was addressed in the following study, yielding a similarly pessimistic conclusion.

Mallar and Thornton (1978) report on a program (LIFE-'Living Insurance for Ex-Offenders') seeking to establish whether transitional aid programs and/or job-placement assistance for ex-prisoners reduce recidivism for theft crimes (also see Myers, 1983). A non-random sample of 432 high-risk prisoners from Maryland's state prisons released into the Baltimore area in the early1970s was randomly partitioned into four treatment groups: one receiving direct financial aid ($60/week for three months); one receiving job-placement assistance (for up to one year); one receiving both; and a control group receiving no assistance of either type.

The authors conclude: 'The provision of financial aid led to a large and statistically significant reduction in theft rearrests, while the provision of job-placement services proved to be singularly ineffective in reducing recidivism' (Mallar and Thornton, 1978, p. 224). Subjects in the financial aid group were less likely to be employed full time, especially during the first quarter after release, and more likely to be enrolled in school or a training program. The authors speculate that this apparent investment in human capital may widen the differential in recidivism response over time. It also appears that the transitional aid group achieved higher paying jobs, leading the authors to suggest that transitional aid permitted subjects to invest more in job search. Finally, the authors demonstrate the benefit/cost viability of the direct aid program.

Broadly similar results with respect to the job-placement component were obtained in an expanded version of the LIFE program (named TARP, 'Transitional Aid Research Project'; see Rossi, Berk and Lenihan, 1980). This program applied a controlled experimental design to all released inmates (not just parolees) from Georgia and Texas state prisons. The transitional aid component also appeared to be unsuccessful, but the authors attribute this to work disincentive effects not in place for the LIFE program (for additional comment see Long and Witte, 1981, pp. 129-130, and Englander, 1983, pp. 28-29). Again, these studies do not address the question whether the prospect of transitional financial aid would eventually reduce the initial deterrent effectiveness of punishment.

The National Supported Work Program (Hollister, Kemper and Maynard, 1984; Couch, 1992) placed subjects in a variety of supportive and subsidized work environments commensurate with their backgrounds. The emphasis was on developing work habits in accordance with a graduated stress concept of job-market preparation. As one author describes it: 'Stress within the working environment increased gradually during the training period until it simulated the workplace norms of the private sector. At that point, not more than 18 months after entry, individuals who received the services... had to attempt a transition to unsubsidized employment' (Couch, 1992, p. 381). Over the period from March 1975 to July 1977, 2,276 ex-offenders, one of four subject groups, were randomly assigned to either an experimental group or a control group, with regular nine-month follow-ups extending to three years.

All subjects had been incarcerated sometime during the six months preceeding enrollment in the program, and the average length of time served was four years. Less than 10 percent of this group exhausted the allowable time in the program. The results indicate no reduction in recidivism among the ex-offender experimental group as a whole, and no measurable labor market effects (Piliavin and Gartner, 1984).

An eight year follow-up (Couch, 1992) indicates no improvement in labor market success for disadvantaged youths (the ex-offender group did not receive the long-term follow-up). Other large-scale studies (for example, the Mathematica Policy Research, Inc. study of the Job Corps (Mallar et al., 1982) and the Abt Associates review of the Job Training Partnership Act (JTPA) programs(Orr et al., 1996)) do not identify an ex-inmate subgroup for analysis.

As the concluding sections of this chapter attest, the rich research possibilities inherent in large longitudinal data sets are ushering in a new era of empirical research on criminal behavior (see, for example, Tauchen, Witte and Griesinger, 1994) and recidivism. At the same time, the research design ofexperimental studies will continue to improve (Witte, 1993). Weitekamp and Kerner (1994) sensibly call for an integration of longitudinal and experimental studies. This method would seem to have considerable potential for evaluating specific programs for inmates and ex-inmates.

Pending the outcome of these hybrid studies, the conflicting results found in even the limited subsample of the literature discussed above suggests that a magic one-size-fits-all rehabilitation bullet does not exist. Offenders differ in their motivations as well asin their abilities, proclivities and backgrounds. Moreover, 'success' itself will onlybe found by choosing carefully from amongst different outcome measures, and then measured only in small magnitudes. Finally, it bears noting that even if 'Something Works', the corresponding implementation may be globally suboptimal either because of high direct program costs, or because of the implicit added incentive for individuals to enter the criminal market.

CRIMINAL AND LEGITIMATE LABOR MARKETS FOR FORMER PRISON INMATES

Resultsobtained from specific in-prison rehabilitation programs and manpower programsfor released offenders have been weak and inconsistent. This, coupled with the substantial increase in the proportion of the US population incarcerated over the last two decades makes the wide-scale implementation of costly rehabilitation programs unlikely. Consequently, recent economic research focuses on the general effects of incarceration, independent of prison programs, on subsequent criminal and legitimate labor market activities of released offenders. Various kinds of empirical information and estimation strategies are employed.

Grogger (1991) uses panel data on California arrestees to attempt to determine the effect of imprisonment on future criminality as well as to estimate the incapacitative effect of prison. Since estimates of the proportion of all young California males arrested at some point reach as high as one-third, the sample of arrestees offers a more representative picture than data on prison releasees alone (see Witte, 1980 and Myers, 1983). Grogger's empirical results suggest that imprisonment has a criminogenic effect ('each additional month spent in prison increases average arrests by about 2 percent' (Grogger, 1991, p. 304)) which may be attributed to either negative training or negative labor market signalling. Moreover, under the assumption that sanction expectations are formed entirely from one's own historical involvement with the justice system(that is, 'specific' as opposed to 'general' deterrence), 'the criminogenic effect of imprisonment is nearly three times as great as the deterrent effect' (ibid.). Prison is also found to have an incapacitative effect-each month reduces the average individual's criminal activity roughly in proportion to the time spent in prison. As Grogger notes (ibid., p. 299), the interpretation of the results depends crucially upon whether arrests are an appropriate measure of criminal activity. In addition, unobserved fixed characteristics could also bias the results. For example, a penchant for violence could be correlated with both longer sentences for any given crime category as well as with greater post-incarceration criminality. The following studies address this type of complication.

Freeman (1992) employs the National Longitudinal Survey of Youth and other surveys to estimate the long-run impact of incarceration on future legitimate employment of young US males. After standardizing for observed personalcharacteristics of individuals in the sample, he finds that incarceration in 1980 had a substantial negative impact on whether one was employed in any given subsequent year (to 1988) and on the total number of subsequent weeks worked. 'For the entire eight-year period, incarceration in 1980 reduced subsequent work weeks by 27 percent for blacks and 22 percent for all youth' (ibid., p. 217). Only one-third of the negative employment effect is attributed to the exclusionary impact of current incarceration on currrent employment. Freeman tests whether his results might be due to some unobserved characteristic correlated with both criminality and labor market fitness (such as functional illiteracy) by utilizing data on the pre-and post-incarceration employment experience of individuals. Adapting an omitted variables regression model, Freeman finds that incarceration continues to have a substantial impact on subsequent employment, although the impact is reduced by up to one-half (ibid., p. 225). Freeman cautions that these results do not implythat a random person assigned a criminal record would necessarily have thepredicted subsequent employment experience. Rather, the statistics indicate what happened to those who *chose* crime. In other words, the data remain consistent with rational decision making by far-sighted individuals facing the risk of incarceration and the potential loss of legitimate income.

Freeman's results may be compared with those of Grogger (1995), who again studies a sample of young male California arrestees. All individuals in the sample were arrested at least once between 1973 and early 1987. Grogger seeks to determine the effects of contact with the criminal justice system on subsequentlegitimate labor market outcomes. He obtains a comparison sample of non-offenders by partitioning the sample in accordance with the date of first arrest. The treatment sample consists of young California males first arrested prior to 1985, and the comparison sample consists of those first arrested in 1985 or later. Quarterly data on earnings and employment from 1980 through 1984 are merged with each individual's criminal justice history. To eliminate theimpact of unobserved variables correlated with arrests, Grogger applies the fixed-effectsestimator to a distributed lag model.

Unobserved correlated factors are found to have a large effect on labour market outcomes, whereas arrests are found to have a relatively modest and short-lived impact on earnings and employment. ('After six-quarters the effect (of an arrest) is insignificantly different from zero' (ibid. p. 61).) The impact of incarceration is also noted, although the results here are somewhat unreliable because the relatively long prison sentences may lead to regression results that simply reflect a contemporaneous enforced exclusion from the labor market. The results relating to jail sentences are more reliable, as their duration is typically of one year or less. Jail sentences are found to have an impact on subsequent earnings and employment, but again these are characterized as relatively short-lasting when compared with Freeman's results. Grogger notes (ibid., p. 70) that this may be due to the differences in sentence lengths for the two sample: long sentences (Freeman's sample) may have long-lasting effects, whereas short sentences(Grogger's sample) have relatively short-lasting effects. Insofar as the empirical results *do* conflict, different rationalizations of criminal activity would be in order. Freeman's results may be interpreted as indicating a relatively moderate impact of arrests and incarceration on labor market prospects. Studies using empirical measures of actual sentence lengths served would be helpful in determining whether the supply-side argument or the demand-side argument is stronger.

Other papers bearing on the impact of incarceration on earnings and employment stress the independent deterrent effect of criminal stigmatization, a byproduct of contact with the criminal justice system. Rasmussen (1996) presents two models of criminal stigmatization. The moral hazard model has employers unwilling to pay the market wage to ex-offenders because of their lower net productivity (contribution to product less thievery from the firm and other destructive behaviors), whereas in the adverse selection model a criminal record signals exogenously lower *gross* productivity (for example, lower intelligence). Applied to the economics of prisons, the moral hazard effect reflects the negative training discussed earlier:

time spent in prison increases theoffender's productivity as a criminal. Any deterrent effect of stigmatization would be expected to be greater for those with the highest education and greatest job market prospects. Lott (1992b) finds for a sample of US federal larcenyand theft offenders (typically involving government property or postal offenses) that 'a one-month increase in sentence length causes a 5.5 to 32 percent greater reduction in postconviction income' (ibid., p. 597).

Waldfogel (1994a) similarly employs a sample of white-collar criminals to demonstrate that the reduction in job market prospects from imprisonment is due primarily to stigma, and not stalled experience growth or job displacement. Waldfogel cautions that his results may not be generalizable to offenders whose pre-conviction jobs do not involve substantial trust, and whose convictions are for crimes other than fraud and larceny. (For example, Lott (1992a) finds that longer sentences do not affect the post-imprisonment legitimate income of drug offenders.) To the extent that crime becomes more concentrated in an underclass composed of individuals who have little in the way of job market aspirations and opportunities, the deterrent effect of any criminal stigma may becomeinsignificant. As well, the stigma measured by the disapproval of one's friends and neighbours will probably fall as the proportion of the population incarcerated increases, thus decreasing the deterrent effectiveness of punishment (Freeman, 1996, pp. 32-33). Other papers more relevant to the impact of conviction than incarceration include Lott (1990), Freeman (1986), Grogger (1992), Waldfogel (1994b) and Nagin and Waldfogel (1995).

PUBLIC POLICY BROADLY CONCEIVED

Is the criminal justice system administering sentence lengths that might be considered efficient? Waldfogel (1993) constructs a static model of optimal sentencing where the planner chooses sentences to minimize the direct social harm from crime and the cost of imposing punishment. Optimal sentences are derived after making strong simplifying assumptions on functional forms and the relationships between variables. The results (corrected to account for an interpretive error noted in Pyle, 1995, p. 13), suggest that actual sentences in theUS for 1984 are somewhat shorter than optimal sentences, but nevertheless are closer to the optimum than would be called for by a strictly retributive (proportionate to the harm) sentencing scheme. Alternatively, using relatively weak assumptions one can infer the social values of the harms imposed by crimes as implicit in current sentences. Waldfogel (1993) finds these implicit valuationscorrespond closely with estimates of actual harms as given by Cohen (1988).

SinceWaldfogel (1993) takes the probabilities of punishment as exogenous, his analysis does not reach the question of whether the optimal number of offenders is incarcerated. A more comprehensive analysis is needed to address what is perhaps the most important public policy issue concerning the economics of prisons: Do prisons pay? Piehl and Dilulio (1995) (also see Dilulio and Piehl, 1991) review the literature and present some estimates. The idea is to use self-reports of incarcerated offenders to estimate the amount of crime such offenders would have committed if not incarcerated, and then, after pricing these crimes, to compare the 'saved' social costs attributable to incarceration with the direct costs (capital and operating) of incarceration. The self-reports come from surveys constructed to minimize biased and inaccurate reporting. (The earliest reliable surveys were completed by the Rand Corporation (see the discussion in Visher, 1986).) Since the distribution of offender reports are heavily skewed, the result depends upon whether the experience of the median, mean or whichever other offender's experience is taken as the basis for the estimate. For example, in one recent report (Piehl and Dilulio, 1995, p. 25, Table 3), the benefit-cost ratio for prisons ranges from 64.02 to 0.07, depending upon where in the distribution the sampling is done.

Moreover, this method does not impart a social value to retribution, nor does it capture deterrent and replacement effects. It takes as a baseline the unlikely prospect that offenders would simply be released unsupervised if not incarcerated.The omission of replacement effects is particularly troubling since it works in an opposite direction to that of the deterrent, retribution and incapacitation effects. The implication is that the derived benefit-cost ratios are not necessarily a lower bound for whatever part of the distribution is sampled. Limiting the estimates to crime categories with low replacement rates should give more reliable estimates, but identifying these categories is a problem. Whereas incarcerated drug dealers are rapidly replaced on the streets, and intra-familial murderers are not, the situation is not so clear with respect to many other crimes. Moreover, there are undoubtedly differences in prison populationsacross geographical jurisdictions.

The age-distribution of offenders, the crime mix, and so on... are all affected by numerous variables (legitimate labor market opportunities, the allocation of police resources) not accounted for in the analysis, thus making inferences for jurisdictions other than that from which the sample was obtained, or indeed for the same jurisdiction at a differenttime, somewhat problematic.

Since age markedly affects the proclivity for crime, the criminal career profile should also be taken into account (Blumstein and Cohen, 1987). For example, a sampled offender on the downward slope of the age-criminality curve will report crime figures that, if extrapolated forward, will lead to an upwardly biased estimate of the benefits from incarceration. Finally, all downstream costs related to incarceration are ignored in this type of analysis.

If offenders form their expectations of the risk and costs of punishment primarily from their own experiences, then failing to incarcerate the sampled offender would lower his perception of the riskiness of criminal activity, and lead to increases in the amount of future crime.

The training effects (whether positive or negative) of imprisonment and any stigma and job-market effects are also included from considaration. Very few self-report studies attempt to adjust for all present concerns except deterrence and downstreams effects. His 'best guess' point estimate of the incarceration elasticity of aggregate crime is 0.16 (Spelman, 1994, p. 220). That is, a 1 percent increase in the prison population is predicted to reduce the level of crime by about 0.16 percent.

An alternative methodology more in keeping with the economic model is presented in Levitt (1996) (also see Marvell and Moody, 1994). Levitt estimates offensesupply functions using (a proxy for) prison population as an explanatory variable. If prison populations were exogenous, in principle the coefficient couldbe used to capture incapacitation, deterrence and replacement effects.

But Levitt rightly notes that prison populations depend to an extent upon the level of offenses, so that simultaneity problems intrude (Hersch and Netter, 1984, and Cameron, 1989, attempt to estimate the impact of offenses on sentence lengths and prison populations). Levitt employs instrumental variables reflecting prison overcrowding legislation, and thus attempts to isolate the one-way impact of incarceration on crime rates.

The estimation indicates that 'each additional prisoner leads to a reduction of between five and six reported crimes. Including unreported crimes raises the total to fifteen' (Levitt, 1996, p. 345). This number is very close to the median numbers obtained from self-reportsurveys, although only incapacitation effects are accounted for in the latter studies.

Levitt demonstrates that his estimates lead to a benefit-cost ratio for the marginal prisoner that exceeds unity, and suggests that the current level of imprisonment (in the US) is 'roughly efficient' (ibid., p. 324).

Levitt's paper will undoubtedly excite controversy (see, for example, Donohue and Siegelman, 1998). If the various subsystems of the criminal justice system do not adjust rapidly to exogenous shifts, then lagged offense rates would be expected to have an impact upon the demand for overcrowding litigation. This would call into question a crucial assumption in the model. Levitt presents numbers indicating otherwise (Levitt, 1996, pp. 334-336), and presents econometric tests supporting the overidentifying restrictions (ibid., p. 340).

Perhaps an equally important consideration is whether Levitt has faithfully interpreted the model he seeks to implement. For Ehrlich (1973) as for Becker (1968), the supply of offenses function includes offender risk variables. Thus the appropriate imprisonment variable included in the offense supply equations is a measure of the expected cost of punishment, conditional upon conviction. Proxies typically used for this theoretical measure are based upon average sentence lengths received or served, not prison populations *per se*. While not implausible, the argument that potential offenders form their sanction expectations on the basis of observations of prison populations requires independent justification.

Donohue and Siegelman (1998) employ both the incapacitation and aggregate offense-supply models to calculate cost-benefit ratios from imprisonment in the U.S. The goal is to establish whether a continuation of the huge run-up in the proportion of the population incarcerated over the last quarter century is cost justified.

The authors, after reviewing the applicable studies,adopt offense elasticities of approximately 0.15 (also see Wilson, 1994). Attaching cost figures to these estimates suggests that further increases in the proportion incarcerated is unjustified for the US, but recent levels may be justified. These calculations do not take into account the possible criminogenic impact of current incarcerations. If imprisonment increases the criminality of released prisoners, then the US may be incarcerating at excessive rates. Donohue and Siegelman (1998) argue that certain pre-school enrichment programs are a more cost efficient alternative for reducing the level of crime.

ADDITIONAL TOPICS

This chapter has not attempted to canvass all topics that could be included in a survey of the economics of prisons. Notable exclusions are prison industries (Barnes, 1921; Auerbach et al., 1988), industrial relations in prisons (Staudohar, 1976; Wynne, 1978; Peterson, 1981; Zimmer and Jacobs, 1981), litigation of prisoner suits (Brown, 1992), racial disparities in the prison population and in recidivism (Myers, 1980a, 1980b, 1992; Freeman, 1986, 1988; Myers and Sabol, 1988; Cameron, 1989; Dilulio, 1994; Langan, 1994), class-based models of prison use (Andrews, 1993), various alternatives to imprisonment and to standard methods of incarceration (fines, community-based sanctions, electronic monitoring, bootcamps, corporal punishments (Langbein, 1977; Polinsky and Shavell, 1984; Waldfogel, 1995; Benson and Rasmussen, 1995; Avio, 1995; Kan, 1996)) and economic factors in the origins of prison systems (Langbein, 1976; Conley, 1981; Lewis, 1988, 1990; Nicholas, 1990).

The economics of prisons has come a long way since Becker (1968) regenerated the interest of economists in crime. Further progress will require developments in both theoretical and empirical spheres, including the specification and estimation of dynamic structural models of criminal behaviour. The many simplifying assumptions of existing models must be relaxed, and the relationships between the various crime categories and between criminal and legitimate labour markets better understood.

Studies of countries other than the US are necessary for establishing the generality of the empirical findings. 'Protracted prospective' longitudinal data sets (Janson, 1994) must be constructed on representative individuals, with information that includes sentence lengths actually served and activities undertaken while imprisoned, as well as on the more standard variables.

In general, one could argue that the punishment theories developed by economistsand within which the economics of prisons is embedded need to pay more attention to the stylized facts uncovered by longitudinal studies:

(i) most crimesare committed by youths;

(ii) only a small number of these youths persist in criminal activity as they age; but

(iii) these same people are responsible for the bulk of serious crimes (for discussion see Farrington, Ohlin and Wilson, 1986; Moffitt, 1994).

The theoretical models developed in economics do not appear to satisfactorily address these facts. One policy implication is that more attention is paid to influencing the lifetime profile of established criminals than attending to the prevention of such careers in the first place. Similarly, the underlyinglegal and social institutions providing the background environment for criminal activity require careful examination (Witte, 1993). Akerlof and Yellen (1994) provide an illustrative model that points in the right direction (also see Becker, 1996), a model which implicates 'community policing' (Campbell,1994). Finally, given their comparative advantage, economists have quite naturally confined themselves to the impact of the law and its administration on the incentives implicit in fixed preferences, that is, to short-run 'carrot and stick' approaches to modifying criminal behavior.

Perhaps a more complete picture of human nature than that depicted in the economic model of crime is warranted. It may now be time to explore the long-run preference-shaping impact of the law (Dau-Schmidt, 1990; Friedman, 1993; Robinson, 1994) and education (Witte, 1996, 1997; Usher, 1997), along with the role of habituation in that process (Wilson, 1994; Dilulio, 1996). We know little about how and why a shared moral order is developed and maintained (Robinson, 1994). This change in perspective, calling as it does for an examination of the relationship between socialization and individuation, suggests a return to a relatively neglected part of the research program laid out in Adam Smith ([1791] 1976). Analysis of the social institutions that inculcate self-command, and which otherwise function as civilizing forces in our society (Muller,1993; Wilson, 1993), should be part and parcel of the research strategy adopted by social scientists to help understand and control crime.

5

The Surveillance Society

INTRODUCTION

In June 2006 the Surveillance Studies Network was commissioned, by the United Kingdom Information Commissioner, to write a report on the surveillance society. This document is a summary of that report. It is split into three sections which cover the essential material in the report. The first maps the terrain of the surveillance society: its definitions, issues and consequences. The second shows how the surveillance society operates. The third examines some of the regulatory challenges posed by the surveillance society.

SUMMARY, HISTORY, DEFINITIONS

We live in a surveillance society. It is pointless to talk about surveillance society in the future tense. In all the rich countries of the world everyday life is suffused with surveillance encounters, not merely from dawn to dusk but 24/7. It is not just that CCTV may capture our image several hundred times a day or that check-out clerks want to see our loyalty cards in the supermarket. It is that these systems represent a basic, complex infrastructure which assumes that gathering and processing personal data is vital to contemporary living.

Some forms of surveillance have always existed as people watch over each other for mutual care, for moral caution and to discover information covertly. However, from about 400 hundred years ago, 'rational' methods began to be applied to organizational practices, that steadily did away with the informal social networks and controls on which everyday business and governing previously relied. People's ordinary social ties were made irrelevant so that family connections and personal identities would not interfere with the smooth running of these new organizations, called 'bureaucracies'. But the good news was that by this means citizens and eventually workers could expect that their rights would be respected because they were protected by accurate records as well as by law. Impersonal and rule-centred practices spawned surveillance. New, post war, information technologies revolutionized bureaucratic administration, enhancing speed, control and co-ordination. This, coupled with improved identification and tracking techniques developed in military and police departments, constitutes the main message of this report. Surveillance grows as part of being modern.

What's Wrong with Surveillance Society?

Understanding surveillance society as a product of modernity helps us avoid two traps: thinking of surveillance as a malign plot hatched by evil powers and thinking that surveillance is solely the product of new technologies (and of course the most paranoid see those two as one). But getting surveillance into proper perspective does not mean that all is well. All it means is that we have to be careful identifying the key issues and vigilant in calling attention to them.

Surveillance is two-sided, and its benefits must be acknowledged. Yet at the same time risks and dangers are always present in large-scale systems and of course power does corrupt or at least skews the vision of those who wield it. Large-scale technological infrastructures are prone to large-scale problems. One inadvertent or ill-advised keystroke can easily cause havoc. Think of the release for 'research' purposes, of twenty million of ordinary peoples' online search queries from AOL in August 2006. Supposedly shorn of identifiers, it took only moments to start connecting search records with names.

It is equally important to consider corruption and skewed visions of power. Again, we do not have to imagine some wicked tyrant getting access keys to social security or medical databases to see the problem. The corruptions of power include leaders who appeal to some supposed greater good (like victory in war) to justify unusual or extraordinary tactics. In the USA, Japanese Americans were singled out for internment during World War Two through the – normally illegal – use of census data. More recently, many Muslim Americans are branded as unfit for travel using no-fly lists or are otherwise subject to racial profiling, condemned in other contexts for its manifest unfairness.

In the world of high technology and global commerce unintended consequences of well-meaning actions and policies abound. For example, in order to remain competitive, corporations, we are told, 'know their customers' and thus pitch their advertising and even locate their plants and stores appropriately. No one suggests that the store manager wishing to lure only the most creditworthy customers is devious in obtaining credit check services from Experian. It simply makes sense in the quest for greater profitability. But the results – the unintended consequences – of sifting through records to create a profitable clientele is that certain groups obtain special treatment, based on ability to pay, and others fall by the wayside.

Most profoundly, all of today's surveillance processes and practices bespeak a world where we know we're not really trusted. Surveillance fosters suspicion.

The employer who installs keystroke monitors at workstations, or GPS devices in service vehicles is saying that they do not trust their employees. The welfare benefits administrator who seeks evidence of double-dipping or solicits tip-offs on a possible 'spouse-in-the-house' is saying they do not trust their clients. And when parents start to use webcams and GPS systems to check on their teenagers' activities, they are saying they don't trust them either. Some of this, you object, may seem like simple prudence. But how far can this go? Social relationships depend on trust and permitting ourselves to undermine it in this way seems like slow social suicide.

Defining Surveillance; Tracing Surveillance Society

The surveillance society is a society which is organised and structured using surveillance-based techniques. To be under surveillance means having information about one's movements and activities recorded by technologies, on behalf of the organisations and governments that structure our society. This information is then sorted, sifted and categorised, and used as a basis for decisions which affect our life chances. Such decisions concern our entitlement and access to benefits, work, products and services and criminal justice; our health and well-being and our movement through public and private spaces. Everyday encounters with surveillance include:

- Video cameras which watch us everywhere we go – in buildings, shopping streets, roads and residential areas. Automatic systems can now recognise number plates (and increasingly faces).
- Electronic tags which make sure those on probation do not break their release conditions, and people arrested by police have samples of their DNA taken and kept whether they are guilty or not. 'Criminal tendencies' are identified earlier and earlier in life.
- We are constantly asked to prove our identity, for benefits, healthcare, and so on. The UK government now plans to introduce a new system of biometric ID cards, including 'biometrics' (fingerprints and iris scans) linked to a massive database of personal information.
- When we travel abroad, who we are, where we go and what we carry with us is checked and monitored and the details stored. Our passports are changing: computer chips carry information, and like ID cards, there are proposals for biometric passports.
- Many schools use smart cards and even biometrics to monitor where children are, what they eat or the books they borrow from the library.
- Our spending habits are analysed by software, and the data sold to all kinds of businesses. When we call service centres or apply for loans, insurance or mortgages, how quickly we are served and what we are offered depends on what we spend, where we live and who we are.
- Our telephones, e-mails and internet use can be tapped and screened for key words and phrases by British and American intelligence services.
- Our work is more and more closely monitored for performance and productivity, and even our attitudes and lifestyle outside work are increasingly scrutinised by the organisations that employ us.

Where we find purposeful, routine, systematic and focused attention paid to personal details, for the sake of control, entitlement, management, influence or protection, we are looking at surveillance. To break this down:

- The attention is *purposeful;* the watching has a point that can be justified, in terms of control, entitlement, or some other publicly agreed goal.
- Then it is *routine;* it happens as we all go about our everyday business.
- Surveillance is also *systematic;* it is carried out according to a schedule that is rational, not merely random.
- Lastly, it is *focused.* Much surveillance refers to identifiable persons, whose data are collected, stored, transmitted, retrieved, compared, mined and traded.

The personal details in question may be of many kinds, including CCTV images, biometrics (fingerprints or iris scans) communication records and content, or most commonly, numerical or categorical data. Because so many data are of the last type referring to transactions, exchanges, statuses, accounts and so on, Roger Clarke has called this 'dataveillance.'

Dataveillance monitors or checks people's activities or communications in automated ways, using information technologies. It is far cheaper than direct or specific electronic surveillance and thus offers benefits that may sometimes act as incentives to extend the system even though the data are not strictly required for the original purpose

Perspectives on the Surveillance Society 1: Processes

We turn now to an inventory of processes and issues that relate to the surveillance society as it has just been outlined. This is intended as a catalogue or check-list of important things to consider when discussing the surveillance society. It is important to note that although these vary in time and place in some form they are crucially significant for understanding the basic contours of surveillance society.

Social sorting is endemic in the surveillance society. In government and commerce large personal information databases are analysed and categorized to define target markets and risky populations.

Once classified, it is difficult to break out of the box. Since 9/11 such sorting might possibly have contributed to safety in the air (we shall never know) but it has certainly led to crude profiling of groups, especially Muslims, that has produced inconvenience, hardship and even torture. Social sorting increasingly defines surveillance society. It affords different opportunities to different groups and often amounts to subtle and sometimes unintended ways of ordering societies, making policy without democratic debate. *Data flow:* Data gathered by surveillance technologies flow around computer networks. Many may consent to giving data in one setting, but what happens if those data are then transferred elsewhere? In order to protect children from abuse, or to reduce fraud in public services, frequent calls are made to draw on more and more varied databases. Yet there is already all-too-little knowledge either among the public or among data-sharing agencies about where exactly those data travel. The idea that policy interventions be 'intelligence-led' has taken hold and this, along with the networking and data-matching potentials of today's digital infrastructures, means that surveillance appears to operate by a logic of its own. That logic needs to be questioned, examined and checked, particularly in regard to processes that involve data-flow from one setting to another.

Function Creep occurs when personal data, collected and used for one purpose and to fulfil one function, migrate to other ones that intensify surveillance and privacy invasions beyond what was originally understood, and considered socially, ethically and legally acceptable. In the case of Oyster cards in the UK, data that begin life in the commercial sphere of public transit, are increasingly required in police inquiries.

Function creep usually happens quietly, as a bit of administrative convenience. Indeed, because new technologies permit increasing amounts of data interchange and because organizational efficiency is frequently seen as a top priority, the human consequences of function creep are all-too-often unknown, ignored or downplayed.

Technologies: Technologies are critical to surveillance, but two important things must also be remembered: One, 'human surveillance' of a direct kind, unmediated by technology, still occurs and is often yoked with more technological kinds. Two, technological systems themselves are neither the cause nor the sum of what surveillance is today. We cannot simply read surveillance consequences off the capacities of each new system. For the surveillance society properly to be understood, we have to understand how technologies work, how they are used (this is an interactive process, involving in-house personnel as well as technology consultants and operatives), and how they influence the working of the organisation. Moreover, we need to understand these things clearly enough to influence policy and practice as our later discussion of impact assessments suggests.

A further concern regard technologies is that many argue (mistakenly, as we shall see) that anxieties about surveillance society may be allayed by technical means. Certainly, some so-called privacy-enhancing technologies (PETs) serve well to curb the growth of technological surveillance and their use should be encouraged where appropriate. But these are at best only ever part of the answer. We are correct to be wary of any offers to fix what are taken to be technical problems with technical solutions. As we shall see, the real world of surveillance society is far too complex for such superficial responses.

Perspectives on the Surveillance Society 2: Issues

Privacy, Ethics, Human Rights: Since the 1970s, much reflection and legal discussion of surveillance has occurred, producing data protection laws in Europe and privacy law elsewhere. Such regulation adopts a specific understanding of privacy. Although the 'Fair Information Principles' (FIPs) have evolved it has proved difficult to persuade policy-makers of the salience of the *social* dimensions of privacy let alone of the need to confront problems associated with the surveillance society as such. Surveillance society poses ethical and human rights dilemmas that transcend the realm of privacy. Ordinary subjects of surveillance, however knowledgeable, should not be merely expected to have to protect themselves. Three key issues are as follows:

Social Exclusion, Discrimination: Surveillance varies in intensity both geographically and in relation to social class, ethnicity and gender. Surveillance, privacy-invasion and privacy-protection differentiate between groups, advantaging some and, by the same token, disadvantaging others. Cradle-to-grave health-and-welfare, once the proud promise of social-democratic governments, has been whittled down to risk management and – here's where the surveillance society comes in – such risk management demands full knowledge of the situation. So personal data are sought in order to know where to direct resources.

Choice, Power and Empowerment: Ordinary people can and do make a difference especially when they insist that rules and laws be observed, question the system or refuse to have their data used for purposes for which they have insufficient information or about which they harbour doubts. But how far can individuals and groups choose their exposure to surveillance and limit personal information collected and used? When the surveillance system is infrastructural, and when its workings are shrouded in technical mystique, it is very hard indeed to make a significant difference. For instance, not until some identity theft scandal breaks do consumers become aware of the extent of personal profiling carried out by major corporations.

Even then, the focus tends to be on security – how to prevent similar fraud – rather than on curbing the power of businesses and state agencies promiscuously and prodigiously to process so much data. Individuals are seriously at a disadvantage in controlling the effects of surveillance.

Transparency, Accountability: Individuals and groups find it difficult to discover what happens to their personal information, who handles it, when and for what purpose. Yet little by little, their personal data are used to help shape their life chances, to guide their choices. Given the power of large organisations with sophisticated surveillance capacities, however, it seems only fair that ordinary people should have a say, even if only at the level of principle. This may be sought, not only through specialized agencies but also through advocacy groups and the mass media.

Accountability should be assumed within organisations, especially when high-powered surveillance occurs routinely, with potentially damaging consequences. Although workplace surveillance offers some salutary examples of poor practices at least in some instances employers have been obliged to curb the excesses of their monitoring by active labour union intervention. And much can be achieved through a transparent process of employers explaining what monitoring entails and obtaining negotiated consent for it from employees. When it comes to consumer surveillance, however, no analogue exists, and yet the massive data-power of a Tesco or a Walmart is almost unparalleled. The emergence of today's surveillance **society** demands that we shift from self-protection of privacy to the accountability of data-handlers. Such work parallels the efforts of regulators to enforce controls and to press for the minimising of surveillance.

A SURVEY OF THE SURVEILLANCE SOCIETY

The Surveillance Studies Network commissioned a number of expert reports which covered: Health and Medicine; Consumption; Work and Employment; Public Services; Citizenship; **Crime** and Justice; Communications; Built Environment and Infrastructure; and, Borders. From these reports, several key themes emerged which can be grouped into four areas: the context of the surveillance **society**; surveillance technologies; the processes by which surveillance operates and is implemented; and finally, how surveillance impacts on individuals and groups in **society**. There is of course, a great deal of overlap between these areas, and even more that could not be included.

The Context of the Surveillance Society

We first outline several underlying trends in western societies that lead to the surveillance **society**. These are: risk and security; the militarization of surveillance; the political economy of surveillance; and finally, the growing personal information economy.

Risk and Security: We live in a **society** obsessed by risk. Risk management techniques dealing with external and internal threats have become a key part of organisational activities. A *pre-emptive* as opposed to a *preventative* approach to risk has emerged.

Significantly, use of data-mining and profiling to identify risks shifts surveillance practices toward the screening of the actions and transactions of the general population.

This screening can then be used to target interventions on people or groups of people who are considered to be at risk or to pose risks for others. Collection and analysis of information, including data on identifiable individuals are vital. This can confer personal and social benefits, but at the same time the conception of safety and security has important implications for liberty, privacy and other social values, as well as for innovation and change Several examples illustrate this trend to risk assessment and pre-emption:

- Epidemiology and modelling within medical surveillance, to identify individual cases, record occurrences for statistical analysis and identify categories of the population who are at risk for particular diseases
- Risk assessment of individuals, families and neighbourhoods in child protection, mental health and criminal justice
- Categorising the risk travellers pose to national security using passenger manifests and financial transactions
- Evaluating the relative value of individual consumers, and their geodemographic profiles

The Militarization of Surveillance: Military surveillance is one of the few phenomena that can be said to be truly global in an age where everything is supposedly being globalised. The Earth is surrounded by a multitude of military surveillance satellites and transnational communications systems are thoroughly infiltrated by military surveillance systems. With the Global Positioning System and the Internet as two contemporary examples of technologies designed with military capability built-in, the entire history of modern surveillance can be traced from early development based in WW2 and Cold War Command Communications, Control and Intelligence (C3I) systems, with the aim being to make the planet a totally defensible and secure space.

This interaction manifests itself not only in the government and technological components, but also in the increasingly military way of talking about everyday safety: state and mass media talk of 'threat assessment', the 'war on drugs', the 'war on **crime**', and indeed 'the war on terror', of toughness in the law, of 'zero tolerance', and so on. 'Information warfare' has come out of the dark shadows of military covert operations and into the bright light of the business world, where corporate espionage is rife and the computer penetration and security specialists are redesignated as 'knowledge warriors'. Many surveillance technology companies are intimately bound up with the military yet sell to civilian users too. For example TRW, a major partner of the US defence contractor became a leader in civilian biometrics; French company Sagem manufactures everything from mobile phones through surveillance algorithms to unmanned aerial reconnaissance systems.

The Political Economy of Surveillance: These new companies along with traditional security providers and the large military suppliers form part of what might broadly be called 'the security industry'. Other industrial sectors are also key to the growth of surveillance, in particular, telecommunications and computing and banking and **insurance**. The security industry has grown massively in recent years. According to the US consultancy Security Stock Watch's 100 company index the growth of the industry as a whole has consistently outperformed both the Dow Jones and the high-technology NASDAQ indices.

At the end of the financial year 2005-6, the index had more than doubled in 3 years, with an estimated market capitalisation for the 100 companies on the index of over $400 Billion US. *Personal Information Economies*: Surveillance is not just conducted by states and organisations but also by ordinary people. After the 2005 London bombings, both television companies and police were encouraging people to use their mobile phone cameras to take pictures of suspicious characters. Growing numbers of people, particularly children and young people, are also putting their lives up for display, and in turn watching others' lives, though online webcams and social networking sites like *MySpace* and *Bebo*. At the same time, those with greater access to knowledge resources are starting to manage their 'data double' found, for example, in the databases of credit referencing agencies such as *Experian* or *Equifax*. These agencies allow individuals online access to their credit-records, enabling them to challenge and correct misleading data. This combination of voluntary corporate openness and the self-educated individual cannot be relied **upon** as a form of regulation, notwithstanding that a new generation of young people may be growing up as citizens used to carrying out, being subject to, and dealing with surveillance.

SURVEILLANCE TECHNOLOGIES

Whilst it is vital not to forget the importance of non-technological surveillance (for example, eavesdropping, spying and surveillance involving direct human judgement), this section will focus on issues connected with surveillance technologies. We will first concentrate on overlapping advances in four areas: telecommunications; video surveillance; databases; biometrics and location, tagging and tracking technologies. We will then consider interconnections between different technologies and the trend for surveillance technology simultaneously to vanish and spread everywhere. We will conclude by considering the limits of technological development.

***Technological Development*:** It is indisputable that new technologies have helped to change the nature of surveillance. There is no inherent 'good' or 'evil' within these technological systems. Efficient national databases can be used for the provision of targeted health care or for the victimisation of political opponents. But it is also not a simple matter of how they are used either. All technologies are developed within particular organisations which have particular aims and interests. Several particular technologies and their capabilities will be examined

***Telecommunications*:** Surveillance in telecommunications refers to the degree to which individuals, organisations and corporate bodies are able to monitor, sort and store information about the occurrence and content of telecommunications exchange, both between technological devices, and between technological devices and people. Since the state began 'wiretapping', technological development has led to more diverse technologies employed for telecommunications, and greater surveillance capability. For example, the location of a mobile device can be ascertained simply by triangulating the signal of the device with its reception by a number of different base stations as the signals are 'handed over' from one to another – this information can be stored for later data-mining. The so-called 'ECHELON' system, the global surveillance network operated by the American National Security Agency (NSA) maintains a huge base at Menwith Hill in North Yorkshire, routinely automatically filters all telecommunications traffic passing thorough the UK for key words and phrases and increasingly employs more sophisticated algorithms for advanced speech and even meaning recognition

Video Surveillance: Photographic surveillance has been in existence since the late 19 th century. Following the most recent surge of CCTV installation from the early 1990s, prompted by attempts to reverse the decline of city centre shopping districts as well as fear of terrorism, crime, there may now be as many as 4.2 million CCTV cameras in Britain: one for every fourteen people, and a person can be captured on over three hundred cameras each day.

During the 1990s the Home Office spent 78% of it crime prevention budget on installing CCTV and an estimated £500M of public money has been invested in the CCTV infrastructure over the last decade.

However a Home Office study concluded that 'the CCTV schemes that have been assessed had little overall effect on crime levels'.

Digitisation has allowed the automated use of CCTV systems to grow. So far this has occurred largely on the roads. Vehicle number plates are being used to identify the registered owner. Camera based enforcement of speed restrictions increased from just over 300,000 in 1996 to over 2 million in 2004 and raising an estimated £113 million in fines per annum.

This increase in state surveillance has received a consistently negative press, despite the fact that speed cameras, unlike open street CCTV have a significant impact in reducing death and injuries cause by traffic accidents.

There are plans to expand capity at the National Automatic Number Place Recognition (ANPR) centre from 35 million reads per day to 50 million by 2008.

***The Database*:** Multiple data can now be gathered, tabulated and cross-referenced far faster and more accurately than with the paper files that were once the characteristic feature of modern bureaucracy. Surveillance which uses databases can be usefully thought of as 'dataveillance.' Databases combined with other surveillance systems also allow algorithmic surveillance, the use of software to work on captured images or data and compare them to those in the database. This has been essential in the development of biometrics. Dataveillance is seen extensively in marketing, medicine, policing and border control.

For example, in *marketing* as the cost of databases has decreased, many private sector corporations seek to gather as much data on their customers as possible and target their marketing more specifically. Transactional data (use of credit cards, mobile phone calls etc) traceable to a person are combined with additional data from loyalty card programmes, customer surveys, focus groups, promotional contests, product information requests, call centre contacts, web site cookies, consumer feedback forums and credit transactions. This *internal* and frequently proprietary data is often 'overlaid' with *external* data from state agencies (e.g.: National Statistics), non-profit organizations or specialist data collection companies. These are most readily connected to postal codes, and given streets are 'profiled' with terms like 'prudent pensioners', 'fledgling nurseries' to 'rustbelt resilience.'

Simple matching techniques and the use of geodemographic profiling is now augmented by more sophisticated 'heuristic' (learning) processes of data mining, often referred to as Knowledge Discovery in Databases (KDD). This further assists in discovering previously unknown and *non-obvious* relationships within sets of information.

The 'product' of these systems is perhaps most visible as the basis for web personalisation systems, such as is employed by Amazon.com, which use multiple sources of data to predict the likely preferences of current shoppers.

Biometrics: All new ID systems use some kind of biometric: fingerprints, iris-scans, facial topography and hand-scans are all used on different passports and ID card systems. The allure of biometrics is the appearance of an 'anchor' for identity in the human body, to which data and information can be fixed. The biometric identifier becomes the access gateway to the data held. It is this convergence of data-mining and information integration with biometric identifiers. The idea is that accuracy will be increased and fraud reduced. PINs and passwords may be forgotten or lost, but the body provides a constant, direct link between record and person. The 'War on Terror' has produced a surge in research funding for and the implementation of biometrics. After 9/11 in the USA, biometric techniques already in commercial use or on the threshold of applicability were fast tracked and heralded as the key to winning this new kind of war.

The US Patriot Act, in a framework that has implications far beyond US soil, established a set of practices for biometric applications that afforded their almost unlimited use in the investigation and identification of terrorist activity. In the UK, the aforementioned shift towards digital CCTV has led to further research into the practicalities of biometric CCTV systems and facial recognition, following early experiments in Newham, Birmingham and other locations.

***Locating, Tracking and Tagging*:** Surveillance practices are increasingly referenced, organised and located through Geographical Information Systems (GISs). Many track the geographical movements of people, vehicles or commodities using RFID chips, Global Positioning Systems (GPS), smart ID cards, transponders or the radio signals given off by mobile phones or portable computers. Some current applications of these technologies are in law enforcement, border management and the workplace: For example, in *law enforcement,* in 2004/5 some 631 adults and 5751 juveniles, some as young as twelve years old, were 'tagged' allowing them to await trial at home rather than be remanded into custody.

Offenders released from prison are also subject to electronic monitoring either as a condition of early release from prison under the Home Detention Curfew Scheme or as a condition of being released on Parole.

In US *border management* RFID-enabled border smart cards are being trialled at the US-Mexico border. The RFID industry is flagging the potential for the technology to allow the tracking or tracing of migrant workers who cross the border for a time-limited period. Starting with animals, living beings are beginning to be implanted with RFID. In the US 70 people with degenerative brain conditions have also been implanted so they are more easily tracked, and one company chipped two of its employees for *workplace* access control. Continued developments in the application of real time geographic data to consumer profiles will provide yet another layer of data to assist corporations in targeting marketing campaigns to particular consumers. These, therefore, are technologies whose functions are highly likely to 'creep.'

***Technological Synergy and Function Creep*:** Whilst the capabilities of individual technologies and systems are important, there is also increasing technological synergy, or convergence of surveillance technologies. This is a long-term trend within computer systems and is also motivated by desires to create economies of scale. More and more systems are designed with interoperability in mind. This also means that new products can emerge out of older technologies, which in themselves had been understood and managed by regulators, coming together to create an entirely unforeseen and unregulated function. For example:

- IDs that work for several purposes – border crossing, fraud control, access to government information and perhaps commercial (video rental) and semi-commercial (libraries) too. When agendas such as the 'war on terror,' curbing the migration of undesirable groups and even the quest for solutions for credit card fraud are shaping the development of ID systems, the 'impersonal' ethos of a classic bureaucracy does seem somewhat undermined.
- ANPR in London was originally developed for military purposes, installed to help identify IRA bombers, and now has a role in traffic management, local government revenue raising and security against a new generation of terrorists.

***Towards Pervasive Surveillance*:** Technologies are at their most important when they become ubiquitous, taken for granted, and largely invisible. Pervasive or ubiquitous computing (Ubicomp), also known as 'ambient intelligence' (AmI), creates the conditions for pervasive or ubiquitous surveillance by being simultaneously embedded in the physical and virtual environment. Electronic services and realms are relatively easy to control compared to physical urban streets, but many urban passage-points now involve *both* electronic and physical parts working closely together. The combination of CCTV, biometrics, databases and tracking technologies can be seen as part of a much broader exploration, often funded with support from the US/UK 'war on terror', of the use of interconnected 'smart' systems to track movements and behaviours of millions of people in both time and space. In industry parlance, this is called multiscale spatiotemporal tracking.

The Limits of Technology: Of course, the promise of technologies is almost never delivered quite as anticipated. The biometric technologies for the USVISIT programme, for example, were downgraded from planned iris scans to digital fingerprints for logistical reasons.

There are also concerns about reliability, 'failure to enrol (FTE)' (the biometric is unrecognisable) and 'false non-match' (subsequent reading does not match the properly enrolled individual biometric). Despite this, major implementation decisions are often made before full trials have occurred. For example in the proposed UK ID system, it has been estimated that as many as one in six persons may not be able to use their ID cards because of the FTE problems.

Similar problems with law enforcement technologies such as facial recognition and ANPR have also been identified

Technological Lock-in and Regulatory Lag: Surveillance technologies frequently get promoted unproblematically as 'the answer' to multiple threats, most recently to the threat of terrorism. However the more that we become dependent on surveillance technologies, the more there is an apparent 'lock-in' which prevents other options from being considered, and a comprehension gap which increases a dependence on expertise outside the democratic system. Regulators are constantly running behind technological innovation, unable to understand 'how it works'. In this constant chase, one has to ask whether states possess the necessary tools to carry out meaningful regulation of complex surveillance practices. The question that frequently arises with all technological development is whether 'the genie can be put back into the bottle'. Patent holders and vendors tend to be silent on the reversibility of devices and systems.

SURVEILLANCE PROCESSES

The importance of pre-emptive risk assessment, and the prescription of surveillance as a solution to all kinds of problems has given rise to a number of processes and phenomena unique to it. Social sorting, unforeseen consequences, information sharing and a blurring of the public and private are four examples.

Social Sorting, Categorisation and Targeting. Social sorting, the sorting of the population into different categories of risk, entitlement or value, can be observed in many areas:

- Consumers continually supply businesses with their transaction data, and are part of an evolving feedback loop that binds acts of consumption with the gathering of data and the generation of profiles.
- Call centres now rank order customer accounts according to their relative spend, and alter their service levels accordingly. The Telecoms industry records traffic data to identify the best routes to market (e.g. marketing by SMS)
- Call centre employees are assessed for social and lifestyle factors which match those of the market segment they are serving.
- At many air, sea and land ports of entry it is now common, for example, to see 'fast track' lanes for expedited crossing, for example the 'Privium' system at Schiphol Airport in the Netherlands, which uses an iris-scan in place of lengthy queues for passport control.

Unintentional Control: Surveillance should not be taken to be identical with direct social control.

The intention of surveillance is often simply to manage efficient and swift flows of goods, people and information.

However, what spells 'efficiency' for one person spells 'social control' for another: this is particularly true for strongly personalised systems like ID records retrieval, which involves consistent and unique identifiers for individual citizens.

Information Sharing: To allow for social sorting, information needs to be accurate and readily available. In many countries, including Britain, there is a trend towards more integrated, 'joined-up' public services, often through partnerships and teamwork across several agencies. Increasingly, a variety of local partnership arrangements bring together a variety of agencies and professions so that their skills can be better focused on providing services to individuals in a more integrated way.

One effect of this key development is that the boundaries that were once thought to have provided certain, albeit fragile, safeguards to privacy and limits to surveillance are called into question, often leaving both the public and the service-providers bewildered about how personal information is, and should be, managed.

This is the case in public services, law enforcement, border management and marketing. For example, the Nectar card operated by Loyalty Management UK has over 50% of the UK population holding one of their loyalty cards. 216 catalogue companies in the UK are signed up to the Abacus data-sharing consortium, with information on 26 million individual consumers enhanced by Claritas' Lifestyle Universe. This overlays income, lifestyle, and life stage data at an individual level for each of these customers.

The Blurring of Public / Private Boundaries: Whilst both public sector and private sector share information, boundaries between state and private sector interests are blurring, as more tasks of government are carried out through a sometimes complex combination of public, private, voluntary-sector and market mechanisms.

Increasingly, a variety of local partnership arrangements bring together a variety of agencies and professions so that their skills can be better focused on providing services to individuals in a more integrated way.

Where state information is available for private use, as has been suggested with the National Identity Register (NIR), concerns have to be raised about the limits to the consent of people as citizens and as consumers, and where those boundaries lie. Questions will continue to be raised with the privatisation of telecommunications, border management (IBM's Project Semaphore, the UK's e-borders programme) and local security (e.g. Citizen Corps in the US who 'look out for unusual activities').

SOCIAL CONSEQUENCES OF SURVEILLANCE

We now turn more overtly to the social consequences of the surveillance technologies and processes we have just discussed. Critiques of surveillance are most frequently framed in terms of privacy and this is undoubtedly a vital area, although we would prefer to discuss it as one aspect of individual autonomy. We would also emphasise the far less frequently discussed outcomes of choice and consent; and most importantly, the sorting, categorisation and targeting processes on the life chances of individuals and whole groups or communities, their relative mobility, and access to opportunities.

Autonomy: Anonymity and Privacy: Surveillance affects autonomy by compromising individual anonymity and privacy. In many ways, a general condition of anonymity allows the individual the ability to make their own identity through their actions and relationships. One of the first casualties of pervasive surveillance, and particularly of ID systems, is the anonymity that allowed people to escape from the intense human surveillance strictures of small communities. The privacy of the vulnerable or marginalised is continually diminishing. In UK prisons, offenders all subject to almost constant surveillance. Even once released from prison, offenders are also increasingly subjected to electronic monitoring either as a condition of early release from prison under the Home Detention Curfew Scheme or as a condition of being released on parole.

Employers' capacities to delve into the private lives of their employees must be continually scrutinised. The coverage of multiple databases by national identification systems, particularly those which span public and private sectors, is a key area of concern. Similarly By the end of 2002, the BBC was reporting that law enforcement bodies had made over 400,000 requests for traffic data from mobile network operators.

As the ACLU have commented in their study of a new surveillance network, businesses and citizens are being 'conscripted into the construction of a surveillance society'.

Choice and Consent: Choice has played a major role in the debates about surveillance and data protection in North America. Yet in the United Kingdom, it has had a somewhat lower profile in contrast other means of protection. Can one chose whether or not to be surveilled if one wants to live a normal life? How is it possible anymore to argue that we have consented to surveillance? The issue of choice can be seen at work throughout the criminal justice system. We do not choose to be monitored by CCTV as we walk though public space, and no one has chosen to have their vehicle movements logged at the ACPO's ANPR Centre.

Arrestees do not choose, and are coerced, into providing fingerprint and DNA samples, which will be permanently logged on the police national database, even if they are released without charge. And, while a person cannot be forced to give a urine sample to test for the presence of drugs, it is hardly a matter of choice, as refusal can result in a fine, imprisonment or both. It is almost impossible for a person to know how information is being used, and how it may, in subtle ways, affect their lives; for instance, by increasing the chances that their vehicle is stopped by the police, or the demand that they pay in advance for goods and services. One answer might be to make state surveillance interactions with citizens non-compulsory where this is possible, which is what has been proposed with ID in Britain. However, this is largely an illusory answer, for once it is needed for a range of service-access it will become *de facto* compulsory. Moreover, existing identifiers relate to single roles, as drivers, consumers or tourists whereas the ID card system gives the government powers to monitor activities across a range of roles that include all of these as well as that of citizen.

Discrimination: Speed, Access and Social Exclusion: Discrimination, in the form of differential speed, ease of access and various degrees of social exclusion is a major outcome of the social sorting processes produced by surveillance. Governmental logic has changed. While older, twentieth century understandings of citizenship stressed the *inclusion* of all eligible persons in systems of health, welfare and legal protection, newer citizenship practices, including ID systems, seem to stress *exclusion* of undesirable elements.

Those with access to resources are highly mobile – international businesspersons, tourists and the like – and their identification systems (from credit cards to frequent flyer cards) tend to accelerate ease of movement. But for others, who are working (or worse, unemployed) migrants, refugees or asylum seekers, not to mention those with distinctive 'Muslim' or 'Arab' names, these systems tend to militate against movement both within and between countries.

The intensified surveillance of urban life also involves powerful processes of social exclusion. This is characterised by the creation of disconnections for those people and places deemed in some way unprofitable or risky. Crucially, then, the new surveillance technologies can thus forcibly *slow down* certain people's lives, making them logistically more, not less, difficult. Once introduced, however, both access and blockage are increasingly policed automatically, threatening a technological lock-in dividing contemporary societies more decisively into high-speed, high-mobility and connected and low-speed, low-mobility and disconnected classes.

Exclusion is also found in the pricing structures for goods. With Amazon.com already shown to be selling DVDs to different customers at different prices, the question is raised whether regulatory intervention might be necessary to ensure that mass commercial price-fixing does not emerge. And whilst it is difficult to draw conclusions about workplace surveillance and social exclusion, mainly because of the pre-existing occupational and social structural determinants of labour markets, one area is beginning to stratify opportunities for employment: e-recruitment. Sifting through large volumes of CVs and searching for potential candidates raises the question of discrimination in two ways. First, because e-recruitment is subject to biases and 'rules of thumb' embodied in professionals' choice of keyword search term, and second, because certain social, economic and ethnic groups do not have easy access to the internet.

This can work itself deep into the very infrastructure of society. With human discretion removed and embedded in code, and when cultural and national identity has become such a contested dimension of life, carrying a heavy freight of life-chances and choices, memories and hopes, it is ironic that parallel efforts are made to reduce it to machine-readable formulae and algorithms for ease of bureaucratic, policing and corporate administration.

Democracy, Accountability and Transparency: There are many questions here: what are the limits of public scrutiny?

How is the boundary between commercial databases and public and state security to be regulated? How are private companies to be made accountable for errors and false hits in their database systems? For example, currently there is extremely limited access for citizens who find themselves on a 'smart border' watch list. While multiple agencies and authorities can access the system or place information on the system, there is restricted capacity to remove or correct data. Finally, there are substantial questions surrounding the accountability of elected governments to their citizens and the 'offshore' nature of many of the private contractors of contemporary surveillance systems. In effect, commercial banks of data such as credit card transactions or mobile phone records that are held by multinational corporations can be 'offshore' and beyond the direct reach of a political jurisdiction. Recent examples of multinationals extraditing information will raise specific challenges for public scrutiny and regulation, particularly when a company holds the commercial data *and* has a contract for surveillance functions.

Under legislation in many countries, citizens have a right to know what information is held about them, and how it is being used, although there are exceptions to this requirement. This right requires a 'data controller' to provide to each individual information on all the data they hold on her and details of any processing it has been subject to. This goes some way to rectifying the asymmetry of power of the surveillance gaze, particularly where consent to use our personal data has been implied, rather than positively granted. However, large numbers of people do not know their rights, fail to exercise them, and receive little help from others in doing so.

Intensified dataveillance is becoming a normal feature in the modern state, and may, in itself, be justifiable – and justified by those who promote them – in the public interest. These activities may often be explicitly empowered by parliament. What makes them problematic is their manipulation of large quantities of personal data in ways that may overstep the mark established by data protection principles and laws (parliament, once again), and by other constraints and guidelines about how information is to be collected, collated and communicated. We may become accustomed to being surveilled, our activities and movements tracked and also anticipated, without noticing it, and – especially in the public services – without the ability to opt in or opt out, or to understand fully what happens to our data. We may well accept as 'reasonable' the limitations on privacy that we might otherwise reject if we were to consider what being a citizen should mean. It is far from certain that the political situation will, at the end of the day, allow privacy rights to stand up strongly to the claims of government organisations made in the 'public interest', even if the public interest seems clear and of greater importance. If surveillance is meant to be 'proportionate', a lot depends on how that terms is interpreted, and on who interprets it. A lot also depends on the safeguards that surround the new, intrusive developments.

REGULATING THE SURVEILLANCE SOCIETY

Surveillance requires regulation. By 'regulation' we do not mean only legal devices for controlling systems and practices, but any techniques that have a regulatory effect: that is, they apply rules to surveillance and data processing by setting limits and controls. Most of the systems for controlling personal data information processing have been developed in the context of data protection, with the aim of safeguarding *privacy*. Our comments in this section deal mostly with these strategies. But regulating *surveillance* could be something else again. It could be argued that surveillance protection must be devised in its own right, because its undesirable effects are not only those that have to do with the invasion of privacy, and that the first line of defence, though not negligible, is vulnerable. In this section of the Report we reflect on the regulatory experience, and assess the adequacy of these efforts. We also suggest possibilities for improvement.

What is Wrong with Regulation?

Regulation of privacy and surveillance has suffered from some common drawbacks. We are able to identify at least six areas of difficulty:

- Regulation has tended to be reactive: response had been made to technological development, implementation and practice after the fact.
- Regulation has had a largely technical and managerial focus, based on codes of practice, the fulfilment of standard legal requirements, and the application of

privacy-protective technologies, leaving little room for anticipation.

- Much regulation has been based on a narrow conception of personal privacy and of its value to individuals alone, (necessarily) reflecting the current thinking of policymakers who often implement a restricted view of what is in the 'public interest'.
- Regulation has been discussed and implemented largely outside of public debate.
- Debate has taken place within expert communities: for example, the world of data protection or law-enforcement. This has meant very little engagement amongst ordinary people with some of the most important issues of our time.
- Regulation is often seen, in political terms, as a burden unfairly placed on business as well as the state, inhibiting initiative, risk-taking and productivity. In Britain, there has been a marked attempt at deregulation, or 'better regulation', to lighten the load. The recognition that business and government may stand to benefit from the public-trust and efficiency gains that regulation may bring is very patchy in practice, although more evident in rhetoric.
- Media discussion concentrates heavily on 'horror stories' about incidents of privacy invasion, and also portrays both utopian and Orwellian views about surveillance technologies. Newsworthy stories are important, but too often, the complex ethical and social issues around surveillance are ignored. When surveillance is discussed, it is often in terms of either simple cause-and-effect ('CCTV will prevent crime') or fear ('we will all be under control'). Similarly, alternative views are countered by the fallacious and dangerous argument that 'if you have nothing to hide, you have nothing to fear'.

The Current State of Regulation

For the past thirty-five or more years, privacy protection has spread round the world. Lying at the heart of these developments have been some totemic principles. They require that an organisation:

- must be *accountable* for all the personal information in its possession;
- should *identify the purposes* for which the information is processed at or before the time of collection;
- should only collect personal information with the *knowledge and consent* of the individual (except under specified circumstances);
- should *limit the collection* of personal information to that which is necessary for pursuing the identified purposes;
- should not use or disclose personal information for purposes other than those identified, except with the consent of the individual (the *finality* principle);
- should *retain* information only as long as necessary;
- should ensure that personal information is kept *accurate, complete and up-to-date*;
- should protect personal information with appropriate *security safeguards*;
- should be *open* about its policies and practices and maintain no secret information system
- should allow data subjects *access* to their personal information, with an ability to amend it if it is inaccurate, incomplete or obsolete.

Imbued with these or similar sets of 'fair information principles' (FIPs), the regulatory world for governing privacy invasion and surveillance has been populated by general laws, laws covering certain sectors (e.g., telecommunications) or practices (e.g., data-matching), and international documents and declarations at the global and regional level, of which perhaps the most prominent is the European Data Protection Directive 95/46/EC, also reflected in the Directive on Privacy and Communications (2002/58/EC). Regulatory authorities such as privacy and information commissioners have been established at national, sub-national, and even regional levels. In addition, private companies, trade associations, and public authorities have formulated their own codes of practice and protocols, and online merchants have adopted privacy statements or policies. Penalties and sanctions have been applied to offenders under the various forms of legal regulation. In recent years, technological solutions – privacy-enhancing technologies, or PETs – have been enlisted in the cause of limiting collection, providing anonymity, and otherwise mitigating the surveillance potential of technology itself. Privacy advocates have been vocal and active in warning of dangers, exposing practices, and raising public awareness of how surveillance and privacy invasions may affect their lives. The media have often responded to surveillance's threats, even as the media itself finds it profitable to invade the privacy of celebrities and 'ordinary' citizens alike.

Building a practical system to control surveillance on the slender foundation of information privacy protection seems, to many, to be misguided. To others, however, privacy and its protection is capable of being extended to cover other, physically intrusive, situations in which there is an asymmetry between the individual and the surveillors, as in video surveillance. New surveillance practices, however, increasingly entail discriminations and other social 'bads' in ways that have powerful and inequitable effects upon life-chances beyond the realm of privacy violations themselves, which have consequences mainly for individuals. It is arguable, therefore, that the regulatory regimes for surveillance and privacy need to be re-thought and modified (at least) to be able to affect the design, implementation, and effects of new, more intensive and extensive, surveillance technologies. But the new surveillance is not just about technologies. It can be claimed that the 'problem' for regulatory regimes is not only how to cope with the technologies, but also how to influence the policies and purposes of those who develop and deploy them, and how to influence societies and populations who are subjected to them.

REGULATORY INSTRUMENTS: PROS AND CONS

The existing repertoire of policy instruments that have been brought into use for privacy and data protection, and therefore apply to large areas of surveillance as well are as follows:

International Instruments: The European Convention on Human Rights, and other international declarations, give legal and moral force to privacy protection that may play a significant part in reining in the excesses of surveillance. These and related documents have shaped specific legislative and implementation activity in a very large number of countries and lesser jurisdictions. Action at the international level is largely responsible for the pre-eminence of the set of principles that have governed data protection, and by extension, surveillance, for a long time.

Laws: The global spread of legislation to control personal-information processing has proceeded rapidly from the 1970s to the present time. Many countries have enacted sectoral and general laws for data protection, and most of these laws have established some form of specific enforcement and supervisory machinery. The latter, in the form of privacy commissioners, are essential to the entire effort to safeguard privacy. The USA remains outside the 'club' of countries with comprehensive laws of this kind, thereby weakening global efforts to regulate surveillance, except in a piecemeal and patchy way. The weakness of many laws and their implementation machinery in the field of personal information processing has long been a matter for complaint. Critics may have reason for impatience with legal solutions that may legitimate surveillance rather than regulate it.

Moreover, privacy and data protection laws do not easily regulate a wide range of surveillance practices, such as those that are part of modern telecommunications, and cannot easily be interpreted expansively to do so. In addition, the harm that surveillance may do to individuals, groups and whole societies do not come within the range of impacts that these individual rights-based laws are designed to remedy or prevent.

Self-regulation: A variety of codes of conduct or practice have been developed by industries or companies, specialist bodies, and states, to regulate surveillance in many domains of activity. There are also online means of self-regulation by merchants who trade over the Internet, in the form of online privacy statements, backed up by organisations who vouch for them. Self-regulation is sometimes written into laws, as are codes of practice in the UK's Data Protection Act 1998 and in the EU's 1995 Data Protection Directive 95/46/EC. Self-regulation is increasingly regarded as a better way of regulation given the 'failure' of laws and the less-regulated business climate that is considered desirable to foster.

Yet it is hard to imagine the existence of codes and the like without the prior and parallel existence of laws or international instruments that are the sources of the very norms and guidelines that codes embody.

Privacy-enhancing Technologies: A major development since the early 1990s has been the realisation that technologies themselves can provide powerful controls over surveillance or privacy invasion. Hence, the surveillance or non-surveillance potentials of specific technologies depend upon how they are designed and deployed. Thus encryption of personal data as it stored or flows across domains and other boundaries can range from the nonexistent to the very strong, network design and software 'code' can have a pronounced regulatory effect.

Encryption, anonymous web-browsing, filtering devices, smart agents, privacy-preference tools and the like may act as empowering instruments for the individual. It is unclear whether they are strong solutions to online surveillance practices by themselves.

Individual self-help: This is a further broad category of regulation. Here, the individual controls their own information disclosure, either through the use of PETs, by opting-in or opting-out of certain information-processing procedures, but also through knowledge, awareness and vigilance concerning the surveillance practices and privacy threats. All these put a premium on the individual having sufficient interest in protection and the 'cultural capital' – the ability and the means to comprehend what is happening, and to assert themselves in controlling inroads or seeking redress once these threats have been realised. In the USA, in the absence of regulatory or supervisory agencies, self-help, including initiating legal action, is the dominant means of privacy regulation, and criticisms of this model are legion. Other data-protection systems rely to some extent on individuals bringing complaints to the regulators and acting as frontline informants about dubious practices. We would also identify the activities of the following as important:

- privacy and anti-surveillance pressure groups, which – along with sections of the media – raise public awareness of issues and dangers, monitor situations, and exert pressure upon governments and businesses which make use of surveillance;

- technologists, who design surveillance and information systems, and whose education, training, and adherence to codes of practice may affect the awareness of their employers and shape the products;
- academic researchers, whose work may bring to light what is happening, explain why it is happening, and develop and test theories about the place and legitimacy of surveillance in the societies of the past, present and future; thus contributing expertise to public debate.

General Problems Concerning Instruments

Three of the most important problems with existing regulatory practices have to do with *fragmentation* and *weak co-ordination*. One problem concerns the main *instruments*; the other concerns the welter of jurisdictional *levels* at which regulation is supposed to take place. For both, the difficulty concerns the potentially more unified and global surveillance challenge that regulation may be expected to face, giving the likely persistence of trends. For both, the question is how matters may be improved. In other words, can fire be fought with fire?: if the forces operating to extend surveillance are increasingly integrated and 'joined up', whether in any one country or internationally, how well integrated are the instruments and the levels of countervailing protective activity? The third problem is that of applying these instruments to the social effects of surveillance – and, perhaps especially, 'new surveillance' – beyond privacy invasion, or of fashioning new tools. For all three, there is room for rethinking the panoply of regulation in terms of how it can be made more coherent and effective. There is also room for considering the possibilities for privacy and surveillance impact assessment to be applied at whatever level and within whatever field, domain or sector of application. This, too, can only be indicated here.

Options for Future Regulation

Privacy Impact Assessment: We believe there may be considerable merit in adopting the approach of privacy impact assessment (PIA) in the regulatory practices of jurisdictions at whatever level happens to be relevant.

PIA may best be seen as an instrument that those who proposing new or revised personal data-processing systems can use to mitigate the potentially harmful privacy effects on data subjects. PIA may help to show how privacy protection can be accommodated within an information-sharing scheme as an important ethical and legal requirement that may contribute to important social and political objectives, such as better, more citizen-oriented public service, or security, and not as an obstacle to them.

From Privacy Impact Assessment to Surveillance Impact Assessment: To encompass the potentially harmful effects of surveillance on a wider basis than that of protecting privacy, we suggest it would be necessary to develop PIA tools beyond their existing configuration, and to develop what could be called *surveillance impact assessment*, or SIA. This, of course, involves a change of meaning, for whereas PIA assesses impacts *of information processing on privacy*, SIA would assess the impacts *of surveillance on a range of values* that may include, but also transcend, privacy itself.

Because PIA has been innovated as a tool for looking at *privacy*, conceived in terms of individual rights, it is not at present best suited to embrace the further ramifications of surveillance in terms of a range of other social and personal impacts. Doing this would require something of a paradigm shift from considering only the effect on *individuals*, as privacy policy tends to do, to considering the value of privacy protection and surveillance limitation in *societal* terms as well.

Privacy is not only an individual value, but is also important for society as a foundation for the common good and for values held in common, such as democracy, trust, sociability, and a free and equal society. Because the value of privacy extends beyond the individual, we all have a stake in the right, and the ability, of any individual to have ones privacy protected. It is a collective value insofar as it is a collective good that cannot be divided, from the protection of which individuals cannot be excluded, and which cannot be efficiently provided by the market.

This is why SIA could play a valuable role by incorporating PIA but transcending it with a range of enquiries aimed at assessing the impact of surveillance, or privacy invasion, upon society itself and upon the other, non-privacy, interests of separate individuals, categories and groups. Questions raised in a SIA might include:

- Does the technique cause unwarranted physical or psychological harm?
- Does the technique cross a personal boundary without permission (whether involving coercion or deception or a body, relational, or spatial border)?
- Does the technique violate assumptions that are made about how personal information will be treated, such as no secret recordings?

Other Options: If SIA builds upon PIA, other options also build upon the present.

- Build a pool of technological knowledge-and-awareness capability to help regulators stay abreast of technological developments.
- Advise managers and technologists on how to design implement surveillance techniques responsibly, paying particular attention to strategy, organizational change, staff training and social responsibility
- Reconceptualise privacy as a collective social value, rather than an individual value.
- Encourage public debate about surveillance in a participative and non patronising way
- Conduct independent assessments of the costs of privacy, surveillance regulation and compliance. Consider whether they are excessive, and whether they inhibit innovation.
- Consider whether this balances the benefits of public trust and efficiency, bearing in mind that the 'balance' test is far from adequate and should be scrutinised in itself.
- Elevate the tone of the media beyond clichés, sensationalism and scare-mongering Finally, something should be said about the way regulation could be improved through a consideration of how adequate the relationships, and the interdependence of tasks, are: between regulatory systems at different levels up to the global, and between different kinds of participant,

including regulatory agencies and groups in civil society. It remains for further discussion how far, for example, the co-operative relationships that were indicated in the EU Directive 95/46/EC have served not only enforcement and compliance purposes, but intelligence-gathering and issue-awareness on the broader front of surveillance practices and technologies. For another example, how far there is a mutually productive relationships between regulatory agencies and civil-society groups that both assist these agencies when the latter draw issues and useful information or knowledge to their attention, and act as a gadfly when regulation appears to falter or when government and business practices seem to extend surveillance. Whether there is room for further innovation of independent roles in the regulatory system, apart from committed regulators and committed anti-surveillance advocates, is another matter for exploration beyond this Report, which perhaps serves as one kind of illustration.

6

Fundamental Principles of Insurance

Some useful terms in Insurance:

INDEMNITY

A contract of insurance contained in a fire, marine, burglary or any other policy (excepting life assurance and personal accident and sickness insurance) is a contract of indemnity. This means that the insured, in case of loss against which the policy has been issued, shall be paid the actual amount of loss not exceeding the amount of the policy, i.e. he shall be fully indemnified. The object of every contract of insurance is to place the insured in the same financial position, as nearly as possible, after the loss, as if he loss had not taken place at all. It would be against public policy to allow an insured to make a profit out of his loss or damage.

UTMOST GOOD FAITH

Since insurance shifts risk from one party to another, it is essential that there must be utmost good faith and mutual confidence between the insured and the insurer. In a contract of insurance the insured knows more about the subject matter of the contract than the insurer. Consequently, he is duty bound to disclose accurately all material facts and nothing should be withheld or concealed. Any fact is material, which goes to the root of the contract of insurance and has a bearing on the risk involved. It is only when the insurer knows the whole truth that he is in a position to judge (a) whether he should accept the risk and (b) what premium he should charge.

If that were so, the insured might be tempted to bring about the event insured against in order to get money.

INSURABLE INTEREST

A contract of insurance effected without insurable interest is void. It means that the insured must have an actual pecuniary interest and not a mere anxiety or sentimental interest in the subject matter of the insurance.

The insured must be so situated with regard to the thing insured that he would have benefit by its existence and loss from its destruction. The owner of a ship run a risk of losing his ship, the charterer of the ship runs a risk of losing his freight and the owner of the cargo incurs the risk of losing his goods and profit. So, all these persons have something at stake and all of them have insurable interest. It is the existence of insurable interest in a contract of insurance, which distinguishes it from a mere watering agreement.

CAUSA PROXIMA

The rule of causa proxima means that the cause of the loss must be proximate or immediate and not remote. If the proximate cause of the loss is a peril insured against, the insured can recover. When a loss has been brought about by two or more causes, the question arises as to which is the causa proxima, although the result could not have happened without the remote cause. But if the loss is brought about by any cause attributable to the misconduct of the insured, the insurer is not liable.

RISK

In a contract of insurance the insurer undertakes to protect the insured from a specified loss and the insurer receive a premium for running the risk of such loss. Thus, risk must attach to a policy.

MITIGATION OF LOSS

In the event of some mishap to the insured property, the insured must take all necessary steps to mitigate or minimize the loss, just as any prudent person would do in those circumstances. If he does not do so, the insurer can avoid the payment of loss attributable to his negligence. But it must be remembered that though the insured is bound to do his best for his insurer, he is, not bound to do so at the risk of his life.

SUBROGATION

The doctrine of subrogation is a corollary to the principle of indemnity and applies only to fire and marine insurance. According to it, when an insured has received full indemnity in respect of his loss, all rights and remedies which he has against third person will pass on to the insurer and will be exercised for his benefit until he (the insurer) recoups the amount he has paid under the policy. It must be clarified here that the insurer's right of subrogation arises only when he has paid for the loss for which he is liable under the policy and this right extend only to the rights and remedies available to the insured in respect of the thing to which the contract of insurance relates.

CONTRIBUTION

Where there are two or more insurance on one risk, the principle of contribution comes into play. The aim of contribution is to distribute the actual amount of loss among the different insurers who are liable for the same risk under different policies in respect of the same subject matter. Any one insurer may pay to the insured the full amount of the loss covered by the policy and then become entitled to contribution from his co-insurers in proportion to the amount which each has undertaken to pay in case of loss of the same subject-matter.

In other words, the right of contribution arises when (i) there are different policies which relate to the same subject-matter (ii) the policies cover the same peril which caused the loss, and (iii) all the policies are in force at the time of the loss, and (iv) one of the insurers has paid to the insured more than his share of the loss.

INSURANCE LAW & REGULATIONS IN INDIA

The concept of insurance has been prevalent in India since ancient times amongst Hindus. Overseas traders practised a system of marine insurance. The joint family system, peculiar t o India, was a method of social insurance of every member of the family on his life. The law r elating to insurance has gradually developed, undergoing several phases from nationalisation of the insurance industry to the recent reforms permitt ing entry of private players and foreign inves tment in the insurance industry. The Constitution of India is federal in nature in as much ther e is division of powers between the Centre and the States. Insurance is included in the Union List, w herein the subjects included in this list are of the exclusive legislative competence of the Centre. The Central Legislature is empower ed to regulate the insurance industry in India and hence the law in this r egard is uniform throughout the t erritories of India. The development and growth of the insurance industry in India has gone through three dist inct stages.

Insurance law in India had its origins in the United Kingdom with the establishment of a British firm, the Oriental Life Insurance Company in 1818 in Calcutta, followed by the Bombay Life Assurance Company in 1823, the Madras Equitable Life Insurance Society in 1829 and the Oriental Life Assurance Company in 1874. However, till the establishment of the Bombay Mutual Life Assurance Societ y in 1871, Indians were charged an extra premium of up to 20% as compared to the Brit ish. The first statutor y measure in India to regulate the life insurance business was in 1912 with the passing of the Indian Life Assurance Companies Act, 1912 ("Act of 1912") (which was based on the English Act of 1909). Other classes of insurance business were left out of the scope of the Act of 1912, as such kinds of insurance were still in rudimentary form and legislat ive controls were not considered necessary.

General insurance on the other hand also has its origins in the United Kingdom. The first general insurance company Triton Insurance Company Ltd. was promoted in 1850 by British nationals in Calcutta. The first general insurance company established by an Indian was Indian Mercantile Insurance Company Ltd. in Bombay in 1907. Eventually, with the growth of fire, accident and marine insurance, the need was felt to bring such kinds of insurance within t he purview of the Act of 1912. While there were a number of attempts to introduce such legislation over the years, non-life insurance was finally regulated in 1938 thr ough the passing of the Insurance Act, 1938 ("Act of 1938"). The Act of 1938 along with various amendments over the years continues till date t o be the definitive piece of legislation on insurance and controls both life insurance and general insurance. General insurance, in turn, has been defined to include "fire insur ance business", "marine insurance business" and "miscellaneous insurance business", whether singly or in combination with any of them.

On January 19, 1956, the management of life insurance business of two hundred and fort y five Indian and foreign insurers and provident societ ies then operating in India was taken over by the Central Government. The Life Insurance Corporation ("LIC") was formed in Sept ember 1956 by the Life Insurance Corporation Act, 1956 ("LIC Act") which granted LIC the exclusive pr ivilege to conduct life insurance business in India. However, an exception was made in the case of any company, firm or persons intending to carry on life insurance business in India in r espect of the lives of "persons ordinarily resident outside India", provided the appr oval of the Central Government was obtained. The exception was however not absolute and a curious prohibition existed. Such company, firm or person would not be permitted to insure the life of any "person ordinarily resident outside India", during any period of their temporary r esidence in India. However, the LIC Act, 1956 left outside its purview the Post Of fice Life Insurance Fund, any Family Pension Scheme framed under the Coal Mines Provident Fund, Family Pension and Bonus Schemes Act, 1948 or the Employees' Provident Funds and the Family Pension Fund Act, 1952.

The general insurance business was also nationalised with effect from January 1, 1973, through the introduction of the General Insurance Business (Nationalisation) Act, 1972 ("GIC Act"). Under the provisions of the GIC Act, the shares of the existing Indian general insurance companies and undertakings of other exist ing insurers were transferred to the General Insurance Corporation ("GIC") to secure the development of the general insurance business in India and for t he regulation and control of such business. The GIC was established by the Central Government in accordance with the provisions of the Companies Act, 1956 ("Companies Act") in November 1972 and it commenced business on January 1, 1973. Prior to 1973, there were a hundred and seven companies, including foreign companies, offering gener al insurance in India. These companies were amalgamated and grouped into four subsidiary companies of GIC v iz. the National Insurance Company Ltd. ("National Co."), the New India Assurance Company Ltd. ("New India

Co."), the Oriental Insurance Company Ltd. ("Oriental Co."), and the United India Assurance Company Ltd. ("United Co."). GIC undertakes mainly re-insur ance business apart from aviat ion insurance. The bulk of the general insurance business of fire, marine, motor and miscellaneous insurance business is under taken by the four subsidiaries.

Since 1956, with the nationalization of insurance industr y, the LIC held the monopoly in India's life insurance sector. GIC, with its four subsidiaries, enjoyed the monopoly for general insurance business. Both LIC and GIC have played a significant role in the development of the insurance market in India and in providing insurance coverage in India through an ext ensive network. For example, currently, the LIC has a network of 7 zones, 100 divisions and over 2,000 branches. LIC has over 550,000 agents and over 100 million lives are covered.

From 1991 onwards, the Indian Government introduced various reforms in the financial sector paving the way for the liberalization of t he Indian economy. It was a matter of time before this liberalization affect ed the insurance sector. A huge gap in the funds required for infrastructure was felt particularly since much of these funds could be f illed by life insurance funds, being long tenure funds.

Consequently, in 1993, the Government of India set up an eight-member committee chaired by Mr. R. N. Malhotra, a former Governor of India's apex bank, the Reserve Bank of India to rev iew the prevailing structure of regulation and supervision of the insurance sector and to make recommendations for strengthening and modernizing the regulatory system. The Committee submitted its repor t to the Indian Government in January 1994. Two of the key recommendations of the Committee included the privat ization of the insurance sector by permit ting the entry of private players to enter the business of life and general insurance and the es tablishment of an Insurance Regulatory Authorit y.

It took a number of years for the Indian Government to implement the recommendations of the Malhotra Committee. The Indian Parliament passed the Insurance Regulator y and Development Act, 1999 ("IRD Act") on December 2, 1999 with the aim "to provide for the establishment of an Authority, to protect t he interests of the policy holders, to regulate, promote and ensure orderly growth of the insurance industry and to amend the Insurance Act, 1938, the Life Insurance Corporation Act, 1956 and the General Insurance Business (Nationalization) Act, 1972". The IRD Act has established the Insurance Regulatory and Development Authority ("IRDA" or "Authority") as a statutory regulator to regulate and pr omote the insurance industry in India and t o protect the interes ts of holders of insurance policies. The IRD Act also carried out a series of amendments to the Act of 1938 and conferred the powers of the Controller of Insurance on t he IRDA.

The members of the IRDA are appointed by the Central Government from amongst persons of ability, integrity and s tanding who have knowledge or experience in life insurance, general insurance, actuarial science, finance, economics, law, accountancy, administration etc. The Authority consists of a chairperson, not more than five whole-time members and not more than four part-time members.

The Authority has been entrus ted with the dut y to regulate, promote and ensur e the orderly growth of the insurance and re-insurance business in India. In furt herance of this responsibilit y, it has been conferred with numerous powers and functions which include prescribing regulations on the investments of funds by insurance companies, regulating maintenance of the margin of solvency, adjudication of disputes between insurers and inter mediaries, supervising the funct ioning of the Tariff Advisory Committee, specifying t he percentage of premium income of the insurer t o finance schemes for promoting and regulating professional organizations and specifying the per centage of life insurance business and general insurance business to be undertaken by the insurer in the rural or social sector.

The Tariff Advisory Committee ("Advisory Committee") is a body corporat e, which controls and regulates the rates, advant ages, terms and conditions off ered by insurers in the general insurance business. The Advisory Committee has the authority to require any insurer to supply such information or stat ements necessary for discharge of its functions. Any insurer f ailing to comply with such provisions shall be deemed to have contravened the provisions of the Insurance Act. Every insurer is required to make an annual payment of fees to the Advisory Committ ee of an amount not exceeding in case of reinsurance business in India, one percent of the total pr emiums in respect of facultative insurance accepted by him in India; and in case of any other insurance business, one percent of the total gross premium written direct by him in India.

All insurers and provident societies incorporat ed or domiciled in India are members of the Insurance Association of India ("Insurance Association") and all insurers and prov ident societies incorporated or domiciled elsewhere than in India are associate members of t he Insurance Association. There are two councils of the Insurance Association, namely the Life Insurance Council and the General Insurance Council. The Life Insurance Council, through its Executive Committee, conducts examinations for individuals wising to qualif y themselves as insurance agents. It also fixes the limits for actual expenses by which the insurer carr ying on life insurance business or any group of insurors can exceed from the prescribed limits under the Insurance Act. Likewise, the General Insurance Council, through its Executive Committee, may fix the limits by which the actual expenses of management incurred by an insurer carrying on general insurance business may exceed t he limits as prescribed in the Insurance Act.

The Ombudsmen are appointed in accordance with the Redressal of Public Grievances Rules, 1998, to resolve all complaints relating t o settlement of claims on the par t of insurance companies in a cost-effective, ef ficient and effective manner. Any person who has a grievance against an insurer may make a complaint to an Ombudsman within his jurisdiction, in the manner specified. However, prior to making a complaint, such person should have made a representation to the insurer and either the insurer has rejected the complaint or has not r eplied to it. Further, the complaint should be made not later than a year from the date of r ejection of the complaint by the insurer and should not be any other proceedings pending in any other court, Consumer Forum or arbitr ator pending on the same subject matter. The Ombudsmen are also empowered to receive and consider any partial or total repudiation of claims by an insurer, any dispute in regard to the premium paid in t erms of the policy, any dispute on the legal construction of the policies in as much such a dispute relat es to claims, delay in settlement of claims and the non-issue of any insurance document to customers after receipt of premium.

The Ombudsmen act as a counsellor and mediator and make recommendations to both par ties in the event that the complaint is settled by agreement between both the parties. However, if the complaint is not settled by agreement, the Ombudsman may pass an award of compensation within three months of the complaint, which shall not be in excess of w hich is necessary to cover the loss suffered by the complainant as a direct consequence of the insured peril, or for an amount not exceeding rupees two million (including ex gratia and other expenses), whichever is lower. Ombudsman within his jurisdiction, in the manner specified. However, prior to making a complaint, such person should have made a representation to t he insurer and either the insurer has rejected the complaint or has not replied to it. Further, the complaint should be made not later than a year from the date of rejection of the complaint by the insurer and should not be any other proceedings pending in any other court, Consumer Forum or arbitrator pending on t he same subject matter. The Ombudsmen are also empowered to receive and consider any par tial or total repudiation of claims by an insurer, any dispute in regard to the premium paid in terms of the policy, any dispute on the legal construction of the policies in as much such a dispute relat es to claims, delay in settlement of claims and the non-issue of any insurance document to customers af ter receipt of premium. The Ombudsmen act as a counsellor and mediator and make recommendations to both par ties in the event that the complaint is settled by agreement between both the parties. However, if the complaint is not settled by agreement, the Ombudsman may pass an award of compensation within three months of the complaint, which shall not be in excess of w hich is necessary to cover the loss suffered by the complainant as a direct consequence of the insured peril, or for an amount not exceeding rupees two million (including ex gratia and other expenses), w hichever is lower. Every insurer seeking to carr y out the business of insurance in India is required to obtain a cer tificate of registration from the IRDA prior to commencement of business. The pre-conditions for applying for such registration have been set out under t he Act of 1938, the IRD Act and the various regulations prescribed by t he Authority.

The following are some of the import ant general registration requir ements that an applicant would need to fulfil:

(a) The applicant would need to be a company registered under the provisions of the Indian Companies Act, 1956. Consequently, any person intending to carry on insurance business in India would need to set up a separate entit y in India.

(b) The aggregate equity participation of a for eign company (either by itself or through its subsidiary companies or its nominees) in the applicant company cannot not exceed twent y six per cent of the paid up capital of the insurance company. However, the Insurance Act and the regulations there under provide for the manner of computation of such twent y-six per cent.

(c) The applicant can carry on any one of life insurance business, general insurance business or reinsurance business. Separate companies would be needed if the intent were t o conduct more than one business.

(d) The name of the applicant needs to contain the words "insurance company" or "assurance company".

The applicant would need to meet with the following capital structure requirements:

(a) A minimum paid up equity capital of rupees one billion in case of an applicant w hich seeks to carry on the business of life insurance or general insurance.

(b) A minimum paid-up equity capital of rupees t wo billion, in case of a person carrying on exclusively the business of reinsurance.

In determining the aforesaid capital r equirement, the deposits to be made and any preliminary expenses incurred in the formation and regis tration of the company would be included. A "promoter" of the company is not permitted to hold, at any time, more than t wenty-six per cent of the paid-up capital in any Indian insurance company. However, an interim measure has been permitted percentages higher than twent y six percent are permitt ed if the promoters divest, in a phased manner, over a period of ten years from the date of commencement of business, the share capital held by them in excess of twent y six per cent.

An applicant desiring to carry on insurance business in India is requir ed to make a requisition for a registration application t o the IRDA in a prescribed format along with all the r elevant documents.

The applicant is required to make a separate requisit ion for registration for each class of business i.e. life insurance business consisting of linked business, non-linked business or both, or general insurance business including health insurance business.

The IRDA may accept the requisition on being satisfied of the bonafides of the applicant, the completeness of the application and that the applicant will carry on all the functions in respect of the insurance business including management of investments *etc*. In the event that the aforesaid requirements are not met with, the Authorit y may after giving the applicant a reasonable opportunit y of being heard, reject the requisition. Thereafter, the applicant may apply to the Authority within thirt y days of such rejection for re-considerat ion of its decision. Additionally, an applicant whose requisition for regis tration has been rejected, may approach the Authority with a fresh request for regis tration application aft er a period of two years from the date of reject ion, with a new set of promoters and for a class of insurance business dif ferent than the one originally applied for.

In the event that the Authorit y accepts the requisition for registr ation application, it shall direct supply of the application for registr ation to the applicant. An applicant, whose requisition has been accepted, may make an application along with the relevant documents ev idencing deposit, capital and other requirements in the prescribed form for grant of a certif icate of registration. If, when considering an application, it appears to the Authorit y that the assured rates, advantages, terms and conditions offered or t o be offered in connection wit h life insurance business are in any respect not workable or sound, he may require that a statement thereof to be submitted to an actuary appointed by the insurer and the Authorit y shall order the insurer to make such modifications as reported by the actuar y. After consideration of the matters *inter alia* capital structure, record of performance of each promoters and directors and planned infrastructure of the company, the Authority may gr ant the certificate of r egistration. The Authorit y would, however, give preference in grant of cert ificate of registration to those applicants w ho propose to carry on the business of pr oviding health covers to individuals or groups of individuals. An applicant grant ed a certificate of r egistration may commence the insurance business within twelve months fr om the date of registration. In the event that the Authorit y rejects the application for registr ation, the applicant aggrieved by the decision of the Authority may wit hin a period of thirt y days from the date of communication of such rejection, appeal to the Central Government for reconsideration of the decision and the decision of the Central Government in this regard would be final.

An insurer who has been granted a cer tificate of registration should renew the registrat ion before st the 31 day of December each year, and such application should be accompanied by evidence of fees that should be the higher of-

- fifty thousand rupees for each class of insurance business, and
- one fifth of one per cent of tot al gross premium writ ten direct by an insurer in India during the financial year preceding the year in which the applicat ion for renewal of certif icate is required to be made, or the application for renewal of certificate is required t o be made, or rupees fift y million whichever is less; (and in case of an insurer carrying on solely re-insurance business, instead of the total gross premium written direct in India, the total premium in respect of facultative re-insurance accepted by him in India shall be taken into account).

This fee may vary according to the total gross premium writ ten direct in India, during the year preceding the year in which the application is r equired to be made by the insurer in the class of insurance business to which the regis tration relates but shall not exceed one-four th of one percent of such premium income or rupees fift y million, whichever is less, or be less, in any case than fifty thousand rupees for each class of insurance business. However, in the case of an insurer carrying on solely re-insurance business, the total pr emiums in respect of facultative re-insurance accept ed by him in India shall be taken into account.

The registration of an Indian insurance company or insurer may be suspended for a class or classes of insurance business, in addition to any penalt y that may be imposed or any action that may be taken, for such period as may be specified by the Authority, in the following cases:

- conducts its business in a manner prejudicial to the interes ts of the policy-holders;
- fails to furnish any information as r equired by the Authorit y relating to its insurance business;
- does not submit periodical returns as required under the Act or by the Authorit y;
- does not co-operate in any inquiry conducted by the Author ity;
- indulges in manipulating the insurance business;
- fails to make investment in the infrastr ucture or social sector as specified under the Insurance Act.

The Authority, in case of repeated defaults of the grounds for suspension of a certificate of registration, may impose a penalt y in the form of cancellation of the cer tificate. The Authorit y is compulsorily required to cancel the r egistration of an insurer either w holly or in so far as it relates to a particular class of insurance business, as the case may be:

- if the insurer fails to comply with t he provisions relating to deposits; or
- if the insurer fails, at any time, to comply wit h the provisions relating t o the excess of the value of his assets over the amount of his liabilities; or
- if the insurer is in liquidation or is adjudged an insolvent; or
- if the business or a class of the business of the insurer has been transferr ed to any person or has been transferred to or amalgamated with the business of any other insurer; or

- if the whole of the deposit made in respect of the insurance business has been r eturned to the insurer;
- if, in the case of an insurer, the standing contract is cancelled or is suspended and continues to be suspended for a period of six months, or
- if the Central Government of India so directs.

In addition to the above, the Authorit y has the discretion to cancel the r egistration of an insurer · if the insurer makes default in complying with, or acts in contravent ion of, any requirement of the Insurance Act or of any rule or any regulation or order made or, any direction issued thereunder, or

- if the Authority has r eason to believe that nay claim upon the insurer arising in India under any policy of insurance remains unpaid for three months af ter final judgment in regular course of law, or
- if the insurer carries on any business other than insurance business or any pr escribed business, or
- if the insurer makes a default in complying with any direct ion issued or order made, as the case may be, by the Authority under the IRDA Act, 1999.
- If the insurer makes a default in complying with, or acts in contravent ion of, any requirement of the Companies Act, or the LIC Act, or the GIC Act or the Foreign Exchange Management Act, 2000.

The order of cancellation shall take ef fect on the date on which notice of t he order of cancellation is served on the insurer. Thereafter, the insurer would be prohibited from entering into any new contracts of insurance, but all rights and liabilities in respect of contracts of insurance ent ered into by him before the cancellation takes ef fect shall continue as if the cancellation had not taken place. The Authority may, aft er the expiry of six months from the dat e on which the cancellation order takes effect, apply to t he Court for an order to wind up t he insurance company, or to wind up the affairs of the company in respect of a class of insurance business, unless the registration of the insurance company has been revived or an application for winding up has alread y been presented to the Court.

The Authority has a discret ion, where the registr ation of an insurer has been cancelled, to rev ive the registration, if the insurer wit hin six months from the date on which t he cancellation took effect:

- makes the deposits, or
- complies with the provisions as to t he excess of the value of his assets over the amount of his liabilities, or
- has his standing contract rest ored, or
- has the application accepted, or
- satisfies the Authorit y that no claim upon him remains unpaid, or
- has complied with any requirements of the Insurance Act or the IRDA Act, or any rule or regulation, or any order made thereunder or any direct ion issued under these Acts, or
- that he has ceased to carry on any business other than insur ance business or any prescribed business.

The main regulations that regulate the insurance business are the Insurance Act, 1938, the Life Insurance Corporation Act, 1956, the General Insurance Business (Nationalisation) Act, 1982, the Marine Insurance Act, 1963 and the Motor Vehicles Act, 1988. The Indian Contract Act, 1872, governs most of the aspects of the insurance contract. Additionally, the Foreign Exchange Management Act, 2000, Income Tax Act, 1961, Indian Stamp Act and the Hindu and Indian Succession Act govern some aspects involved in insurance.

Every insurer should, in respect of the insurance business carr ied on by him in India, deposit with the Reserve Bank of India ("RBI") for and on behalf of the Central Government of India the following amounts, either in cash or in approved securities est imated at the market value of the securities on the day of deposit, or partly in cash and par tly in approved securities:

- in the case of life insurance business, a sum equivalent to one per cent of his total gr oss premium st written in India in any financial year commencing after the 31 day of March, 2000, not exceeding rupees hundred million;
- in the case of general insurance business, a sum equivalent to three per cent of his t otal gross st premium

written in India, in any financial year commencing after the 31 day of March, 2000, not exceeding rupees hundred million;

- in the case of re-insurance business, a sum of rupees two hundred million.

If business done or to be done is marine insurance only and relates exclusively to country craft or its cargo or both, only rupees one hundred thousand should be deposited with the RBI.

These deposits will be held by the RBI though for the credit of the insurer and are returnable to the insurer in the event the provisions of the Insurance Act mandate such return. Interest accruing, due and collected on deposited securities will be paid to the insurer, subject to any deductions of the normal commission chargeable for the realization of interest. In addition, it is important to note that the deposits will:

- not be susceptible to any assignment or charge; or
- not be available for the discharge of any liability of the insurer other than liabilities arising out of policies of insurance issued by the insurer so long as any such liabilities remain undischarged, or
- not be liable to attachment in execution of any decree except a decree obtained by a policy-holder of the insurer in respect of a debt due upon a policy which debt the policy-holder has failed to realize in any other way.

Where the insurer has ceased to carry on all classes of insurance business in India, the deposit made with the RBI shall, on an application being made to the Court, be returned to the insurer after satisfaction of all his liabilities in India in respect of all classes of insurance business. Every insurer is required to invest and keep invested certain amount of assets as determined under the Insurance Act. The funds of the policyholders cannot be invested (directly or indirectly) outside India.

An insurer involved in the business of life insurance is required to invest and keep invested at all times assets, the value of which is not less than the sum of the amount of its liabilities to holders of life insurance policies in India on account of matured claims and the amount required to meet the liability on policies of life insurance maturing for payment in India, reduced by the amount of premiums which have fallen due to the insurer on such policies but have not been paid and the days of grace for payment of which have not expired and any amount due to the insurer for loans granted on and within the surrender values of policies of life insurance maturing for payment in India issued by him or by an insurer whose business he has acquired and in respect of which he has assumed liability.

Every insurer carrying on the business of lif e insurance is required to invest and at all times keep invested his controlled fund (other than funds relating to pensions and general annuit y business and unit linked life insurance business) in the following manner, free of any encumbrance, charge, hypothecation or lien:

For the purposes of calculating the investments, the amount of deposits made with t he RBI by the insurer in respect of his life insurance business shall be deemed to be assets invested in Government securities. In computing the assets to be inves ted by the insurer, any investment made with reference to the cur rency other than the Indian rupee which is in excess of t he amount required to meet the liabilities of the insurer in India with r eference to that currency t o the extent of such excess and any investment made in purchase of any immovable propert y outside India or on account of any such property shall not be taken into account.

Further, an insurer should not out of his controlled fund invest any sum in the shares or debentures of any privat e limited company. Where an insurer has accepted reassurance in respect of any policies of life insurance issued by another insurer and maturing for payment in India or has ceded reassurance to another insurer in respect of any such policies issued by himself, the assets to be invested by the insurer shall be increased by the amount of the liabilit y involved in such acceptance and decreased by the amount of the liability involved in such cession.

In case of an insurer incorporated or domiciled outside India or an insurer incorporated in India whose share capital to t he extent of one-third is owned by, or the members of whose governing body to the extent of one-third consists of members domiciled elsewhere than in India, the assets required to be invested should, (except to the extent of any part w hich consists of foreign assets held outside India) be held in India by way of a trust for the discharge of the liabilities.

Every Insurer shall invest and at all times keep invested his segregated fund of unit linked life insurance business as per pattern of investment of fered to and approved by the policy-holders. The insurer is permitted t o offer unit linked policies only where the units are linked to categories of assets that are both marketable and easily r ealizable. However, the total investment in other approved category of investments should at not t ime exceed twenty f ive per cent of the fund. An insurer carrying on general insurance business is requir ed to invest and keep invested at all times his total assets in approved securit ies in the following manner:

Every insurer is required to invest and at all times keep invested assets of pension business, general annuity business and group business in the following manner:

Every re-insurer carr ying on re-insurance business in India is required to invest and at all t imes keep invested his total assets in the same manner as specif ied for the general insurance business. An insurer should maintain, at all times, an excess of the value of his assets over the amount of his liabilities of not less than the relevant amount arrived at in the f ollowing manner ("required solvency margin"):

(a) in the case of an insurer carrying on life insurance business, t he required solvency margin shall be the higher of rupees five hundred million (one billion in case of re-insurers) or the aggregate sum arrived at based on the calculations specified in the Insurance Act.

(b) in the case of an insurer carrying on general insurance business, the required solvency margin, shall be the highest of the following amounts:-

  (i) rupees five hundred million (rupees one billion in case of a re-insurer); or

  (ii) a sum equivalent to twenty per cent of net premium income; or

  (iii) a sum equivalent to thirty per cent of net incurred claims.

This shall be subject to credit for re-insurance in computing net premiums and net incurred claims being actual but a percentage, determined by the regulations, not exceeding fifty per cent.

An insurer who fails to maint ain the required solvency margin will be deemed to be insol vent and may be wound up by the court. An insurer is requir ed under the IRDA (Assets, Liabilities and Solvency Margin of Insurers) Regulations, 2000, to prepare a statement of solvency margin in accordance with Schedule III-A, in respect of life insurance business, and in Form KG in accordance with Schedule III-B, in respect of general insurance business, as the case may be.

Every insurer is required to prepare a statement of the value of assets in accordance with the provisions of the aforesaid r egulations. Every insurer should prepare a s tatement of the amount of liabilities in accordance with the prov isions of Schedule II-A of the aforesaid regulations, in respect of the life insurance business, and in Form HG in accordance with Schedule II-B, in respect of the general insurance business. The aforesaid forms should be furnished separat ely for business within India and the total business transacted by the insurer.

In the event that an insurer transacts insurance business in a country outside India and submits the statements or returns or any such par ticulars to a public authorit y of that country, he is required to enclose such particulars along with the Forms specified in the aforesaid regulations and the IRDA (Actuarial Report and Abstract) Regulations, 2000. Every insurer should submit to the Authorit y the following returns, showing that as of 31 day of December of the preceding year the assets held and invested, investments made out of the controlled fund and all other particulars necessary to establish that the requirements of the Insurance Act have been complied with.

An insurer carrying on the business of insurance or reinsur ance in India is required, under the IRDA (Appointed Actuary) Regulations, 2000, to appoint a person fulfilling the eligibilit y requirements, to act as an appointed actuary, after seeking the appr oval of the Authority in this regard. It is mandatory for an insurer carrying on the business of life insurance in India to appoint any actuary. An appointed actuary has access to all such informat ion and documents of an insurer for the performance of his duties and obligations. An appointed actuary may also attend the meetings of the insurer and discuss matters relat ed to the actuarial advice and solvency of margin.

An appointed actuary, in addition to rendering actuarial adv ice to insurer (in particular in the areas of product design and pricing, insurance contract wording, investments and reinsurance), is also required *inter alia* to ensure the solvency of the insurer at all t imes, certif y the assets and liabilities that have been valued and maintain the solvency margin.

In case the insurer is carrying on life insurance business, an appoint ed actuary should also *inter alia*-

- certify the actuarial report, abs tract and other returns required under the Insur ance Act,
- comply with the provisions wit h respect to the bases of premium,
- comply with the provisions with respect to recommendation of interim bonus or bonuses payable by the life insurer to policyholders whose policies mature for payment by reason of death or otherwise during the inter-valuat ion period, and
- ensure that the policyholders' reasonable expectations have been considered in the matter of valuation of liabilities and distribution of surplus to the participating policyholders w ho are entitled for a share of surplus.

In case of an insurer carrying on general insurance business in India, the appoint ed actuary is required to ensure that the r ates are fair in respect of those contracts that are governed by the insurer's in-house tariff and t hat the actuarial principles, in the determinat ion of liabilities, have been used in the calculation of reserves for incurred but not reported claims and other reserves where actuarial advice is sought by the Authority.

Every insurer carrying on life insurance business should every year cause an investigation to be carried out by an actuary with respect to financial condition of the life insurance business, including a valuation of his liabilities and should cause an abstract of the report to be made. This provision shall apply in the event that an investigat ion into the financial condition of the insur er is made with a view to the distribution of profits or an investigation is made of which the results are made public. The IRDA (Insurance Advertisements) Regulations, 2000, seeks to regulate and control every insurance advertisement issued by the insurer, intermediary or insurance agent. For this purpose, every insurer, intermediary or insurance agent is required to establish and maintain a system of control over the content, form and method of dissemination of all advertisements concerning its policies and such advertisement should be filed with the Authority as soon as it is first issued. An advertisement issued by an insurer should not fall in the category of an unfair or misleading advertisement. An '*unfair or misleading advertisement*' means and includes any advertisement:

- that fails to clearly identify the product as insurance;
- makes claims beyond the ability of the policy to deliver or beyond the reasonable expectation of performance;
- describes benefits that do not match the policy provisions;
- uses words or phrases in a way which hides or minimizes the costs of the hazard insured against or the risks inherent in the policy;
- omits to disclose or discloses insufficiently, important exclusions, limitations and conditions of the contract;
- gives information in a misleading way;
- illustrates future benefits on assumptions which are not realistic nor realizable in the light of the insurer's current performance;
- where the benefits are not guaranteed, does not explicitly say so as prominently as the benefits are stated or says so in manner or form that it could remain unnoticed;
- implies a group or other relationship like sponsorship, affiliation or approval, that does not exist;
- makes unfair or incomplete comparisons with products which are not comparable or disparages competitors.

Every advertisement should disclose the full particulars and identity of the insurer, and that insurance is the subject matter of solicitation. In the event that such advertisement describes any benefits, the form number of the policy and the t ype of coverage should be fully disclosed. In case of Internet advertisements, the website or portal of the insur er or intermediary should contain disclosure statements which outline the site's specific policies vis-à-vis the privacy of personal information for the protection of both their own businesses and the consumers they serve and should also display the registration or license numbers. In addition to these requirements, every insurer or intermediary is also required to follow recognized standar ds of professional conduct as prescribed by the Advertisement Standards Council of India.

If an advertisement is not in compliance with the aforesaid regulations, the Authorit y may take action in one or more of the following ways:

- issue a letter to the adver tiser seeking information within a specific t ime, not being more than ten days from the date of issue of the let ter;
- direct the advertiser t o correct or modify the adver tisement already issued in a manner suggested by the Authorit y with a stipulation that the corrected or modified advertisement shall receive the same type of publicit y as the one sought to be corrected or modified;
- direct the advertiser t o discontinue the advertisement;
- any other action deemed fit by the Authorit y, keeping in view the circumstances of the case, to ensure that he interests of t he public are protected.

Every insurer who begins to carry on the business of insurance in India should ensure that he undertakes the following obligat ions to provide life insurance or general insur ance policies, during the first five financial years, to the persons residing in the rural sector or social sector, workers in the unorganised or informal sector or for economically vulnerable or backward classes of the society and other categories of persons and such insurance policies shall include insurance for crops.

A policy of insurance is a contract of a personal nature and hence cannot be transferred by the insured without the consent of the insurer. In the case of life and personal accident insurances, the subject matter of the insurance is a life and is not amenable t o transfer. An assignment of the policy in such cases is just an assignment of the right to receive the pr oceeds of the policy. The Insurance Act lays down the mode of assignment and transfer of a life insurance policy. An assignment or transfer may be made only on satisfaction of the following conditions:

(i) an endorsement upon the policy itself or by a separate instrument;

(ii) the endorsement or instrument should be signed by the transferor or his agent and should be attested by at least one witness;

(iii) it should specifically set forth the fact of transfer or assignment.

The aforesaid conditions need to be complied with irrespective whether the transfer or assignment is made without consideration or not. The insurer, on being given notice of the assignment or transfer, shall recognize the assignee or transferee as the only person entitled to the benefit of the policy and such a person shall also be subject to all the liabilities and equit ies to which the transferor or assignor was subject to.

Additionally, an assignment may be (a) absolute, or (b) conditional that it shall be inoperative or that the interest shall pass t o some other person on the happening of a specific event during the lifetime of the person insured, or (c) in favour of the sur vivor or survivors of a number of persons. However, the term "policy holder" does not include an assignee whose inter est in the policy is defeasible or is for the time being subject to any condition. Hence, an assignee of a policy subject to any condition shall not be entitled to t he rights of a policy holder.

A policy holder of a life insurance policy on his own life has the right, either w hile effecting the policy or before it matures, to nominate a person to whom the money secured by the policy should be paid in the event of the death of the policy holder. An insurer is not bound by such nomination unless it is brought to his notice, endorsed on the policy and regis tered in the records of the policy.

It is pertinent to not e that a transfer of assignment of a policy automatically leads t o cancellation of a nomination. Additionally, these provisions relating to nomination under the Insurance Act do not 16 apply to any policies under the Married Women's Propert y Act, 1874. The Reserve Bank of India ("**RBI**") is the apex bank of India established in 1935 under the Reserve Bank of India Act, 1934.

The Exchange Control Department within the RBI is responsible for the regulation and enforcement of exchange controls. Prior t o 1999, India had stringent exchange control regulations under the Foreign Exchange Regulation Act, 1973 ("FERA"). The Foreign Direct Investment ("FDI") regime in India has been progressively liberalized in the ninet ies with the passage of the Foreign Exchange Management Act, 1999 ("FEMA"), which replaced FERA. Most restrictions on foreign investment have been removed and the procedur es have been simplified. Non-residents can invest directly in India, either w holly or as a joint venture. Foreign investment is allowed in vir tually all sectors including the services sect or, subject to Government permission in cert ain cases. Insurance companies that are register ed with the IRDA, are permitt ed to issue general insurance policies denominated in foreign currency and are also permitted to receive pr emiums in foreign currency without the prior approval of the RBI. However, this is permitted only for cer tain kinds of cases such as marine insurance for vessels owned by foreign shipping companies and chartered by Indian companies, aviation insurance for aircraf ts imported from outside India on lease/hire basis for the purpose of air taxi operations *etc.*

Authorised dealers are also permitted t o settle claims in foreign curr ency on general insurance policies subject to certain condit ions such as the claim has been made for the loss occurred during the policy period, the claim has been settled as per t he surveyors report and other substantiating documents, claims on account of reinsurance are being lodged with the reinsurers and will be received as per the reinsurance agreement, the remittance is being made to the non-resident beneficiary under the policy *etc.* However, in the case of resident beneficiaries, the claim is required to be settled in rupee equivalent of the foreign currency due and under no circumstances can payment be made in foreign currency to a resident benef iciary.

As per the provisions of the Foreign Exchange Management (Insurance) Regulations, 2000, no person resident in India is permitted t o take any general or life insurance policy issued by an insurer outside India. However, the RBI may permit, for sufficient r easons, a resident in India to take any life insurance policy issued by an insurer outside India. However, an exemption has recently been made only for units located in Special Economic Zones ("**SEZs**") for general insurance policies taken by such units. Therefore, remittances towards premium for general insurance policies taken out by units located in SEZs from insurers outside India are permit ted provided that the pr emiums are paid out of the foreign exchange balances.

A person resident in India but not permanently resident therein is permitted to continue holding any insurance policy issued to him by an insurer outside India, if the premium on such policy is paid out of foreign currency resources outside India. A person resident in India may take a general insurance policy issued by an insurer outside India, provided that, befor e taking the policy he has obtained a no objection cert ificate from the Central Government of India. Fur ther, a person resident in India is also permitted to cont inue to hold any insurance policy issued by an insurer outside India when such person was resident outside India, subject to fulfilment of cer tain conditions. A foreign company may enter the insurance business in India in either of the f ollowing ways:

- FDI is permitted in India primarily either under t he 'automatic route', or with prior government approval. Where FDI does not fall under the 'automatic r oute', the foreign invest or would require the approval from the Foreign Investment Pr omotion Board ("FIPB"). Indian companies are generally permitted t o accept FDI without prior approval, provided cer tain sectoral policies and investment limits are met. In the insurance sector ther e is 26% sectoral cap on FDI, subject to obtaining license from the IRDA, which means that a f oreign company can invest up to only 26% in an Indian insurance company (calculated in the manner specified in the Insurance Act and regulations thereunder), while 74% would have t o be invested by an Indian company.
- In the event that a foreign insurance company is not desirous of directly investing in an Indian insurance company, it may, in the beginning, set up a branch or liaison office, subject to the approval of the RBI and/or the Government of India in this regar d. The branch

office in India is permitted to under take only a cert ain set of activities such as carr ying our research work for the parent company, representing the parent company in India etc. A liaison of fice is also permitted to under take only a certain set of activities such as acting as a communication channel between the parent company and Indian companies. Insurance companies and insurance agents, in India, are subject to tax for the premiums and the commissions received by them respectively, under the Indian Income Tax Act, 1963 ("Income Tax Act").

The Income Tax Act deals with the computation of the income of the f ollowing insurance companies:

- Companies carrying on life insurance business which ar e resident in India;
- Companies carrying on any other kind of insurance business, which ar e resident in India; and
- Non-resident persons carrying on the business of insurance in India thr ough a branch.

There is no recognized business method of ascert aining the profits derived from life insurance business. This would depend on the actuarial calculations and valuations. The Income Tax Act lays down provisions with respect to t he income received by an assessee from the business of insurance, whether the company which receives such business income is resident in India or not. These special provisions exclude the operation of other sections under the Income Tax Act dealing with computation of income. Therefore, the profits and gains from the insurance business are t o be computed artificiall y in accordance with these rules. The First Schedule of the Income Tax Act overrides the other provisions r elating to computation of income under separat e and distinct heads of income. The income is therefore, not to be computed under t he different heads and in accordance with the provisions of the Income Tax Act, but the income from all the sources should be computed as one figure on the basis laid down in this schedule.

The profits and loss of a person carrying on the business of insurance are to be computed separately from the prof its and gains from any other business. Though the profits of life insurance business are to be computed separately from the profits of non-life insurance business or other business carried on by the assessee, any loss incurred in life insurance business can be set off against profits of non-life insurance business or other business. In comput ing the profits of life insurance business, the profits and gains of the business is taken t o be the annual average of the "surplus".

This surplus is arrived at by adjusting the surplus or deficit disclosed by the actuarial valuation made in respect of the last inter-valuat ion period ending before the commencement of the assessment year. The tax payable, computed in the manner stat ed above, will be reduced by tax withheld at source for income from interes t on securities in respect of annual average of income tax. In computing the profits of any business other than lif e insurance, the profits and gains is taken to be the balance of the profits disclosed in the annual accounts.

In case of non-resident companies carrying on the business of insurance in India, in the absence of reliable data, the profits and gains is taken to be that proportion of the world income which corresponds to the propor tion of the premium income derived from India. A branch of a foreign insurance company is subject to income tax at the rate of 42% (including 5% surcharge on tax) while a subsidiar y of a foreign insurance company is subject to tax at the r ate of 38.75% (including 5% surcharge on tax).

The Finance Act, 2002 has brought insurance within the service tax net. The insured is thus liable to pay service tax at the r ate of 5%.

The Income Tax Act provides that the income tax payable on t he profits and gains arising from the life insurance business will be calculated at the rate of 12.5% of such prof its and gains. An insurance company is required to deposit an amount equal to one-third of the tax, in a Social Securit y Fund as notified by the Central Government.

Further, the insurance company is required to deposit an amount of not less than 2.5% of the profits and gains of the insurance business in such a Securit y Fund. Where the insurance company has deposited such an amount, the income tax payable by the insurance company will be reduced by that amount and the amount to be deposited in t he Security Fund would also be calculated on the income tax so reduced.

The Income Tax Act has laid down provisions for the taxat ion of insurance commissions. 'Insurance Commission' has been defined to mean any income (remuneration or reward) by way of commission or otherwise for soliciting or procuring insurance business. The effect of the prov ision is that any person responsible for paying any such income to a resident individual will be r equired to deduct income tax at the prescribed rates. The pr ovision applies only in the event that the individual is a resident of India. This provision is not applicable for an indiv idual who is not a resident of India. Tax for such payments made to a non-resident will have to be deducted under in accordance with the provisions of Section 195 of the Income Tax Act.

An insurance policy needs to be duly stamped in accordance with the stamp dut y prescribed for each kind of policy under the Indian Stamp Act, 1899 ("Stamp Act"). The rates of stamp duty on insurance policies are the same throughout the t erritories of India. Generally, the stamp dut y on a life insurance policy or group insurance is borne by the person effecting t he insurance. In the case of a fire insurance policy, the insurer is liable to bear the st amp duty. Non-payment of stamp dut y, is a punishable offence with a fine w hich may extend up to rupees two hundred if an insur er receives the premium for an insurance policy and does not execute a policy or executes a policy which is not stamped.

All persons who desire to act as an insurance agent for any insurer would have to be regist ered as such under the provisions of the Insurance Act and the IRDA (Licensing of Agents) Regulations, 2000. A license issued under the provisions of the Insurance Act entit les the holder to act as an insurance agent for any insurer.

Any person ("applicant"), desirous of being an insurance agent or a composite insurance agent, may make an application for a license to act as an insurance agent to the Author ity. The applicant should possess the minimum qualifications of twelf th standard or equivalent examination conducted by any recognized Board or institution, in cases w here the applicant resides in a place with a population of five thousand or more as per the last census; and passed the tenth standard or equivalent examination from a recognized Board or inst itution if the applicant resides in any other place. Such an applicant should also not suffer from any of the following disqualif ications:

- that the person is a minor;
- that he is found to be of unsound mind by a Court of compet ent jurisdiction;
- that he is found guilty of cr iminal misappropriation or criminal breach of trus t or cheating or forgery or an abetment of or att empt to commit any such offence by a Cour t of competent jurisdiction.
- Provided that where at least five years have elapsed since the completion of the sentence imposed on any person in respect of such person that his conviction shall cease to oper ate as a disqualification;
- that in the course of any judicial proceeding relating t o any policy of insurance or the winding up of an insurance company or in the course of an investigation of the af fairs of an insurer it has been found that he has been guilty of or has knowingl y participated in or connived at any fraud, dishonesty or misrepresentation against an insurer or an insur ed;
- that he does not possess the requisite qualifications and practical training for a period not exceeding twelve months;
- that he has not passed the examination;
- that he violates the code of conduct.

However, any license that had been issued prior to the commencement of the IRDA Act, 1999 shall be deemed to have been issued in accordance with the IRDA (Licensing of Agents) Regulations, 2000 and the provisions of the regulat ion in relation to the pract ical training, qualifications and examination shall not be applicable to such existing insurance agents. No insurance agent can be paid by way of commission or as remuneration, in any form, an amount exceeding,-

- in case of life insurance business, fort y per cent of the first year's premium payable on any policy or policies effected thr ough him and five per cent of a renewal premium payable on such a policy. However, the insurer may, during the first ten years of their business, pay f ift y-five per cent of the first years' premium payable on any policy or policies eff ected through them and six per cent of the renewal premiums payable on such policies.

- in the case of business of any other class, fift een per cent of the premium. An insurance surveyor is a technical expert who inspects the damage or loss of an insurance company. The insurer, based on the estimation of damage of the sur veyor, arrives at the amount of compensation payable to the assured.

Every individual, who int ends to act as a surveyor and loss assessor in respect of the general insurance business, may make an application to the Authorit y for a license. The Authority may grant a license (which shall be valid for a period of five years) af ter he is satisfied that the applicant:

(i) satisfies all the applicable requirements of the Insur ance Act and rules thereunder;

(ii) has furnished evidence of payment of fees for grant of license, depending upon the categorization;

(iii) has undergone a period of practical training, not exceeding twelve months; and

(iv) any other information that may be requir ed by the Authority.

A surveyor and loss assessor is required to spend a major par t of his time in investigating and managing losses arising from any contingency and prepare repor ts. He is required to carry out his duties in compliance with the code of conduct. A surveyor and loss assessor has inter alia the duty and responsibilit y to ensure that he discloses whether he has any int erest in the subject matter in question or w hether it pertains to any of his r elatives, business partners or through material shareholding; or maintaining confidentiality and neutralit y without jeopardizing the liability of the insurer and claim of t he insured; or conducting inspection and re-inspection of the propert y in question suffering a loss; or recommending applicability of depreciation, or the percentage and quantum of depreciation etc. Under the provisions of the IRDA (Third Party Administrators Health services) Regulations, 2001, ("TPA Regulations")the Third Party Administrator ("TPA") means a third part y administrator, who has obtained a license from the Authorit y, and is engaged for a fee or remuneration, as specified in the agreement with the insurance company, for the provision of health services.

An insurance company may engage more than one TPA and similarly, one TPA may serve more than one insurance company. The TPA is required to maintain professional confidentialit y of records, books, evidence etc. of all transactions that it carries out. In addition, the TPA is required to furnish t o the insurance company and the Authority, an annual repor t and any other return as may be required by the Authority. The TPA is prohibited from charging the policyholders with any separ ate fees.

Only a company, with a share capital and register ed under the Companies Act, 1956, can function as a TPA. In addition, the company is also required to fulfil the following conditions to be eligible to act as a TPA:

- The main or primary object of the company should be to carr y on business in India as a TPA in the health services, and on being licensed by the Authorit y.
- The minimum paid up capital of the company shall be in equity shar es amounting to rupees ten million.
- The TPA should, at no point of time, have a working capital of less than rupees ten million.
- At least one of the directors of the TPA should be qualified medical doctor registered with the Medical Council of India;
- The aggregate holdings of equity shares by a foreign company shall not at any time exceed twenty-six per cent of the paid-up capital of a third par ty administrat or.
- Any transfer of shares exceeding five per cent of the paid up capital shall be int imated by the TPA to the Authorit y within 15 days of the transfer indicating the names and par ticulars of the transferor and transferee.

Every license granted by the Authorit y shall remain in force for three years. The Authority may revoke or cancel a license gr anted to a TPA for any of the following reasons:

- The TPA is functioning improperly and or against the interests of the policyholders or insurance company.
- The financial condition of the TPA has deteriorated and that the TPA cannot function effect ively or that the TPA has breached any of the conditions of the TPA Regulation.
- The character and ownership of the TPA has changed significantly since the grant of license.
- The grant or renewal of license was on the basis of fraud or misrepresent ation of facts and that there is a breach on the par t of the TPA in following the procedure or acquiring the qualifications under the TPA Regulation.
- The TPA is subject to winding up proceedings under the Companies Act, 1956.
- Thcro is a breach of code of conduct.
- There is violation of any direct ions issued by the Authority under the Insurance Act or the TPA Regulations.

Every insurer re-insures himself t o protect against the risks t o which it subjects himself in the conduct of insurance business. The general insurance company has been designated as the sole re-insurer in India. Every insur er is required to re-insure wit h an Indian re-insurer such percentage of the sum assured on each policy as specified by the Author ity in this regard.

The insurer is free to chose any re-insurer subject t o the condition that such a re-insurer should enjoy a credit rating of a minimum of BBB of Standard and Poor or equivalent rating of any international rating agency. However, the placement of business by the insurer with any other re-insurer can be made only after obtaining the prior approval of the Authorit y. Every insurer is mandatorily required to retain the maximum premium earned in India commensurate with his financial strength and volume of business.

Every insurer should draw up a re-insurance programme in respect of all the lives covered by him. However, a programme of reinsurance on an original premium basis can be drawn only after obtaining the approval of the Authority. Further, a life insurer is not permitted to make any treaty arrangements with its promoter company or its associate or group company, except on terms, which are commercially competit ive in the market and the prior approval of the Authority.

The profile of the programme, duly cert ified by the appointed actuary, should be filed with the Authorit y at least fort y-five days before the commencement of each financial year. Additionally, the insurer should also submit the statist ics relating to its reinsurance transact ions with the annual accounts to the Authority.

Every insurer who wants to w rite inward reinsurance business should adopt an underwriting policy for the purpose of underwrit ing inward reinsurance business. A note on the underwriting policy indicating the classes of business, geographical scope, underwriting limits and profit objective should be filed with the Authority.

Every insurer is required to maintain a retention, which is commensurate with its financial strength and volume of business. The Authority may requir e an insurer to justif y its retention policy and may give directions to ensure that t he Indian insurer is not merely fronting for a foreign insurer. Every insurer should cede such percentage of the sum assured on each policy for dif ferent classes of insurance writt en in India to the Indian re-insurer as may be specified by the Author ity in accordance with the provisions the Insurance Act.

Every insurer is required to submit its reinsurance programme to the Authorit y for the forthcoming year within forth-five day s before the commencement of the financial year. Additionally, the insurer should also file with the Authorit y a photocopy of every reinsurance treat y slip and excess of loss cover note in respect of that year together with a lis t of re-insurers and their shares in the reinsurance arrangement.

Insurers are permitt ed to place their reinsurance business outside India with only t hose re-insurers who have over a period of the past five years count ing from the year preceding for which the business has to be placed, enjoyed a rating of at least BBB (with St andard and Poor) or equivalent rating of any other international rating agency. It is obligatory for all insurers to of fer an opportunity to other Indian insurers including the Indian re-insurer to participate in its facult ative and treaty surpluses before placement of such cessions outside India.

Any surplus over and above the domestic reinsurance arrangements class wise may be placed by the insurer independently with any of the r e-insurers, subject to a limit of ten per cent of the total reinsurance premium ceded outside India being placed with any one re-insurer. In the even that the insurer would like to cede a share exceeding such limit to any par ticular re-insurer, in respect of specialized insurance, the insurer should seek the specific approval of the Authority in this regard.

Every insurer should also make an outstanding claims pr ovision for every reinsurance arrangement accepted on the basis of loss information advices received from brokers/cedants and in cases where such advices are not received, on an actuarial estimation basis. In addition, ever y insurer should also make an appropriate provision for IBNR claims on its reinsurance accepted portfolio on actuarial estimation basis.

The Indian re-insurer is required to organize domestic pools for reinsurance surpluses in fire, marine hull and other classes in consultation with all insurers and should also assist in maintaining the retention of business within India. Such arrangements are required to be submitted to the Authority for appr oval. Further, the Indian re-insurer is required to retrocede at least fift y per cent of the obligatory cessions received by it to the ceding insurers after pr otecting the portf olio by suitable excess of loss covers.

Every insurer wanting to w rite inward reinsurance business should have an underwriting policy for underwriting r einsurance business, which should be filed with the Authorit y stating the classes of business, geographical scope, underwriting limits and pr ofit objective.

Where there is a positive enactment of the Indian legislature, the language of the statute is applied t o the facts of the case.

However, the common law of England is often relied upon in consider ation of justice, equit y and good conscience.

A contract of insurance is a contract uberrimea fidei i.e. a contract of utmost good faith. This is a fundamental principle of insurance law. Both the parties t o the contract are required to observe utmost good faith and should disclose every material fact known to them. There is no difference between a contract of insurance and any other contract except that in a contract of insurance there is a requirement of utmost good faith. The burden of proof to show non-disclosure or misrepresentation is on the insurance company and the onus is a heavy one. The duty of good faith is of a continuing nature in as much no material alteration can be made to the terms of the contract without the mutual consent of the parties. Just as the assured has a dut y to disclose all. the material facts, the insurer is also under an obligation to do the same. The insurer cannot subsequently demand additional premium nor can he escape liability by contending that the situation does not warrant the insurance cover.

The Insurance Act lays down that an insurance policy cannot be called in question two years af ter it has been in force for two years. This was done to obv iate the hardships of the insured w hen the insurance company tried to avoid a policy, which has been in force for a long time, on t he ground of misrepresentation. However, this provision is not applicable when the statement was made fraudulently. The Marine Insurance Act, 1963 ("Marine Insurance Act") lays down that the insured must disclose all the material facts before t he contract is concluded.

The disclosures by the assured or by his agent should be true. The insured is deemed to know every circums tance, which in the ordinary course of business, ought to be known by him. The insurer may avoid the contr act if the assured fails to make such disclosure or if the representation made is untrue. However, circumstances which diminish the risk, or which are presumed to be known by the insurer or information which is waived by the insurer or any circumstance which is superfluous to disclose by reason of any express or implied warrant y need not be disclosed, in absence of any enquiry. In India the post contractual dut y of good faith is very strict. The situat ion, though, has changed in England through a recent decision of the House of Lords. The decision in the Star Sea Case lays down that the duty of good faith in insurance contracts continues after the inception of the policy, but the duty is far less strict than it was prior to the commencement of the contract. This is because it would enable the insurers to avoid the whole policy ab initio for a post-contractual breach, which had no effect when the policy was drawn initially. However, this position has yet to be accepted by the Indian courts.

Representations are statements, made by one party to the other, either prior to or while entering into an insurance contract, of some matter or circumstances relating to it and which is not an integral part of the contract. These statements are said to have fulfilled their obligations when the final acceptance on the policy is conveyed.

A mere recital of representations made at the time of entering into the contact will not make then warranties. However, if representations are made an integral part of the contract they become warranties, and, in case of their being untrue, the policy can be avoided, even if the loss does not arise from the fact concealed or misrepresented. A policy of life insurance cannot be called in question on the ground of misrepresentation after a period of two years from the commencement of the policy.

In dealing with representations as circumstances invalidating a contract, consideration should be paid as to whether such representations are wilful or innocent and whether they are preliminary or for part of the contract. The Insurance Act lays down three conditions to establish that the misrepresentation was wilful; (a) the statement must be on a material matter or must suppress facts which it was material to disclose; (b) the suppression must be fraudulently made by the policy holder; and (c) the policy-holder must have known at the time of making the statement that it was false or that it suppressed facts which it was material to disclose. The burden of proof of establishing that the insured had in fact suppressed material facts in obtaining insurance is on the insurer and all the aforesaid conditions are required to be proved cumulatively.

In determining whether there has been suppression of a material fact it is necessary to examine whether the suppression relat es to a fact which is in the exclusive knowledge of the person intending to take the policy and also that it could not be ascer tained by reasonable enquiry by a prudent person.

A warranty may be distinguished from a representation in as much a representation may be equitably and substantially answered but a warrant y must be strictly complied with. A breach of warranty will avoid the policy, although it may not relat e to a matter mater ial to the risk insured. Warranties may be express or implied, if it is condition implied by law. However, implied warranties are mostly confined to marine insurance. The Marine Insurance Act defines a warrant y as a promise whereby the assured under takes that some particular thing shall or shall not be done, or that some condition shall be fulfilled, or affir ms or negatives the existence of a par ticular state of facts.

The statements must be true in fact wit hout any qualification of judgement, opinion or belief. The warranty should be in the policy or must be incorporated by reference. If any of the s tatements or representations made by the assured in the proposal have been made the "basis" of the contract and they are found to be untrue, the contract of insur ance would be void and unenforceable in law, irrespective of the question w hether the statement, concerned is of a material nature or not. However, non-compliance of a warranty is excused w hen, by reason of a change of circumstances, the warranty ceases t o be applicable to the circumstances of t he contract, or when compliance with the warranty is rendered unlawful by any subsequent law or when such a warranty has not been mentioned in the policy.

Conditions are terms which pr escribe the limitations under which an insur ance policy is granted and which specify the duties of the assured. They can be either conditions precedent or subsequent. Conditions precedent are those, which ar e essential for the creation of a valid contract, the non-satisfaction of which makes the contract void *ab initio*. Conditions subsequent relate to the continuance of a valid contract, the non-fulfilment of which leads t o the avoidance of the contract from the date of the breach.

They can be further classified into expr ess conditions and implied conditions. Implied conditions are those, which are implied by law to apply t o every contract of insurance irrespective of any specific inclusion or reference to them such as insurable int erest, good faith *etc.* A condition, which seeks to reduce or curtail the per iod of limitation and prescribes a shor ter period than that prescribed by law is void. However, the insured is absolved once it is shown that he has done everyt hing in his power to keep, honour and fulfil the promise and he himself is not guilty of a deliberate breach.

An insurer cannot take recourse to a condition, w hich has not been mentioned in the policy to reduce his liability. However, an insurance policy may not curtail the right but may mer ely provide for forfeiture or waiver of any such right and such a right would be enforceable against either party. Most kinds of insurance policies other than life and personal accident insurance are contr acts of indemnity wher eby the insurer undertakes t o indemnify the insured for the actual loss suf fered by him as a result of the occurring of the event insured against. Even wit hin the maximum limit, the insured cannot recover more than what he es tablishes to be his actual loss. A contract of marine insurance is an agreement whereby the insurer undertakes to indemnify the insured to the extent agreed upon.

Although the insured is to be placed in the same position as if the loss has not occurred, the amount of indemnity may be limited by cer tain conditions:

- Injury or loss sustained by the insur ed has to be proved.
- The indemnity is limited t o the amount specified in the policy
- The insured is indemnified only for the proximat e causes.
- The market value of the propert y determines the amount of indemnity.

Indemnity is a fundamental principle of insurance law, and the principle of Subrogation is a corollary of this principle in as much the insured is precluded from obtaining more than the loss he has sustained. The most common form of subrogation is when an insurance company pays a claim caused by the negligence of another. The doctrine of subrogation confers two specific rights on the insurer. Firstly, the insurer is entitled to all the remedies which the insured has against the third part y incidental to the subject matt er of the loss, such that the insurer can take advant age of any means available to extinguish or diminish, the loss for which t he insurer has indemnified the insured. Secondly, the insurer is entitled to the benefits received by the assured from the thir d part y with a view to compensate himself for the loss.

The fact that an insurer is subrogated to t he rights and remedies of the insured does not *ipso jure* enable him to sue third part ies in his own name.

It will only entitle the insurer t o sue in the name of insured, it being an obligation of the insured to lend his name and assis tance to such an action. An insurance policy may contain a special clause whereby the insur ed assigns all his rights, against third parties, in f avour of the insurer. In case of subrogation, which vest by operation of law rather than as the product of express agreement, the insur ed would be entitled to only to t he extent of his loss. The excess amount, if any, would be returned to the insured.

The doctrine of proximate cause is expressed in the maxim 'Causa Proxima non remota spectator', which means that the proximate and not the remote cause, shall be taken as the cause of loss. The insurer is thus has to make good the loss of the insured that clearly and proximately results, whether directly or indirectly, from the event insured against in the policy. The burden of proof that the loss occurred on account of the proximate cause, lies on the insured.

As per the Marine Insurance Act, unless the insurance policy stat es otherwise, the insurer is liable for any loss proximately caused by a peril insured agains t, but he is not liable for any loss which is not proximately caused by a peril insured against. An insurer would therefore be exempted fr om liability when the cause of loss falls within the except ions of the policy. The Marine Insurance Act further states that the insur er is not liable for any wilful misconduct of the insured i.e. the assured cannot recover for a loss where his own deliberat e act is the proximate cause of it. Further, in the event of loss caused by the delay of the ship, the insurer cannot be held liable, irrespect ive of the proximity of the cause.

The Consumer Protection Act, 1986 ("Consumer Protection Act") is one of the most important socio-economic legislation for the protect ion of consumers in India. The provisions of this Act are compensatory in nature, unlike other laws, w hich are either punitive or preventive. Insurance services fall within the purview of the Consumer Prot ection Act, in as much, any deficiency in service of the insurance company would enable the aggrieved to make a complaint. Disputes between policyholders and insurers generally pert ain to repudiation of the insurance claim or the mat ters connected with admission of the claim or computation of the amount of claim. In the case of assignment of all rights by the insured to the insurer, the consumer forum and he courts generally refuse to accept the locus standi of t he insured.

The courts have held that insurance companies do not fall under the def inition of "consumer" under the Consumer Protection Act, as no serv ice is rendered to them direct ly. Neither the subrogation nor the transfer of the right of action would confer t he legal status of a 'consumer' on the insurer, nor can the insurer be regarded as any beneficiar y of any service. Therefore, the remedy available to the insurer is to file a suit in a civ il court for recover y of the loss To constitute insurable interest, it must be an interest such that the risk would by its proximate effect cause damage to the assur ed, that is to say, cause him to lose a benefit or incur a liability. The validity of an insurance contract, in India, is dependent on the existence of an insurable interes t in the subject matter. The person seeking an insurance policy must establish some kind of interest in the life or property to be insured, in the absence of which, the insur ance policy would amount to a wager and consequently void in nature.

The test for determining if ther e is an insurable interest is whet her the insured will in case of damage to the life or proper ty being insured, suf fer pecuniary loss. A person having a limited interest can also insure such interest.

Insurable interest varies depending on the nature of the insurance. The controversy as to the existence of an insurable interest between spouses was settled by the cour t, which held that such an interest could exist as neither was likel y to indulge in any 'mischievous game'. The same analogy may be extended to parents and children. Further, the courts have also held that such an insurable interest would exist for a cr editor (in a debtor) and for an employee (in an employer) to the extent of the debt incurred and the remuneration due, respectively.

The existence of insurable interest at the time of happening of the event is another important consideration. In case of life and personal accident insurance it is suff icient if the insurable interest is present at the time of taking the policy. However, in the case of fire and motor accident insurance the insurable interest has to be present both at the time of taking the policy and at the time of the accident. The case is completely different with marine insurance wherein there need not be any insurable interest at the time of taking the policy.

The general rule on the formation of a contract, as per the Indian Contract Act, is that the part y to whom the offer has been made should accept it uncondit ionally and communicate his acceptance to the person making the offer. Whether the final acceptance is to be made by the insur ed or insurer really depends on the negotiations of the policy.

Acceptance should be signified by some act as agreed upon by the part ies or from which the law raises a presumption of acceptance. The mere receipt or retention of premium until after the death of the applicant or the mere preparation of the policy document is not acceptance. Nonetheless, acceptance may be presumed upon the retention of the premium. However, mere delay in giving an answer cannot be construed as acceptance. Also, silence does not denote consent and no binding contract arises until the person to whom an offer is made says or does something to signify his acceptance.

When the policy is of a particular dat e, it would cover the liability of the insur er from the previous midnight preceding the same date. However, where there is a special contract t o the contrary in the policy, the terms of the contract would prevail. Hence where the time of the issue of the insurance policy is mentioned, then the liabilit y would be covered only from the time w hen it was issued.

7

The Law of Insurance Contracts

The implementation of China's economic reforms, beginning in the early 80's, and the formal establishment of a "Socialist Market Economy" in the following decade, stimulated substantial changes and improvements in the Insurance Laws and Regulations of the People's Republic of China (hereafter: PRC). The need for a modern and sophisticated legal framework aimed at regulating rights and remedies arising out of insurance contracts, as well as the insurance business in general, became clear and compelling as soon as the Communist State began its slow but inexorable retreat and it ceased to take care of every aspect of the life of the Chinese People.

In the new socialist market context, the insurance contract is predestined to become the most important legal and economic tool available to those individuals who are not willing and/or able to bear the entirety of the risks associated with the implementation of the modern economic reforms.

Against such backdrop, this paper is aimed at exploring the history of insurance in China as well as the framework of insurance laws and regulation enacted in the PRC during the recent years. In particular, the focus of this essay will be upon the legal principles and rules that currently govern insurance contracts and the relationship thereby established between the insurance company and the insured.

Hence, the analysis of the legal protection of policyholders' rights and interests in China will center around the rules of insurance contracts interpretation, integration and performance at present in force. In light of the international nature of the contract of insurance, this paper will also offer a comparison of different approaches to policyholders' protection adopted in various legal systems belonging to both the common law and the civil law tradition.

INTRODUCTION

The implementation of China's economic reforms, beginning in the early 80's, and the formal establishment of a "Socialist Market Economy" in the following decade, stimulated substantial changes and improvements in the Insurance Laws and Regulations of the People's Republic of China (hereafter: PRC). The need for a modern and sophisticated legal framework aimed at regulating rights and remedies arising out of insurance contracts, as well as the insurance business in general, became clear and compelling as soon as the Communist State began its slow but inexorable retreat and it ceased to take care of every aspect of the life of the Chinese People. In a market-oriented economy, individuals are entitled to property rights, they enjoy some degree of freedom to choose what transactions to enter into and they are able to extract private profits and benefits from their own work and activity.

Thus, the ideal of a socialist market economy can be perceived as the embodiment of freedom, autonomy and equality, but also as an improvement of the quality of life of individuals and of the overall economic prosperity of the nation. On the other hand, however, the retreat of the State has increased the risks that private individuals are required to bear. As a consequence of the dismissal of Work Units, for example, many Chinese workers are currently facing new types of risks, such as the risk of loosing their job, the risk of becoming sick or invalid and, consequently, of loosing their ability to work and earn a salary, the risk of suffering a severe financial loss due to property damage and so on and so forth.

Such risks, of course, were once taken care of by the State, through the social structures of the Communist Party. From a theoretical viewpoint, indeed, the State's duty extended to providing social security and economic support to everyone. In the new socialist market context, however, the insurance contract is predestined to become the most important legal and economic tool available to those individuals who are not willing and/or able to bear the entirety of the risks associated with the implementation of the modern economic reforms.

Against such backdrop, this paper is aimed at exploring the history of insurance in China as well as the framework of insurance laws and regulation enacted in the PRC during the recent years.

In particular, the focus of this essay will be upon the legal principles and rules that currently govern insurance contracts and the relationship thereby established between the insurance company and the insured. Hence, the analysis of the legal protection of policyholders' rights and interests in China will center around the rules of insurance contracts interpretation, integration and performance at present in force.

In light of the international nature of the contract of insurance-a feature that characterized such private arrangement since its early developments in Europe, during the Middle Ages-and with a view to better understanding the legal rules recently promulgated in the PRC and the role that they will be called to play in the near future (especially with respect to the business pursued by foreign invested insurance companies), this paper will also offer a comparison of different approaches to policyholders' protection adopted in various legal systems belonging to both the common law and the civil law tradition2.

To this purpose, an overview of the legal solutions accepted in the United States of America appears to be the most appropriate start. In a country where the insurance business has been playing a prominent and sometimes overwhelming role in the quotidian life of the people, courts have designed peculiar rules of contract interpretation and have developed a new body of law, namely the law of Bad Faith, in order to protect the interests of policyholders.

A different social and legal context has determined the adoption of divergent solutions in English law, and this further approach will be therefore briefly considered. After having reviewed the position of the two most important common law countries with respect to policyholders' protection, this paper will analyze the recent developments in Italian law, as an example of a civilian legal system, as well as in the law of the Republic of India, an Asian developing country in which the culture of rights and remedies of the People is profoundly rooted and constitutionally protected.

A BRIEF HISTORY OF THE INSURANCE BUSINESS IN CHINA

The modern practice of insurance in China traces its roots back to the late Qing Dynasty, when it was introduced by foreign businessmen that imported policies commonly used in their own countries of origin. In 1805, the Canton Insurance Company was established in Guangzhou by foreign merchants and in 1885 the Bureau of Ships and Commerce founded the earliest Chinese insurance companies, the Renhe Ins. Co. and the Jihe Ins. Co., in Shanghai.

In 1929 the Nationalist government enacted the Insurance Law of the Republic of China and in 1935 the Insurance Enterprise Act, both amended in 1937 but never implemented in mainland China. At the beginning of the XIX century, in any event, China had a very advanced insurance industry and the market was largely dominated by foreign insurance companies, based in different parts of the country. With the establishment of the PRC in 1949, however, the situation evolved in a peculiar way.

In October 1949 the Chinese government set up the People's Insurance Company of China (PICC), a state-owned enterprise, in Beijing. During the first decade of its operations, the PICC made rapid and steady progress, establishing regional branches and offices in all the provinces, autonomous regions and municipalities (except Tibet and Taiwan), and using branches and sub-branches of banks as its agents. By 1956, all other insurance companies in the PRC ceased to operate and the foreigners had to move out of China.

The nationalization of the industry was eventually achieved and the PICC became a monopoly dominating the market. In this way, the State ultimately bore the risks of most hazards against which insurance would normally be sought in other countries: basic social welfare schemes covered the needs of individuals. Thus, prior to the introduction of economic reforms in the late 1970s, the PICC was the sole insurance company in China and was the market and the regulator all in one. However, political upheaval and State planning both hindered the development of the domestic industry: after 1958, the insurance business was openly denounced by left ideologues.

As a consequence, domestic insurance was virtually suspended and the PICC limited its operations to foreign trade, international cargo and aviation insurance, under the supervision of the People's Bank of China.

During the last two decades, the picture has cha nged dramatically. After the Cultural Revolution, and with the advent of economic reform in 1979, the domestic insurance business resuscitated and the PICC, being the sole insurance carrier in the whole China, enjoyed the strong and increasing demand for insurance products and services and consequently reported significant growth and profitability.

In 1983 the PICC became an economic entity under the direct control of the State Council. On July 23, 1996, in accordance with the 1995 Insurance Law3, it was restructured and renamed as the China Insurance Group (PICC); the group comprised three subsidiaries: PICC Property, PICC Life, PICC Reinsurance.

The most recent reform of China's insurance industry, culminated with the promulgation of the Insurance Law of 1995, has transformed the role of the State in risk bearing and has ended the PICC's monopoly of more than 40 years. As at the end of 1998, China had a more than 25 insurance companies constituted in different legal form (state-owned enterprises, regional joint ventures between PICC Group and local investors and companies involving foreign insurers such as AIA, Tokio Marine and Fire, Manulife and Winterthur), offering a wide variety of coverage.

Since China resumed the insurance business in 1980, the market has grown steadily, at an average rate of 37.6% per annum. Insurance premiums hit 124.73 billion yuan in 1998 and raised to 139.3 billion yuan in 1999.4 Among these premiums, 52.1 billion yuan was from property insurance, up nearly three percent from 1998, and 87.2 billion yuan from life and health insurance, up 15 percent.

As the China's insurance sector developed rapidly and healthily in the last two decades, more than 150,000 people are currently employed by the industry. The growth rate is much higher than the growth rate of the national economy in the same period.5 During the period 1989-1998, the insurance companies operating in the country paid a total of 262.2 billion yuan of compensation and payment to their customers. In 1998 alone, 55.6 billion yuan were paid, including 3.3 billions yuan paid as compensation for the loss caused by floods.

Since 1992 when an experiment was carried out to open the Chinese insurance market to the outside world, nine insurance companies from eight countries including the United States, Canada, Japan and Britain have set up agencies in Shanghai and Guangzhou and a large number of insurance institutions from 17 countries have set up representative offices in China. Preparations for establishing four branches of foreignfunded insurance companies and Sino-foreign joint insurance ventures are now underway.

In November 1998, the China Insurance Regulatory Commission was set up. Most recently, the China Insurance Group Corporation (PICC) was disbanded and four insurance companies including the China People's Insurance Company (the new PICC), the China Life Insurance Company (CLIC), the China Reinsurance Company (CRC) and the China Insurance Co., Ltd. were re-established. August 1999 marked the end of restructuring of China's insurance industry.

190 billion of life insurance. The insurance premium should occupy 2.3% of gross domestic products (GDP). The insurance premium per person is 230 yuan.

It is learned that after five years of development, an insurance market with Chinese characteristics will emerge with six features:

I) Diversified operation bodies. State owned and state hold insurance firms take the lead in market. Nongovernmental capital is allowed in insurance firms. Agency companies and broker companies will be developed to expand marketing channels. Special insurance companies undertaking one certain insurance will be built. As for auxiliary services, actuarials, accounting firms and insurance rating institutions will be set up.

II) Market-oriented operation mechanism. The market bodies, such as insurance firms, agencies and policyholders, act with one another through market mechanism. The operators enjoy equal competition status. The products, charges, capital and human resources are through market mechanism.

III) Intensified operation mode.

IV) Establishing legal system for governmental supervision.

VI) Professionalization of the staff.

VII) Internationalization of the industry. The operation of China's insurance industry got closer to international practice. China insurance is gradually stepping into international market. China's insurance firms actively develop overseas services."

Source from: *Shanghai Securities News*, as reported by *Business Weekly*, March 17, 2000 The founding of four above-mentioned insurance companies is a measure taken to prepare for the opening-up of the insurance market and to prepare the domestic insurance companies for the challenges and opportunities resulting from the market opening.

China Reinsurance Company (CRC), the only Chinese reinsurance company, was founded on March 18, 1999, on the basis of the former PICC Reinsurance. China Reinsurance Company has an independent corporate organization and is funded by the Ministry of Finance. CRC's monetary assets increased from $114 million in 1996 to $904 million in 1998. Its long-term reserves increased from $588 million in 1996 to $730 million in 1998. China Reinsurance Company's business includes all areas of national and international property and life insurance. It handles reinsurance for personal accident insurance, long-term life insurance, health insurance, motor vehicle insurance, property insurance and reinsurance for special insurance lines such as aviation, oil drilling platforms, and nuclear power plants.

On March 19, 1999, China Life Insurance Company (CLIC), the largest Chinese life insurance company, was established in Beijing. It was set up on the basis of the former PICC Life. CLIC is a national commercial life insurance company under the direct leadership of the State Council. It is a wholly state-funded commercial life insurance company specializing in life, health and accident insurance. It will assume life insurance policy liabilities of the former PICC and PICC Life. It ranks first in terms of business scale and market share of China's national life insurance companies. China's largest property insurance company, the new People's Insurance Company of China (PICC) was established in Beijing on March 20, 1999. It was founded on the basis of the former PICC Property. PICC has $930 million in registered capital. It specializes in all insurance services except personal insurance. PICC is a wholly state-owned commercial insurance company. In 1998, its premium income was $4.86 billion, accounting for 80% of the domestic property insurance market.

The China Insurance Company Limited announced its new leadership team on August 19, 1999, marking the end of the restructuring of the People's Insurance (Group) Company of China. China Insurance Company Limited is the state-owned holding company overseeing the China Insurance (Group) Company Limited of Hong Kong (which manages the overseas assets and operations of the former PICC Group). The restructured China Insurance Company Limited has approximately 30 entities operating worldwide, with operations in life and property insurance, international reinsurance and securities and fund management. The company has total assets of $2.17 billion.

As shown by this synthetic overview, China's insurance industry had already fulfilled an important and historical mission of transition to comply with the law of the market economy.

Nevertheless, China still has one of the world's lowest pro capita spending rates per annum on insurance: in 1995 it was a mere US$ 6.1, compared to US$ 39.1 in Mexico, US$ 90.1 in Brazil, US$ 141.5 in Argentina and US$ 146.5 in Chile. Moreover, insurance penetration in China was just 1.17% of GNP in 1995, far lower than most other countries, even developing countries. Untapped demand, particularly for life insurance, is enormous. Currently, two-thirds of insurance is devoted to property insurance, and over half of this is directed to vehicle insurance. There is no legal obligation for Chinese companies to take out insurance, except for employeerelated social security and third party motor purposes. This may indicate that even a small increase in individual spending on insurance will greatly expand the domestic market.

A substantial portion of the urban population began to purchase some life insurance, but most of the rural residents-about 80% of the entire population-are still basically unaware of its availability. Nonetheless, the situation is gradually changing, as a result of several factors, among which: increasing education, birth control, the enactment social reforms, the diminishing of traditional superstitious fears of insuring against death, the breakdown of extended families with the consequent growing need for alternative sources of support during the retirement period and the reduced State's 'cradle to grave' provision.

In conclusion, Chinese attitudes to insurance are changing and an augmenting appreciation of risk, along with greater profitability, can quickly create a local market for property, personal as well as commercial insurance, thereby drastically increasing the relevance of the legal rules aimed at regulating rights and obligations arising out of insurance contracts.

CHINESE LEGISLATION

Before the implementation of the economic reforms twenty years ago, there were substantial gaps and incompleteness in China's insurance laws and regulations. With a view to fostering the reformation process, the State Council promulgated regulations on September 1 1983 on contracts of property insurance, setting the standards for contractual drafting, rights, liability and procedures for insurance companies and the obligations of the policyholder7.

Few years later, in 1985, regulations on the standards for establishing and operating an insurance business were issued by the same authority. After a period of approximately five years of work by various committees, which involved liaison and in depth observations and visits to some thirteen countries to study various approaches to insurance legislation in both Western and Asian environments, the National People's Congress finally enacted the Insurance Law of 1995, which is the PRC's first comprehensive piece of legislation governing insurance contracts, insurance business operating rules, supervision of the insurance industry, standards for agents and brokers and liability matters. The Insurance Law applies to the establishment of an insurance company with foreign shareholders and branches of foreign insurance companies inside the territory of the PRC, pursuant to Article 148, and both domestic and foreignfunded insurance companies are subject to its rules (Article 3).

It is a worth noting, however, that the China Insurance Group (PICC), until its recent reorganization in 1999, remained the principal player in the Chinese insurance market, with a national network of over 4,000 branches and offices and the control of almost 90% of the PRC market.

a) The 1995 Insurance Law-Chapter II: Insurance Contracts

The new Insurance Law of the PRC was ratified at the14th Session of the Standing Committee of the Eighth National People's Congress on June 30, 1995 and promulgated by Presidential Decree n°51 for implementatio n commencing on October 1, 1995. The Insurance Law, with respect to the discipline of the contractual aspects of the business, is widely considered8 as a codification of internationally recognized insurance principles such as: *uberrima fides* (utmost good faith), insurable interest, subrogation9, double insurance benefits, *interpretatio contra proferentem* (interpretation against the drafter) and the killer beneficiary exclusion. As a general principle, "those who engage in insurance activities must observe the laws and administrative regulations and abide by the principles of voluntariness, honesty and good faith." (Article 4). The signing of an insurance contract between the Applicant and the Insurer, moreover, "shall be based upon the principles of equality, mutual benefit, voluntariness and friendly consultation, and shall not harm public interest." (Article 10).

Chapter II of the Insurance Law deals with the set of rights and obligations arising out of the insurance agreement. Article 11 states that the insured must have an insurable interest in the subject matter covered by the policy. In the absence of such insurable interest-defined as a legally acknowledged interest toward the subject matter insured-the insurance contract is considered null and void and is not effective. Once the contractual relationship is established, the policyholder enjoys a general right to terminate the insurance contract, while the insurer does not. However, if the insurer finds out that, at the time the contract was concluded, the insured intentionally withheld the truth or failed to perform the obligation of informing truthfully due to negligence and such was sufficient to have a bearing on the Insurer decision to underwrite insurance or to increase the premium, the insurer may terminate the insurance contract.

Moreover, where the applicant intentionally fails to perform the obligation of informing truthfully, the insurer is not liable for any loss or payment arising from the perils insured against before the contract is terminated and does not bear any obligation to refund the premiums already paid by the policyholder (Article 16). In the event the insured or the beneficiary, where no insured event has occurred, falsely claims that an insured event has occurred and demands compensation or payment of insurance money from the insurer, the insurer enjoys the right to terminate the insurance contract without refunding the insurance premium (Article 27).

Insurance contracts and all amendment thereof must be made in writing and the insurance policies are required to contain at least the following information: (a) Name and address of the insurer; (b) Names and addresses of the policyholder and the insured party, and the name and address of the Beneficiary if any; (c) Insurance subject matter; (d) Insured liabilities and liabilities exempted or excluded; (e) Duration of insurance coverage and the commencement time of insurance liabilities; (f) Insured value; (g) Total sum insured (limits of coverage); (h) Insurance premium and method of payment; (i) Methods of paying compensation or claims; (l) Liabilities for breach of contract and settlement of dispute; (m) Date the contract is executed. All terms in the insurance contract related to the exemption or exclusion of the insurer's liabilities must be brought to the attention of the prospective insured at the time of entering into the insurance contract. If the insurance company fails to make exclusions and exemptions clear and intelligible to the insured, such terms shall be considered null and void (Article 17). Article 30 embodies the widely accepted principle of interpretation known as *interpretatio contra stipulatorem* (or *contra proferentem*): in the event of a dispute between the insurer and the policyholder with respect to the terms of the insurance contract, the People's Court or the arbitrators are in fact required to offer interpretations favorable to the insured. Upon learning the occurrence of an insured event, the insured is required to promptly notify the insurer and to provide the insurance company with as much evidence and information as possible relevant to the ascertainment of the nature and causes of such event and to the extent of the loss thereby incurred (Article 22). The Insurer is required to bear all necessary and reasonable expenses incurred by the both parties in investigating and ascertaining the nature and causes of the event and the extent of losses to the subject matter insured (Article 48).

Upon receipt of a claim from the insured for compensation or payment of insurance money, the insurer is expected and required to make prompt verification (Article 23). If such claim is not covered by its insurance liability, the Insurer must issue a letter of advice to the policyholder of the beneficiary declaring its refusal to make compensation or payment (Article 24). Where the claim is an insured liability, instead, the insurer must perform its obligation to make compensation or payment within ten days after reaching agreement with the insured or the beneficiary concerning insurance compensation or payment amount (Article 23). If the insurer fails to perform his obligations to settle promptly and fairly, he shall indemnify the losses arising therefrom to the insured, in addition to making insurance payment. The insurer is also required to reimburse all the mitigating expenses incurred by the insured to prevent or reduce losses suffered because of the occurrence of the insured event.

The last paragraph of Article 23 declares that no unit or individual is entitled to interfere with the insurer in performing his obligation of indemnification or payment, nor to restrict the right of the insured or the beneficiary to obtain insurance money: this provision becomes crucial and extremely important when analyzed in the context of the transition form a communist to a market economy.

b) The 1983 Regulations on Contracts of Property Insurance

Together with Chapter II, Section 2 of the 1995 Insurance Law, the 1983 Regulations of the PRC on Contracts of Property Insurance outline the rules and standards applicable to property insurance contracts. A substantial part of the provisions in the regulations, promulgated by the State Council on 1 September 1983, have been substantially repeated in the more recent Insurance Law.

Parallel to Article 23 of the Insurance Law, Article 18 of the Regulations-for example-declares that the insurer is required to make payment within ten days of the agreement with the insured on a legitimate claim. In case of failure to pay within the prescribed time, however, the regulations state that the insurer faces a liability for breach of contract and is subject to a penalty commencing from the eleventh day following the date in which the amount of indemnity is determined, according to the interest rate set by the People's Bank of China for short term loans to enterprises.

c) The 1999 Uniform Contract Law

The Second Session of the Ninth National People's Congress adopted and promulgated the new Contract Law of the PRC on March 15, 1999, for implementation commencing on October 1, 1999. The new Contract Law-enacted in order to protect the lawful rights and interests of contract parties, to safeguard social and economic order and to promote socialist modernization-comprises basic principles and detailed provisions on contracts in general as well as various rules pertaining to specific (or, according to the civil law terminology, "nominated") contracts, such as sales, loan, donation, leasing, construction, carriage and transfer of technology.

The conceptual structure of Chinese private law is derived from the civil law tradition and, in particular, from the Germanic model. China, however, has never promulgated a Civil Code and, prior to the enactment of the new Contract Law of 1999, the rules and principles constituting the Chinese law of contract were located in part in the General Principles of Civil Law of 1986 and in part in the Economic Contract Law, the Foreign Economic Contract Law and the Technology Contract Law. The civilian systematic approach to contracts and obligations, characterized by the constant reference to general and abstract concepts, is therefore complicated in China by the fact that a comprehensive Civil Code is still missing from the panorama of the relevant sources of law.

Keeping this in mind, it becomes clear that the new Law of Contract of 1999 is called to play a very important role, because it provides: (a) some general and basic principles applicable as a background to all contractual obligations, (b) a set of default rules aimed at integrating and supplementing the express will of the parties, (c) mandatory provisions aimed at limiting party autonomy and, indirectly, at protecting the interests of weaker contractual parties, (d) specific rules aimed at governing certain frequent transactions (i.e. the mentioned "nominated" contracts). It is important to note that this last feature of the Law of Contract does not limit the ability of the parties to freely determine the content of their agreements, because their private arrangements do not necessarily have to fit in one of the predetermined legal types.

The 1999 Contract Law is fundamental to the analysis of the rules applicable to the contract of insurance in the Chinese legal system. According the civilian hierarchy of sources, in fact, the Insuranc e Law of 1995 is considered a special law and the Contract Law of 1999 a general law, which is applicable also to the contract insurance as long as it does not conflict with the special provisions of the Insurance Law. In particular, several rules and principles comprised in the new Contract Law are worth mentioning for the purposes of the present analysis:

(1) The general principle of good faith in contract performance, announced in very broad terms by Article 6 and reinstated by the provision of Article 60, according to which: "The parties shall fully perform their respective obligations in accordance with the contract. The parties shall abide by the principle of good faith, and perform obligations such as notification, assistance, and confidentiality, etc. in light of the nature and purpose of the contract and in accordance with the relevant usage."

(2) The principle of fairness, that parties to a contract are required to follow in prescribing their respective rights and obligations (Article 5). An important corollary to this general principle is stated in Article 39, concerning standard contracts (such as insurance policies): " Article 39 Standard Terms; Duty to Call Attention

Where a contract is concluded by way of standard terms, the party supplying the standard terms shall abide by the principle of fairness in prescribing the rights and obligations of the parties and shall, in a reasonable manner, call the other party's attention to the provision(s) whereby such party's liabilities are excluded or limited, and shall explain such provision(s) upon request by the other party.

Standard terms are contract provisions which were prepared in advance by a party for repeated use, and which are not negotiated with the other party in the course of concluding the contract.."

(3) The general rules on contractual language interpretation and construction. Article 125 states that in case of dispute between the parties concerning the construction of a contract term, the true meaning thereof shall be determined according to the words and sentences used in the contract, the relevant provisions and the purpose of the contract, and in accordance with the relevant usage and the principle of good faith. Articles 41, moreover, dealing with contracts of adhesion, acknowledges the rule of interpretation *contra stipulatorem* (against the drafter): "Article 41 Dispute Concerning Construction of Standard Term In case of any dispute concerning the construction of a standard term, such term shall be interpreted in accordance with common sense. If the standard term is subject to two or more interpretations, it shall be interpreted against the party supplying it. If a discrepancy exists between the standard term and a nonstandard term, the non-standard term prevails."

These general rules and principles stated in the new Contract Law of 1999, as mentioned, are applicable also to the contract of insurance. Chinese courts will therefore be able to use them as powerful tools to enforce and protect the contractual rights and interests of the policyholders against insurance companies doing business in the PRC.

ON GOOD FAITH AND POLICYHOLDERS' PROTECTION

a) United States Bad Faith Insurance Law

In the United States, insurance plays a very important social role. A substantial part of the basic human needs for security, protection and peace of mind are satisfied by American people through the purchase of private insurance coverage. This result springs from a social and political context that appears to be theoretically very distant from the welfare state ideal.

Insurance companies, however, are often private, for-profit, commercial enterprises and sometimes this may cause problems in the relationship with their customers, especially if policyholders are individual consumers. In addition, the terms of the policies are unilaterally predetermined by the insurance company for several reasons and the insured is merely offered a standard form, very frequently on a take-itor-leave-it basis.

In this context, the legal rules governing insurance contract interpretation and performance are therefore extremely important. With respect to the construction of insurance policies, American courts have developed two special doctrines applicable to the contract of insurance, namely the doctrine of ambiguities and the doctrine of reasonable expectations. According to the former, whenever a term of the policy is unclear it has to be interpreted against the drafter (*contra proferentem*). The latter doctrine, instead, states that a standard clause in an insurance policy (often an exclusion of coverage aimed at limiting the contractual liability of the insurance company), even if not ambiguously drafted, is not enforceable when it contravenes the reasonable expectations of the insured, according to an objective test.

As for the rules on performance, it has to be noted that an implied duty of good faith and fair dealing in contract performance has been recognized by American case law in almost every jurisdiction, by the Restatement (Second) of Contracts at § 205 and by the U.C.C. at § 1-203. In the field of Insurance Law, in particular, it has assumed a great relevance. American courts, in fact, have employed the contractual duty of good faith and fair dealing as the legal basis for the implementation of a policy aimed at monitoring and discouraging the opportunistic behavior of those insurance companies that too often disregarded the legitimate rights and interests of their policyholders.

The most frequent cases involve artificially delayed payments or unreasonable denials of claims in the field of first party insurance (e.g. fire insurance policies etc.). The insurance companies often misbehave in this way, because they try to exploit the transitional financial need of the policyholder (at the time the insured event occurred) in order to negotiate a settlement for a lesser amount. In case of liability insurance (i.e. third party insurance), instead, the typical circumstances involve the insurer's refusal of a reasonable settlement offer advanced by the third party claimant, with a subsequent judgment in excess of policy limits and the consequential personal financial exposure of the insured. If the insurance company merely face a liability limited to the amount insured, it will never agree to settle with the third party claimant for an amount equal to the policy limits, unless the chances of a favorable judgment *ex ante* equal zero and the insurer has sufficient information.

In sum, the perverse economic incentives for the insurer to misbehave in the above situations are numerous and manifold. Courts in the United States have intervened and, with a view to solving such problems, they have held insurance companies liable for bad faith breach of contract, a cause of action that sounds both in tort and contract. As a consequence, policyholders in first party cases have been able to recover consequential damages, compensation for emotional distress and, in some instances, also punitive damages, in addition to the insurance payment due. In third party cases, moreover, insurance companies found liable for bad faith have been required to bear the entire amount of the judgment entered against the policyholder because of their misconduct, also for the portion in excess of the policy limits, and insured parties have been awarded damages for emotional distress and, sometimes, even exemplary damages.15

b) The English Common Law Perspective

The perspective of the English common law on the factual and legal circumstances outlined in the preceding section is quite different from the American one. In the English legal system there is no general duty to perform a contract in good faith and the law of insurance contract interpretation and construction is much less favorable to policyholders. This may depend on several factors, among which the different social role and responsibilities of insurance companies and the longstanding reputation of English insurers (especially the Lloyds of London) with respect of their claims handling practices.

In the recent years, however, English courts have been called to resolve insurance disputes based on the same factual circumstances that led to the development of the law of first party insurance bad faith in the United States. The results, again are very different: in a recent case, for example, the Civil Division of the Court of Appeal has refused to award consequential damages to the insured (a small family business owner and operator) who was forced out of business by an unreasonable delay in the payment of the insurance proceeds.

c) The Italian Approach: Mala Gestio and the Codified Duty to Perform in Good Faith

In the Italian legal system, the rules on insurance contract interpretation and enforcement are comprised in the Civil Code and, in particular, in the XX Section on Insurance of III Title of the IV Book on Obligations, Articles 1882 to 1932. In addition to the detailed discipline of specific or "nominated" contracts covered by the III Title, the IV Book of the Italian Civil Code (hereafter: c.c.) includes also a Title on contracts in general, 17 where rules on requisites, interpretation, effects, discharge, rescission, assignment and validity of a contract are enumerated. As mentioned *supra* with respect to the analysis of the Chinese legislation, in a civil law system the hierarchy of sources renders the general part applicable to nominate contracts as long as it does not conflict with the specific rules set forth for the individual contract at issue.

For the purposes of the present analysis, it is interesting to note that Article 1375 c.c. (in the general part on contracts) states that a contract must be performed according to good faith and Article 1175 c.c. (on obligations in general) declares that debtor and creditor are required to abide by the principle of fair dealing. The general rule of interpretation against the drafter (*contra proferentem*), moreover, is fully recognized in Italy and codified in Article 1370 c.c..

In several recent cases, Italian courts have applied the good faith and fair dealing test to the behavior of insurance companies that assumed the defense of their policyholders in court. The violation of the good faith standard by the insurance company (often due to a reckless disregard of the legitimate interests of the insured) is identified by the Latin terminology "*mala gestio*" and it allowed courts to award consequential economic damages in excess of the policy limits to the insured party. No damages for emotional distress or punitive damages, however, can be granted in these cases according to the Italian contract law rules at present in force.

d) Consumerism, Constitutional Rights and Policyholders' Protection in India

A new legislation, the *Insurance Regulatory and Development Authority* (IRDA) *bill*, recently came into force in the Republic of India. One of the most important features of such legislation is that it opened up the insurance sector to foreign and private investors.

Before January 2000, in fact, the insurance business in India was a government monopoly. After independenc e, the life insurance business was nationalized in 1956 and the general insurance sector followed the same path in 1972. Since then, the market is dominated by two state-owned entities, the Life Insurance Corporation (LIC) and the General Insurance Corporation (GIC), with its four subsidiaries based in Bombay (National Insurance), New Delhi (New India Assurance), Calcutta (Oriental Insurance) and Madras (United India Insurance).

In the absence of national schemes of social safety nets and due to the increasing level of risks associated with modern society in urban areas and the ongoing process of industrialization of the economy, the LIC and the GIC have come under growing pressure to satisfy various demands for insurance. The availability of adequate insurance coverage is also crucial for the 72% of the Indian population who lives and works in the rural areas, where months of hard work and the security of an entire family are often jeopardized by the occurrence of natural events such as a fire or a cyclonic typhoon. Despite a fairly good reputation enjoyed by the nationalized insurance companies, they have been recently challenged on the basis of indiscipline and lack of sincerity in the services provided. LIC and GIC, in fact, have both come under fire during the past few years for delays in payments, rigid and legalistic approaches adopted to defeat the claims of policy holders and to deny benefits. There have also been complaints that policies are issued on unfair terms and conditions and beneficiaries are harassed whenever claims are made for indemnities under insurance policies.

In view of the social responsibilities of the business of insurance to provide reasonable security to policyholders, the courts have passed strictures against the insurers for rejecting claims on frivolous and technical grounds.

Their standards of behavior in dealing with the policy holders are currently subject to strict checks by the judiciary and a new insurance jurisprudence has developed in the recent years. The fundamental concerns for the welfare and benefit of the Indian society have been used by the judiciary as powerful dialectical tools to keep under rigorous control the behavior of the two state-owned insurance companies and of their subsidiaries.

In a welfare state, law has a prominent role as a means of social engineering in constructing a mutually beneficial framework of relations between the insurer and the insured. Thus, courts in India have held the two corporations to be instrumentalities of state for the purposes of art. 12 of the Constitution, and imposed on them duties to act fairly and in consonance with the principles laid down in the Directive Principles of State Policy.24 Judicial decisions in this field have been very often guided by the implementation of the goal of social and economic justice, clearly stated in the Preamble to the constitutional charter.

It is worth noting that such line of arguments shall not necessarily be limited to the misbehavior of LIC and GIC, in their peculiar capacity as instrumentalities of state for the purposes of art. 12 of the Constitution. The protection of the insured-consumer from the manipulative economics indulged in by large business corporations, in fact, is one of the fundamental constitutional duties imposed on the State and the Indian courts firmly consider it necessary to promote the welfare of the people and the common good25.

In *L.I.C. of India v. Consumer Education and research Center*26, the Supreme Court of India-affirming that insurance is a social security measure and therefore it should be consistent with the constitutional animation and conscience of socioeconomic justice-stated that an unfair and untenable clause in an insurance policy is unjust and is amenable to judicial review.

The idea of multidimensional welfare of all the people was certainly among the important features of the new society established by the Constitution of 1950 and it is expressed in the Preamble as well as in articles 38 and 39. In India, therefore, consumer (and insured) justice is clearly part of a broader constitutional policy of social and economic justice. Consumer protection, of course, plays a key role in the implementation of the principle of socio-economic justice.

Keeping this in view, under the auspices of the 1985 UN Resolution on Consumer Protection, the Indian Parliament promulgated the Consumer Protection Act in 1986. This legislation is very peculiar for several reasons. It is important to note that the notion of consumer is quite broad in India. The 1986 Act recognizes the role of consumer organizations in assisting private individuals in seeking justice.

The consumer legislation applies to all goods and services in private, public or the cooperative sector. Thus, the consumer can initiate an action under the Consumer Protection Act against the defective goods or deficient services rendered even by the public sector or government undertakings such as railways, telephones, airlines, banks and, of course, insurance companies.

One of the most important aspects is that it provides a three-tier quasi-judicial machinery at the National, State and District levels for redressing in a simple, speedy and inexpensive way consumer grievances. Consumer Protection Councils at the State and Central levels have also been established, to promote and protect the rights of consumers.

Consumer claims can be brought before the Consumer Disputes Redressal Agencies (CDRA), set up by Section 9 of the Consumer Protection Act. There are three levels of agencies: a Consumer Disputes Redressal Forum (District Forum), a Consumer Disputes Redressal Commission (State Commission) and a National Consumer Disputes Redressal Commission (National Commission). Clauses (4) and (5) and Section 22 of the Act invest the CDRA with the powers of a civil court in respect of several procedural and substantial matters, thereby setting up an effective method of alternative dispute resolution.

In the very recent decision of the case *Spring Meadows Hospital v. Harjot Ahluwalia*, the Supreme Court of India held that the Consumer Protection Act confers jurisdiction on the National Commission in respect of matters where either there is a defect in goods, a deficiency in service, an unfair and restrictive trade practice or the charging of excessive price.

Moreover, the court stated that the Act being a beneficial legislation intended to confer some speedier remedy on a consumer from being exploited by unscrupulous traders, the provisions thereof should receive a liberal construction.

Several policyholders' claims, being actions for deficiency in services rendered by the insurance companies, are therefore brought before the CDRA. The CDRA and, particularly, the National Consumer Dispute Redressal Commission (NCDRC) consequently has developed an interesting jurisprudence in dealing with the same factual problems that American courts few decades ago addressed by creating the law of first party bad faith insurance.

Instead of referring to the covenant of good faith and fair dealing that U.S. courts found implied in every insurance contract, however, the NCDRC reached analogous operational solutions basing its decisions, in accordance with the guidelines established by the Supreme Court of India, on the well recognized constitutional principle of socio-economic justice.

In particular, the NCDRC has widely granted significant money awards for consequential economic loss and mental damages suffered by the insured in connection with unfair and unreasonable insurance claim practices.

e) The Relevant Provisions in the Chinese Insurance Law and Regulations

As shown by the brief comparative inquiry outlined in the preceding sections, several problems arise out of the interpretation and performance of the contract of insurance and it seems that the Chinese legislator was well aware of most of them. The protection of policyholder, at least in theory, is clearly a central concern of the modern Chinese insurance legislation.

As for the issues related to the policy language, it is interesting to note that, according to Article 16 of the Insurance Law of 1995, an insurer is required to explain the contents of the contract to the prospective insured at the time of entering into the agreement.

In case of an exclusion of exemption of liability, moreover, the insurer has the duty to bring it to the attention of the applicant and failure to do so renders the clause ineffective and unenforceable (Article 17 of the IL). There is no requirement to write the contractual clauses in plain language, but the rule of interpretation against the drafter (*contra proferentem*) is clearly stated in Article 41 of the Contract Law of 1999 and reinforced by Article 30 of the Insurance Law of 1995.

The principles of good faith and fairness govern contractual relationships in general (Articles 5, 6 and 60 of the CL) and the contract of insurance in particular (Article 4 of the IL). The fair and prompt settlement of claims is a major cornerstone of sophisticated markets worldwide and China seems to have at least partially recognized the potential problems arising out of defective claim handling practices.

Pursuant to the provision of the Chinese Insurance Law of 1995, an insurance company must promptly and fairly adjust a claim for compensation. If the claim is legitimate, the insurance company is required to make the payment within 10 days of reaching an agreement on the matter with the person entitled to obtain the policy benefits.

The insurance company is required to make an advance payment within sixty days of receipt of the relevant information and evidence rela ted to the claim, if the amount of compensation is not still fully determined.34 According to Article 23 of the IL, if the insurance company fails to perform its obligations and delays or denies valid claims, it is liable for the economic loss caused to the insured party. In addition, according to Article 18 of the Regulation on Contracts of Property Insurance of 1983, it seems that the insurance company would also be liable for a penalty (in the form of interests on the amount due) in case of late payment of the proceeds.

Some problems, however, still remain unresolved. The insurer, for example, is required by the statute to verify the claim promptly and to pay within ten days of reaching an agreement with the policyholder, but there is no express duty to reach a fair agreement within a reasonable time of the verification.

Of course, the civilian juridical logic would suggest that such additional duty on the part of the insurer is mandated by the general principle of good faith and fair dealing in contract performance. If and when the Chinese courts will decide that time has come to abide by the principle of transparency and will publish more extensively their opinions, we will finally apprehend the solution.

CONCLUSIONS

The law of insurance contracts will be of increasing importance in the Chinese legal system during the process of transition from a state-centric planned economy to a new socialist market economy.

This essay has explored the current situation of the insurance market in the PRC as well as the new legislation enacted following the implementation of the open-door policy and the modern economic reforms started in the early 1980s. The focus of the analysis has centered around the legal protection of the policyholders, both in the context of third party liability insurance and in the context of first party property insurance.

In order to better understand the Chinese rules on contract interpretation, integration and performance and with a view to comparing the different solutions adopted in vario us legal systems, a brief overview of the legal experience of the United States, England, Italy and the Republic of India has been offered.

The results of this comparative analysis point out that the strongest protection of the interests of the insured is granted by the United States federal and state courts, followed by the courts and the quasi-judiciary consumer dispute resolution bodies in India, the Italian Court of Cassation and, lastly, by the English courts. The principle of good faith in contract performance and its applicability to the insurance contracts are recognized by all systems but for the English and the Indian ones. The Indian common law in theory still follows the English precedents; as it has been show, however, Indian courts have found their way around the theoretical lack of a general principle of good faith, and have reached the desired operational results by referring to the constitutional goal of socio-economic justice.

The modern Chinese insurance legislation deals extensively with the problems arisen elsewhere in the world during the last few decades and it appears to be deeply concerned with the protection of the legitimate interests of the insured party. In theory, this position is fully coherent with the role assigned to insurance companies in the new socialist market economy. In practice, the material implementation of such statutory rules and principles requires that Chinese courts take an active part in the transitional process. It is still unclear whether today Chinese judges and lawyers, together with the legal system of China as a whole, are ready to make such a crucial institutional step.

8

Crime Insurance-Fidelity Insurance

CRIME INSURANCE

Crime insurance is said to fall in the category of fidelity coverage. Fidelity insurance might also refer to the loss caused by the dishonest ways of the employees. Crime insurance coverage specialist's advice people to ensure that they are adequately insured against:

- Credit card fraud
- On-premises theft
- Off-premises theft
- Kidnap and ransom
- Computer theft

Many companies have efficient crime *fidelity insurance* programs. Crime insurance coverage helps to protect the following organizations, among others:

- Financial institutions
- Manufacturers
- Service industries

Crime insurance policy covers losses to a business organization due to criminal activities. The term 'criminal activity' is exhaustive and refers to situations ranging from employee dishonesty to burglary and robbery, embezzlement, fund transfer fraud, computer fraud and forgery. Small businesses are particularly vulnerable to these crimes and can suffer severe financial consequences due to employee dishonesty. According to a research conducted by the Association of Certified Fraud Examiners (ACFE), business organizations in the United States lose approximately $400 billion per annum to employee fraud, and an average organization suffers a loss of about 6% of its total annual revenue due to misdemeanors by its employees. These facts prove that white collar crime is on the increase. It should be taken into account that the given figures do not include crimes like robbery and burglary. Thus, the statistics mentioned above coupled with the fact that crime related losses are not covered by property insurance policies, makes crime *fidelity insurance* coverage protection an absolute necessity for most businesses. The liabilities covered by fidelity insurance coverage are:

- Money and Security Coverage-Covers losses due to burglary and destruction.
- Employee Dishonesty Coverage-Covers losses due to dishonesty of employees.

Many insurance policies combine both these categories. Business can opt for either a mono line policy for customized liability coverage or a package policy offered by insurance agencies. The premium for crime insurance coverage is decided by the insurance agencies based on the criminal track record of the organization. A small-to-mid-sized organization pays an average premium of about $1000 for a $100,000 insurance coverage. Most of the insurance agency's websites have online forms, where details of the business can be entered for the approximate premium to be calculated.

Hacker insurance also falls under the *crime insurance*. Many companies seek the hackers insurance to protect themselves and their customers online. Business owners should always anticipate emergencies and should have a plan in place to tackle a crime or burglary occurring in their office. This is where an insurance policy will help. The victim of burglary should always make sure that the burglary in his office or house has been registered with the police. This is when he becomes eligible for the fidelity insurance policy.

COMMENTS BY THE NATIONAL INSURANCE CRIME BUREAU

Insurance companies and other financial institutions provide the National Insurance Crime Bureau ("NICB") various types of data deemed "financial" under the Gramm-Leach-Bliley Act of 1999 ("the GLBA")1 and the Commission's proposed rule ("the Privacy Rule"). All such data, including information that would also be protected "health information" under privacy standards recently proposed by the Department of Health and Human Services ("HHS")("HHS Standards"), is used solely for the purpose of reporting, investigating and preventing insurance fraud.

To combat sophisticated, interstate insurance fraud rings, which inflict much of the almost $30 billion in fraudulent claims paid by property and casualty insurers each year, it is essential that the NICB have access to several types of individually-identifiable information. NICB guards such data tightly to assure it is never used for any other purpose.

Congress has repeatedly and consistently recognized the compelling need for NICB to look for fraud indicator "links" across a broad pool of neutral insurance claims information. Most recently, in the GLBA, Congress declared that "investigating or preventing fraud" is "necessary to... administer" a "consumer's insurance" policy and emphatically stated its intention *not* to restrict disclosure and use of information "to protect against or prevent actual or potential fraud."

The Commission's proposed rule, accordingly, specifically exempts communications by, between or among insurance carriers, the NICB and law enforcement from the notice and opt-out requirements.

Under the proposed Rule, insurers will need to inform customers only that they "make disclosures to other non-affiliated third parties as permitted by law." The Commission invited comment "whether such a notice would be adequate." In these responsive comments, NICB explains why the proposed customer notice is consistent with the GLBA and provides adequate notice without creating unnecessary burdens or confusion.

The National Insurance Crime Bureau ("NICB") is a not-for-profit organization, formed in 1992, dedicated to providing unique solutions to the problems of detecting, preventing and deterring insurance-related crime. NICB is supported by nearly 1,000 member property-casualty insurers and self-insured companies and works with insurers and law enforcement in identifying and prosecuting organized criminal conspiracies dealing in insurance fraud and vehicle theft. The NICB is not a "financial institution" or an "affiliate" under the GLBA and the Privacy Rule. It is not significantly engaged in financial activities; it does not provide insurance; nor does it transact any business with "consumers" or "customers." It does, however, receive and use various types of "nonpublic personal information" from insurance carriers and other "financial institutions" with which NICB is not affiliated.

Insurance fraud is the second most prevalent and costly form of white-collar crime. Recent studies have estimated that insurance fraud costs Americans between $35 and $80 billion per year. This amounts to a $100 per year premium surcharge for the average ratepayer. More than $30 billion is lost annually to property/casualty insurance fraud.

Organized insurance fraud rings have existed in major cities across the country for years. The most sophisticated of these gangs have formed interstate fraud rings and ingeniously avoid suspicion by filing false injury claims under different types of insurance policies with different carriers in different states.

The infrastructure of a fraud ring is a network of dishonest lawyers and doctors who stage accidents and file dishonest claims with insurance companies. In some cases, the accident is real but the injuries are bogus. Middlemen, known as cappers or runners, monitor police radios closely and swarm to the scene of a genuine accident before the police arrive. They show up with business cards of personal injury lawyers, chiropractors, and clinics and promise cash payments for anyone willing to file a false insurance claim.

In other cases, a cast of participants in a fraud ring will stage an accident in front of honest witnesses or purposefully hit a driver of a new luxury car they assume is fully insured. For example, an uninsured participant will intentionally hit a car carrying four insured participants.

The insured participants will then present themselves to a participating physician who will prepare an extensive medical history. Following the "accident", the doctor or clinic will prepare detailed medical records consisting of visits that were never made and treatments that were never performed. To obtain payment and defraud the insurer, the claimants' attorney will then submit a demand package to the insurance carrier that includes, among other things, the name of the claimant, a description of the accident, statements of honest witnesses showing clear liability, the details of medical treatment and the basis for compensating the claimant for pain and suffering. Even where the medical records are nearly an exact duplicate of ones submitted previously for a different patient, nothing in an individual demand packet will make it obvious that the claim is fraudulent.

In fact, in one recently prosecuted case, the fraud ring submitted the exact same medical records for thirteen different claims with the name of the original patient "whited out" and new names written in.

The increasing sophistication of fraud rings make it difficult for insurance carriers to decide whether claims should be paid quickly or investigated more thoroughly. By looking for links across a broad pool of neutral claims information, NICB offers predictive fraud solutions. Red flags arise if the claimant has been involved "coincidentally" in too many similar incidents, has filed claims for the same accident with multiple insurance carriers or if the attorney, doctor or other professional has a history of involvement in insurance fraud. Insurance carriers can thereby detect fraudulent activity, block payment of bogus claims and, even after payments have been made, prosecute participants and obtain restitution.

Access to insurance databases is restricted to authorized users and law enforcement officials who are investigating or prosecuting an insurance fraud crime. Authorized users can only retrieve the information in the databases with controlled passwords and do not receive a password unless they register with the database managers and sign a confidentiality and compliance agreement. All the information contained in the database is encrypted to ensure that it cannot be seen or used by unauthorized parties.

In addition, database managers maintain logs of authorized users and illegal or unauthorized attempts to access the databases. They do not permit the sale or use of information contained in the database for marketing or other unauthorized purposes. To ensure compliance with confidentiality standards, the database managers regularly audit the use of their databases.

CONGRESS AND FEDERAL AGENCIES HAVE REPEATEDLY AND CONSISTENTLY RECOGNIZED THE COMPELLING NEED FOR NICB'S FRAUD DETECTION AND DETERRENCE EFFORTS

Congress acted in 1994 to protect the privacy of individuals' motor vehicle-related records, but it made clear its intention that States nevertheless permit driver license and similar personal information to be used to fight fraud. The law specifically allows disclosure to "[f]or use by any insurer or insurance support organization... in connection with... anti-fraud activities."

When Congress tightened those restrictions in 1999 by barring most disclosures of driver information absent express consent by the subjects of those records, it once again specifically exempted use by an insurance support organization in connection with anti-fraud activities. Federal agencies also recently have avoided restricting NICB's access to insurance claim information. For example, in its ongoing efforts to implement privacy provisions in Title II of the Kassebaum-Kennedy Act, HHS implicitly recognized that NICB is not covered by the statute. The agency proposed Standards that impose no restrictions on NICB's use of otherwise protected health information.

In the GLBA, Congress was equally careful not to restrict NICB's anti-fraud activities. Congress affirmatively declared that "investigating or preventing fraud" is "necessary to effect, administer or enforce" a "consumer's insurance" policy and emphatically stated its intention not to restrict disclosure or use of information needed "to protect against or prevent actual or potential fraud." In keeping with the intent and express terms of the statute, the Commission's proposed rule expressly exempts from the basic operative prohibitions and requirements of the statute, including the notice and opt-out requirements, information used for the purpose of "reporting, investigating or preventing fraud" or "to protect against or prevent actual or potential fraud...."

THE PROPOSED CUSTOMER NOTICE IS CONSISTENT WITH THE GLBA, PROVIDES CONSUMERS WITH ADEQUATE NOTICE AND AVOIDS UNNECESSARY BURDENS AND CONFUSION

The Privacy Rule generally requires insurers to provide a detailed explanation to consumers and policyholders concerning the types of information they plan to disclose and the categories of affiliates and non-affiliated third parties with whom such information will be shared. However, disclosures for fraud-fighting purposes are, as explained above, exempt from the operative provisions of the statute and the Commission therefore advises insurers that "[t]he requirements for initial notice... [and] the opt-out do not apply if you disclose... for... reporting, investigating or preventing fraud...." The alternative, presumably, would be to require each insurance writer to list every federal state and local law enforcement agency, every insurance company, the NICB and every other insurance support organization with which it may share access to insurance claims information. That approach would make no sense. It would unduly burden insurance companies and confuse their customers. The Commission's proposal imposes reasonable requirements on insurers and provides adequate notice to consumers and customers. The Privacy Rule provides that privacy notices are required *only* if an insurer discloses "other than as authorized by Secs. 313.10 and 313.11." Insurers who disclose information "as authorized under Secs. 313.10 and 313.11... are not required to list those exceptions in the initial or annual privacy notices.... [Y]ou are only required to state that you make disclosures to other non-affiliated third parties as permitted by law."

As noted above, access to insurance fraud-fighting data is tightly controlled and use is strictly limited to anti-fraud activities. NICB is already in full compliance with the Commission's requirement that it may use "information... in accordance with... an exception... only for purposes of that exception." The Commission also has effectively prohibited improper re-disclosure of protected information by holding the NICB to the same restrictions it has imposed on the financial institutions from which the information was initially received. In addition to the privacy policies that have been implemented by carriers and the NICB, many states have adopted model privacy legislation approved by the National Association of Insurance Commissioners.

Individuals who are the subjects of the records already can avail themselves of a variety of safeguards, including the right to obtain copies of their records and to seek correction of any erroneous information.

The Commission correctly adheres to the GLBA by exempting the disclosure of fraudfighting information from the notice and opt-out provisions of the Privacy Rule. The proposed customer notice serves the public interest and should be adopted in the final regulations as written.

INDUSTRY MUST SURF TIDAL WAVE OF CRIME

The short-term insurance industry is facing many challenges brought about by South Africa's transformation. LEE-ANNE SMITH looks at how the industry is adapting and dealing with problems like rising crime

CRIME has rocketed onto a new plateau since 1994, forcing short-term insurance companies to fork out astronomical amounts in claims.

"It is difficult for the insurance industry to come up with innovative solutions to address the massive crime wave that is rocking the country," says Rory Gainsford, general manager of operations at Fedsure General. "There is a limit to what we can do with what is really a government and police problem. Until the unemployment situation improves and the current attitude towards crime control and heavier sentences is addressed, the industry is limited in what it can offer. All we can do is insist on better levels of protection for businesses, houses and motor vehicles."

Steve Whitty, managing director of Glenrand Insurance Brokers, agrees that the insurance industry can only treat the symptoms of crime, but believes it could also co-operate more in pooling and sharing important information, especially with the strides it has made in the information technology arena.

Bram Field, executive chairman of Compass Insurance, says short-term premiums will continue to rise while crime and violence escalate.

"Perhaps it is time... we use the money being spent on commissions of inquiry, seminars and investigations towards putting in place a larger police force and impose heavier sentences, with faster court action, and above all, take positive action in curtailing the number of firearms so easily obtainable by the criminal element."

He says more people are dispensing with insurance cover mainly as a result of the increasing cost. In 1974, annual insurance premiums represented 1,2% of annual salary. This figure increased to 9,8% in 1996.

However, he says it is short-sighted to cancel insurance as serious losses resulting from fire, storms, and burglaries can be financially crippling.

"What is called for over and above an aggressive fight against crime, is for insurers to make cover against catastrophe risks more affordable (this is already being done) and also for consumers to adopt their own stringent risk-management principles," says Field.

Whitty says rates in the corporate market are soft with plenty of additional capacity from overseas companies. "South Africa has been through its worst history of fire losses in recent times so this time next year insurance companies could be faced with an entirely different agenda from a re-insurance point of view."

Keith Kennedy, general manager operations at Guardian National, believes that if crime could be tackled successfully so that claims were reduced, market forces would bring premiums down.

"What we see and hear in the media about crime, especially white-collar crime, is only the tip of the iceberg. It's time companies took a firm stand."

Turning to those who put in fraudulent claims, he says: "People forget the basic principle of insurance-that the many pay for the misfortunes of the few. If premiums go up as a result of genuine losses it is one thing, but when fraudulent claims contribute to pushing premiums up, it is quite another. In the event of multiple claims, the insurance company has every right to impose higher premiums or cancel cover as it has a duty to protect the pool of policyholders."

Unprecedented crime levels have spawned a new underwriting agency whose core business it is to cover companies against theft by employees. Gregg Smith, managing director of Fidelity Guarantee Acceptances, says conventional insurers transact this business but the extent of crime is leading many companies to rely on the expertise of specialist fidelity guarantee underwriters.

"Fidelity guarantee business has generally been transacted unprofessionally by the South African industry with most of the cream flowing into overseas markets. Conventional insurance companies do not always have the necessary expertise to address this market, and if cover is available at all, it is generally so expensive that it is unaffordable for many companies.

Brian Peck, managing director of Prestasi Brokers, says challenges faced by the short-term insurance industry can be summed up as a result of the evolution of the spiralling of these interconnected issues:

The combination of inflation and the impact of crime on the average claim amount has caused premiums to soar during the first half of the decade.

The average premium began to rise faster than the average individual's ability to pay and precipitated a fundamental shift in the market. More consumers either dropped out of the market or reduced the amount of risk they asked insurers to carry (either self-insuring, risk managing or not insuring at all) which caused the pool of premium income to shrink.

The traditional short-term insurance product was crudely priced. The major determinant of the initial base rate and subsequent rate increases within a group scheme policy was the underwriting performance of the entire block rather than of individuals. In the case of an individually underwritten policy, the pricing was usually obtained by a combination of a few fairly basic causal variables. Peck says these pricing mechanisms have become outmoded and the consumer has become more price conscious.

More intense competitive pressure has developed both from within the insurance industry as traditional players sought to hold onto or build market share, and from the entry of new players (the banking industry saw diversified earnings potential). "Insurers responded by introducing more competitively priced and flexibly structured products. Flexibility was a result of allowing consumers to construct a contract by selective exclusion of certain risk events or elements."

In addition, in an era of escalating claim frequency and amounts, insurers were forced to become more stringent with the settlement of claims in order to keep loss ratios in line with finer pricing of more flexible agreements.

"More expensive insurance resulted as an element the market began inflating claims to 'compensate' either for a prior loss not covered or simply to justify the payment of substantially higher premiums. A more sinister fraudulent element, in conjunction with criminal elements, came to the fore, with people being paid an incentive to allow crime to take place if they had insurance in place to cover the loss.

"Insurers were again forced to respond with more sophisticated pricing, underwriting and claim adjudication procedures to prevent such abuses from taking place, and the consumer now resents the process of both buying and having to claim on an insurance policy," he says.

Peck says there are three major areas of focus where insurers are bringing visible change to the consumer marketplace: "The first is bringing down the costs of acquiring and servicing the business; the second is ensuring that risks are priced and underwritten using the most advanced techniques; and thirdly ensuring the costs of settling claims are managed as closely as possible."

Traditional thinking about the uses of short-term insurance has begun to change, both in terms of the services provided and the market's demands, says Judi Priday, managing director of Quantum Insurance.

"Insurance is increasingly seen as a financial service and is inextricably linked with banking and other financial products. The international market is beginning to merge banking and insurance industries closer together and is investigating alternative ways of managing and financing the risk in conjunction with the insured, offering an all round financial service as opposed to conventional insurance services.

"I believe we must align the South African industry with international trends," she says.

The needs of the corporates can be met by risk financing mechanisms which encompass participation in both the benefits and disadvantages of the cover. There is now no risk that cannot be insured but the cost of certain insurance is still prohibitive. "The challenge in this market must be to offer a product that the company requires at a reasonable cost," she says.

The insurance industry still has a way to go in meeting the needs of customers. The key is to be aware of international trends, remain service-orientated, flexible and sensitive to the challenges facing customers, says Priday.

9

Identity Crime

OVERVIEW

This profile considers identity theft, identity fraud and identity management, supplementing guides elsewhere on the site.

It covers-

- historical background-ID fraud/theft before the dot
- contemporary cons-contemporary conmen and women, compulsives and appropriation of military honours.
- paper and plastic money-cheque and credit card fraud
- resumes-resume massaging in a credentialist society
- the digital era-online ID theft and fraud, including 'joe jobs', appropriation of email addresses and phishing
- statistics-Australian and overseas estimates of the incidence and severity of identity crimes
- costs-an analysis of the cost of identity crime
- responses-verification, education, document disposal, 'identity management', biometrics and other mechanisms for managing identity crime
- Aust law-Australian federal and state/territory legislation regarding ID theft/fraud
- overseas legislation-law in New Zealand, UK, Canada, US and other jurisdictions
- fiction-identity crime in literature and film... and by authors
- forensics-identifying and prosecuting identity crime
- shadows-ubiquitous identification, missing people and other perspectives

- true lies-the business of selling fake identities
- landmarks-major ID thefts and frauds from the early Middle Ages to 2005

INTRODUCTION

The supposed mutability of identity in the digital era-encapsulated in the famous *New Yorker* cartoon "on the internet no one knows that you are a dog"-and the pervasiveness of payment systems that do not require fact to face contact (or much authentication) has been reflected in concern about "identity theft" and "identity fraud".

The US Federal Trade Commission for example claimed that identity-related offences cost cost US consumers and businesses around US$53 billion in 2002. Estimates of the cost in Australia vary from around $2 billion to $6 billion in 2002-03. The Australian Institute of Criminology estimated the overall cost of fraud in Australia as more than $5 billion per year, almost a third of the $19 billion "total cost of crime".

In addition to readily identifiable financial costs, identity fraud/theft affects-

- victims (whose identities have been stolen)
- financial and other institutions
- law enforcement agencies

It facilitates the commission of other types of crime such as people smuggling and of course has been associated with problems such as drug trafficking and terrorism.

IDENTITY THEFT

Characterisation of identity crime varies widely, with inconsistent use of terms such as identity theft, impersonation, fraud, forgery, false pretences, spoofing, misappropriation and even identity pollution, vandalism and assault.

Identity Theft may be characterised as assuming the identity of someone else. As such it has a long and often colourful history, from the days when individuals claimed to be the Son of God (or other relatives) or royalty-typically having miraculously survived murderous attention by Ivan the Terrible, Boris Godunov, Richard III or Robespierre and emerged to claim the throne of France, Russia or England. Difficulty with authentication and the desire to believe (irrespective of signs to the contrary) meant that multiple imposters were often common.

A classic example is the thirty of so individuals claiming to be the Dauphin Louis-otherwise thought to have perished in prison during the French Revolution after his father Louis XVI met Madame Guillotine. One claimant was described as improbably "of negro appearance, with frizzy hair and slightly mad", although presumably more sane than some of his advocates.

The bureaucratisation of Western cultures over the past two hundred years has seen a shift from blood to signifiers of authority (eg the second-hand army uniform that successfully allowed tailor Wilhelm Voigt to commandeer Kopenick town hall at the beginning of last century) and thence to mundane identifiers such as AFNs and Social Security Numbers.

Economically significant ID theft now does not involve supposed heirs of Nicholas II or missing English baronets, miraculously emerging in Australia after drowning off Patagonia. It instead involves misuse of your credit card or cheque book, since in the digital era your identity is embodied in information rather than flesh-something that is explored in the Privacy guide and Surveillance & Authentication profile on this site. We are also starting to see what is generously described as 'spoofing' or 'joe jobs': email or even sites that purport to emanate from a public figure or private individual. That misuse of someone else's name and email address may be used to defeat restrictions on spam. It may also be used to damage a reputation, with the supposed author being incorrectly assigned responsibility for racist or other offensive comments.

Various typologies of ID crime have been suggested, reflecting different positions in the enforcement (or academic/ media feeding) chain. One of the more useful categorisations suggests that in relation to financial services we can differentiate between

- short-term Identity Access
- Account Theft
- Application Fraud
- broader Identity Appropriation

Identity Access involves appropriating someone's identity for quick access to existing financial or other accounts. Typically the thief uses an individual's information to purchase services or products through either a physical credit card (eg stolen from the individual and used to rack up purchases before the financial institution queries unusual spending patterns) or that card's account number and expiration date (eg carbons from credit card slips), with the victim discovering that the account has been access when studying a monthly billing statement or online report.

Account Theft may occur over a longer time frame when a stolen identity is used to take possession of an existing account by changing existing address details. The theft has typically involved mechanisms such as thieves intercepting mail from letterboxes or removing it from an individual's possessions, thereby gaining information needed to change the address on credit card and bank accounts. Victims often attribute missing statements to loss in the postal system and discover the theft when a credit card is declined because the thief has maxed out the card.

Application Fraud involves unauthorised creation of new accounts through a stolen identity, with the victim sometimes not aware of the theft because financial statements are mailed to a new address used by the thief. The theft is often discovered only when a collection company seeks recovery action or applications for new credit are rejected because of the hidden debt.

Identity Assumption has been a literary and Hollywood favourite, with the thief assuming the victim's identity, sometimes as a cover for the commission of non-financial crimes. Proponents of biometrics and identity reference/validation services have claimed for example that criminals have used forged driver registration documents-the de facto official and commercial ID papers in countries such as Australia-that feature the victim's name and other characteristics but the villain's photo.

Such victims supposedly most often discover the imposture when law enforcement agencies approach them about offences that they have supposedly committed. Other offenders have 'rebirthed' dead children, assuming an identity after obtaining death certificates. Other observers have argued that damage to reputation may be as important as any pecuniary loss through misuse of a bank account or credit card, with for example long-term damage to consumer credit ratings (discussed in a separate profile) or loss of esteem in a particular community through appropriation of a real name or avatar used in an online forum.

IDENTITY FRAUD

Identity Fraud, an associated offence, has attracted less media attention. It can take two forms

Most commonly, it involves an individual 'massaging' data: adding a degree or two, deleting a conviction or a divorce, adding a few years of age (popular among teenagers facing age-based access restrictions) or taking a few years off once the individual reaches a certain age.

As such it is popular among all classes, from highschool kids enhancing ID passes to get into nightclubs through to company directors and members of parliament buffing their profiles.

More rarely, some individuals have created a new identity altogether-one that is sometimes used to live an otherwise law-abiding existence rather than as the basis for theft. Self reinvention is arguably a central theme of US culture, where-like people in the rest of the world-many have dreamed of shucking off an inconvenient past and starting afresh, often with the aid of a glossier resume and fewer wrinkles.

As discussed later in this profile, statistics about theft/fraud are problematical. In 1985 the US Congress for example noted indications that up to 500,000 false tertiary degrees are in 'use' in the USA (eg were cited for employment purposes), that 10,000 false medical degrees are in use and that 30% of employees were hired with 'massaged' credentials.

The Australasian Centre for Policing Research has suggested uniform definitions-

- Identity crime is a generic term with broad scope to describe a wide range of identity-related offences in which a defendant uses a false identity to commit, or facilitate the commission of, a crime.

- Identity fraud describes the gaining of money, goods, services or other benefits, or the avoidance of obligations, through the use of a false identity. It includes fraudulently obtaining a financial benefit (eg by credit card skimming), avoidance of taxes or financial loss, and intangible benefits, such as access to citizenship, professional affiliation, and medical services.
- Identity theft describes the theft or assumption by one person of another person's identity, whether the other person is alive or dead. It may also extend to the use of a fictitious identity

IMPACTS

What are the impacts of identity theft and fraud?

The shape of identity crime means that impacts encompass-

- the deeply personal (parents of dead children discovering that someone has appropriated their child's identity)
- erosion of someone's good name (use of an email address for spam) without direct economic impact
- evasion of behavioural restrictions (using a doctored ID card to enter a nightclub while underage)
- illegal receipt of welfare benefits
- scams against consumers and businesses (eg a forged cheque or stolen credit card) that result in direct financial loss
- erosion of someone's profile, with theft of identity resulting an individual losing a good credit rating or even employment opportunities
- evasion of surveillance and law enforcement (eg fake identities for terrorists and other criminals)
- exploitation of 'credentialism' for economic or other benefit.

Later pages of this profile explore estimates of economy-wide economic impacts.

ID Crime before the Dot

This page considers identity theft and identity fraud before the digital era, highlighting some major incidents and issues

It covers-

- introduction
- gods and monsters
- great pretenders
- the confidence man
- clothes maketh the man?
- sages, spooks and scions

As Gilbert & Sullivan lamented in *HMS Pinafore* (1878) "things are seldom what they seem: skim milk masquerades as cream". The history of identity-related deception before the internet reflects the willingness of the deceived to believe and diffficulties in readily determining what is skim milk, what is the genuine article.

The extent of ID theft/fraud over time is not clear... and arguably is not knowable. The instances that remain in popular and scholarly memory survive because they relate to feats of particular audacity or had political significance; mundane deceptions were frequent but have not attracted lasting attention.

As suggested on the preceding page of this profile, a basic trajectory is evident, from identity crime involving sacred or royal identity to deception concerning bureaucratic actors, a shift from blood to uniforms and paper.

Gods and Monsters

Matthew vii 15 warns of false prophets "who come to you in the clothing of sheep, but inwardly they are ravening wolves". In the pre-Christian and early Christian eras it is common to find charismatic figures such as Simon Magus, Alexander of Abonoteichos or Theudas who claimed divine or quasi-divine powers. In appropriating an identity, where better to start than that of God?

Some people were less ambitious. Eusebius for example notes the supposed memoirs and counter-memoirs of Pontius Pilate-for example the *Memoirs of Pilate and Our Savior* of around 312AD exhibited on bronze tablets in public squares.

Confusion about who is who continued in the Middle Ages. Gregory of Tours' *Historia* features an enthusiast who at the end of the sixth century declared himself to be Christ, travelling in the neighbourhood of Arles in company of Mary, performing miracles and gathering followers until struck dead by a representative of Bishop Aurelius.

False bishops Adelbert and Clement, active in Germany around the year 744, gained attention for unorthodoxy (Adelbert told his followers it was unnecessary to confess their sins because he already read their hearts) and claims that their authority was confirmed by a miraculous letter from Jesus Christ that had supposedly fallen from heaven and been picked up by the Archangel Michael. The letter was read aloud by Pope Zachary at the Council of Rome in 745 but was apparently unconvincing as the 'bishops' were subsequently terminated. Franciscan friar James of Jülich was boiled alive in 1392 after the bad career move of pretending to be a bishop and falsely ordaining numerous priests.

Ecclesiastical fraudster Paulus Tigrinus successfully conned Pope Boniface IX (1389) and Antipope Clement VII into colluding in his assertion that he was the wandering Patriarch of Constantinople, lucratively milking minor potentates such as the Duke of Savoy.

The shape of the historical record, which for example like television centres on action rather than providing detailed information about the perceptions of ordinary people, means that it is difficult to be sure why some frauds were successful.

One reason is presumably the 'charisma' of the fraudsters. Another is contemporary expectations that identity was signified and validated by appearance: if you wore the right clothing and displayed the appropriate hauteur you were likely to be who you claimed to be, a case of clothes making the man.

Anxiety about identity and signifiers was reflected in a succession of sumptuary laws in most jurisdictions, seeking to underpin social hierarchies and morality by regulating the clothing of classes and occupations (eg prostitutes). Elizabeth I of England for example decreed that

None shall wear in his apparel any Cloth of Gold, Cloth of Silver or cloth mixed with gold or silver, nor any sables, except Earls, and all of superior degrees, and Viscounts and Barons in their doublets and sleeveless coats

A Scottish law of 1433 had more plaintively prohibited provision of pies to anyone under the rank of baron.

An introduction is provided by Alan Hunt's excellent *Governance of the consuming passions: a history of sumptuary law* (New York: St Martins 1996), superseding Frances Baldwin's 1926 *Sumptuary Legislation & Personal Regulation in England* (rpr New York: AMS Press 1994), and Valentin Groebner's *Der Schein der Person: Steckbrief, Ausweis und Kontrolle im Mittelalter* (Munich: Beck 2004), available as *Who Are You? Identification, Deception & Surveillance in Early Modern Europe* (New York: Zone 2007).

Great Pretenders

Exotic imposters were not restricted to Western Europe or the Church. Byzantine politics had been bedevilled by pretenders such as the Alexis Comnenus who undermined emperor Isaac Comnenus II.

The sudden death of Holy Roman Emperor Frederick Barbarossa in 1190 saw a slew of false Fredericks, followed by more imposters in the 1280s following the death of Frederick II Hohenstaufen (the 'Stupor Mundi' emperor). The death of Baldwin of Antioch saw appearance of a false Baldwin in Flanders in 1225.

In the UK John of Powderham claimed in 1318 that he and not the reigning Edward II should be king, explaining that a nurse had swapped babies after a pig had gnawed on his ear. He later retracted the claim, saying the Devil in the guise of a cat had inspired him. Both John and the cat were then hanged; Edward was deposed in 1327. Misadventures with livestock are recounted in Wendy Childs' 'Welcome, My Brother': Edward II, John of Powderham, and the Chronicles, 1318' in *Church & Chronicle in the Middle Ages: Essays presented to J. Taylor* (London: Hambledon 1991) edited by Ian Wood.

Jack Cade, who claimed descent from the Earls of Mortimer, momentarily gained control of London before being slain in 1450. The demise of the 'princes in the tower', attributed to Richard III, was followed by revolts centred around Lambert Simnel (who claimed in 1486 to be the Duke of Clarence and crowned in Dublin as Edward VI) and Perkin Warbeck (who announced himself in 1497 as Richard, Duke of York).

They are profiled in *Rebels, Pretenders, & Impostors* (New York: St Martins 2000) by Clive Cheesman & Jonathan Williams, Ann Wroe's more detailed *Perkin: A Story of Deception* (London: Cape 2003), Michael Bennett's *Lambert Simnel & the Battle of Stoke* (Stroud: Alan Sutton 1987) and Ian Arthurson's *The Perkin Warbeck Conspiracy, 1491-1499* (Stroud: Alan Sutton 1993).

Dispute about the demise in Africa of King Sebastian of Portugal in 1578 saw a succession of four pretenders, each claiming to be the king.

Problems with succession in Russia after the death of Ivan the Terrible and Boris Godunov (1605) saw four pretenders who claimed to be Ivan's son Dimitri. As Gyula Szvak in *False Tsars* (Boulder: East European Monographs 2001) and Maureen Perrie in *Pretenders & Popular Monarchism in Early Modern Russia: The False Tsars of the Time of Troubles* (Cambridge: Cambridge Uni Press 1995) note, 'comebacks' by dead Russian royalty were recurrent, with multiple false Tsar Peters (following death of Catherine the Great's husband in the 1762 palace coup) and false Constantines (assuming the identity of Nicholas I's older brother Constantine).

The death in a Paris prison of the Dauphin Louis, son of Louis XVI, resulted in over thirty self-proclaimed Louis XVIIs, including one who was implausibly black and frizzy-haired. Ex-forger Karl Wilhelm Naundorff, undeterred by an inability to speak French, convinced enough true believers to fund his 'court' in Brussels until 1845. Recent DNA tests are discussed in Deborah Cadbury's *The Lost King of France: A True Story of Revolution, Revenge, and DNA* (New York: St Martins 2002).

Mary Carleton-born Mary Moders in 1642-married Canterbury shoemaker John Steadman, entered a bigamous marriage with a surgeon named Day following an abortive flight to the Bahamas, bigamously married a bricklayer and then moved to London where she claimed to be a rich German princess named Maria de Wolway. Her supposed wealth evaporated after yet another marriage, which resulted in a bungled trial for bigamy at the Old Bailey. After acquittal she went on stage (failing to wow Samuel Pepys) and manufactured documents to support new identities.

In 1670 she was caught stealing a silver tankard, escaping hanging by transportation to Jamaica. Escaping from that colony she returned a career in London as a 'lady of quality' but while in Newgate prison for theft of silver was recognised as the 'German Princess' and thence hanged at Tyburn in 1673. Presumably now she would be appearing alongside Germaine Greer on the set of *Big Brother*.

Milkmaid Mary Baker (1791-1864) became exotic Princess Caraboo of Javasu, a career change described in John Wells' *Princess Caraboo: Her True Story* (London: Pan 1994) and John Gutch's 1817 *Caraboo: A Narrative of a Singular Imposition Practiced Upon the Benevolence of a Lady Residing in the Vicinity of Bristol.*

Contemporary Olivia Serres (1772-1834) claimed to be Princess Olive, supposed daughter of George III's feckless brother the Duke of Cumberland. Arrested in 1821, she unsuccessfully claimed that as a member of the royal family she could not be thrown into a debtors' prison. Her eldest daughter (1797–1871), falsely claimed to be a member of the British royal family, calling herself "Princess Lavinia of Cumberland" and in 1844 unsuccessfully sought to take the Duke of Wellington to court for having "overlooked" a bequest of £15,000. Undeterred, she brandished forged documents as part of bold but similarly fruitless legal action in 1866 for official recognition.

Sir Gregor MacGregor (1786-1845) merely invented the Central American state of Poyais, pocketing the proceeds of a £200,000 development loan. His exploits are recalled in David Sinclair's *Sir Gregor MacGregor and the Land That Never Was* (London: Review 2003).

In 1833 John Dow (aka John Luttrel)-a former convict from Van Diemen's Land-appeared in Sydney in the guise of Edward, Viscount Lascelles. He audaciously claimed that he was conducting an official investigation for the UK Secretary of State, eloped with a minor heiress and then sued in the NSW Supreme Court for her return when she was rescued by her parents

More recently John Gawsworth (1912-1970), a bibulous London poet and bibliophile, is chiefly remembered as claimant to the make-believe throne of the tiny uninhabited West Indies island of Santa Maria la Redonda. Tiny islands are of course useful because they are so very hard to find on the map, especially by a travel agent. Franz Weber-Richter claimed to be Hitler's son, an assertion just slightly more credible than the revelation that he had spent several months living with aliens on Mercury.

Bolshevik execution of Tsar Nicholas II and his family was followed by various imposters claiming to be the Grand Duchess Anastasia-eg Eugenia Smith and Anna Anderson in 1922, highlighted in Peter Kurth's *Anastasia: The Riddle of Anna Anderson* (New York: Little Brown 1985) and more recently Georgian Natalya Petrovna Bilikhodze-or the Tsarevitch, eg Michael Goleniewski and Nikolai Chebotarev, promoted in Guy Richards' *Imperial Agent: The Goleniewski-Romanov Case* (New York: Devin-Adair 1966) and Michael Gray's *Blood Relative* (London: Gollancz 1998).

At a less elevated level the Martin Guerre case has formed the basis of two films, three plays, a musical, an opera, a novel by Alexandre Dumas-author of royal ID theft tale *The Man In The Iron Mask*-and Natalie Zemon Davis' exemplary *The Return of Martin Guerre* (Cambridge: Harvard Uni Press 1983).

Unpleasant French villager Martin Guerre disappeared after going off to the wars, returning in 1556 as harder-working, more popular and more pleasing to his wife (albeit with smaller-size feet). Property disputes led to claims that he was an imposter, with litigation resolved in 1560 when a one-legged man hobbled into the Parlement of Toulouse claiming that *he* was the real Martin. That claim was successful: the penalty for identity fraud in the Guerre case was public execution.

Two centuries later, amid the chaos of the French Revolution, Anne Buiret claimed to be the Adelaide-Marie de Champignelles, Marquise de Douhault, supposedly imprisoned by her grasping relatives from 1786 to 1789. They claimed that she'd died and been properly buried. The case was not clearly resolved-the court ruled that she was neither Buiret not the Marquise-and the claimant has gained attention as a model of a 'stateless' person ("la femme sans nom") or the basis for Wilkie Collins' thriller *The Woman In White* (1858).

Harry Domela (1905-1978?) persuaded people that he was successively Graf Korf, Prince Lieven of Latvia and Prince Wilhelm of Hohenzollern before starring as himself in an early talkie. Runaway indentured servant Sarah Wilson (b1754) persuaded people in colonial Virginia that she was Susanna Caroline Matilda, sister of Queen Charlotte and thus sister-in-law of George III. The scam ended when she was retrieved by her master.

Palermo urchin Guiseppe Balsamo (1743-1795) reinvented himself as the fantastic Count Alessandro di Cagliostro-alchemist, lover, magnetic healer, muse, freemason and party animal. He is profiled in Iain McCalman's *The Last Alchemist: Count Cagliostro, Master of Magic in the Age of Reason* (London: HarperCollins 2003).

C. Wyatt Evans' *The Legend of John Wilkes Booth: Myth, Memory, and a Mummy* (Lawrence: Uni Press of Kansas 2004) examines the belief that Lincoln assassin John Wilkes Booth escaped and lived until 1903 using the assumed identity of David George. *The Truth About Jesse James* (Scotts Valley: CreateSpace 2008) by enthusiast Betty Duke claims that Jesse James pulled off one of the biggest hoaxes in American history by getting away with his own murder, assuming the alias of James Courtney, and hightailing it to Texas where he died of old age.

The Confidence Man

The age of paper money and social volatility produced adventurers such as French swindler Madame Therese, profiled in Hilary Spurling's superb *La Grande Therese: The Greatest Scandal of the Century* (London: HarperCollins 2000) and Arthur Orton, who claimed to be wealthy UK baronet Roger Charles Tichborne.

Tichborne had disappeared, presumed drowned off South America in an 1854 shipwreck. In 1865 his mother was advised that a man "answering to the description of her son" was working as a butcher at Wagga Wagga, Australia. Any resemblance was tenuous but that man-aka Tom Castro and Arthur Orton-embarked on litigation to claim the inheritance, ultimately being convicted in 1874 of perjury. Orton's claims were championed by disbarred lawyer Edward Kenealy, who modestly claimed he was the "Twelfth Messenger" of God(in a line that began with Adam and included Jesus, Mohammed and Genghis Khan).

The case is featured in *The Tichborne Trial* (London: Grant Richards 1899) by J B Atlay here, Rohan McWilliam's *The Tichborne Claimant* (London: Continuum 2007) and Robyn Annear's *The Man Who Lost Himself: The Unbelievable Story of the Tichborne Claimant* (Melbourne: Text 2002).

Thirty years later, as Partha Chatterjee describes in *A Princely Impostor? The Strange and Universal History of the Kumar of Bhawal* (Princeton: Princeton Uni Press 2002), the ailing Kumar (prince) of a leading Bengali family supposedly died during a trip to Darjeeling in 1909. His body apparently disappeared, fuelling disagreement when the Kumar supposedly reappeared in 1921 as a holy man with an interest in the family estates. Litigation lasted until an appeal to the Privy Council in 1946. Harriet Muraev's *Identity Theft: The Jew in Imperial Russia and the Case of Avraam Uri Kovner* (Palo Alto: Stanford Uni Press 2003) discusses the bizarre Kovner, friend of Dostoyesky, fraud, nihilist and fantasist.

Most identity crime, of course, involved the departure of money rather than bodies, something discussed in Karen Halttunen's *Confidence Men & Painted Women: A Study of Middle-Class Culture in America, 1830-1870* (New Haven: Yale Uni Press 1986), James Cook's *The Arts of Deception: Playing with Fraud in the Age of Barnum* (Cambridge: Harvard Uni Press 2001) and Timothy Spears' *100 Years on the Road: The Traveling Salesman in American Culture* (New Haven: Yale Uni Press 1995). Confidence men claimed expertise, formal qualifications, wealth and family-inspiring anxiety about legitimacy and the recognition of 'real' experts, underpinning moves towards the bureaucratisation of knowledge through formal training and certification.

Clothes Maketh the Man?

Signifiers of expertise, gender or authority could, however, be misread. Four of the more spectacular instances are the Kopenick, Dreadnought, Snell and Barry cases.

Ex-crim Wilhelm Voigt (1849-1922), trading on German deference to anyone in a uniform, bought a second-hand captain's suit in 1906 and commandeered a detachment of grenadiers. Marching to Kopenick town hall, he arrested the burgomaster (who was sent to Berlin military headquarters) and after examining the municipal accounts departed with 4,000 marks-equivalent to A$300,000.

Voigt was arrested five days later after getting drunk on the proceeds; the troops went unpunished because they had "unquestioningly obeyed the command of an officer". The exploit features in a 1932 Carl Zuckmayer play and the 1956 *Der Hauptmann von Köpenick* film.

In England Virginia Woolf starred as the Emperor of Abyssinia when a group of friends disguised as potentates and Foreign Office officials arrived unannounced at Portsmouth naval base in 1910 and persuaded staff to provide an official tour of *HMS Dreadnought*, the Royal Navy's most powerful warship.

Hannah Snell (1723-1792) adopted her brother-in-law's name, borrowed his clothes and joined the Royal Navy. Her career is discussed in Julie Wheelwright's *Amazons and Military Maids: Women Who Dressed as Men in Pursuit of Life, Liberty & Happiness* (London: Pandora 1994). Mary Anne Talbot (1778-1808) served as a cabin boy, drummer boy and celebrity. A successor is described in *Colonel Barker's Monstrous Regiment* (London: Virago 2002) by Rose Collis.

Lillias Valerie Arkell-Smith (1895-1960), aka Lillias Barker, left husband and Australian soldier Ernest Pearce Crouch in 1923 to begin a life as a man under the assumed identity of Victor Barker. She checked into the Grand Hotel in Brighton as Sir Victor Barker and as Colonel Victor Barker married Elfrida Haward later that year before pursuing careers as an actor, boxing club manager, dog kennel manager, dairy farmer, cafe owner and fruit picker. In 1927 she became involved with the National Fascisti, running its boxing programme. Two years later as Captain Leslie Ivor Victor Gauntlett Bligh Barker she found work as a hotel clerk. After service in the Home Guard as Jeffrey Norton she lived as the husband of Eva Norton.

A post-mortem examination of eminent British army surgeon Dr James Barry (1792-1865) revealed that he was a woman, indeed one who had given birth to a child. The Barry case is discussed in *Scanty Particulars: The Scandalous Life & Astonishing Secret of Dr James Barry, Queen Victoria's Preeminent Military Doctor* (New York: Random 2003) by Rachel Holmes and *Impostors: Six Kinds of Liar* (New York: Viking 2000) by Sarah Burton. There is a faint echo in *Self-Made Man: My Year Disguised As A Man* (London: Atlantic 2006) by Norah Vincent.

Francis Wheen's *The Irresistable Con: The Bizarre Life of a Fraudulent Genius* (London: Short 2004) considers the deceptions of guru 'Charlotte Bach', aka Karoly Hadju (1920-1981)... the sort of person who gives transvestism a bad name but apparently impresses Colin Wilson fans.

Closer to home Eugenia Falleni (1875-1938) adopted the appearance of a young man and ran away to sea at age 16, working as a male on vessels in the Pacific before giving birth in 1899 to a daughter and then resuming her identity as a male under the name Harry Crawford. In 1914 'Crawford' married widow Annie Birkett in 1914, apparently living harmoniously until 1917, when Birkett discovered "something amazing about Harry". He battered her to death but failed in a bid to throw her son off The Gap at Watsons Bay. Bizarrely, he successfully wooed and married another woman in 1919 before being convicted of murder in 1920.

British MP and former Aviation Minister John Stonehouse (1926-1988) simply shed his clothes and his identity in 1974, faking his own death by drowning as his business group collapsed and investigators were about to discover that a fund for Bangladeshi hurricane victims was missing £600,000. Stonehouse disappeared to Australia on a false passport in the name of Joseph Markham, a dead constituent. He was discovered in Melbourne, happily living with his mistress and masquerading as Clive Mildoon, another dead constituent. In 1976 he was sentenced to seven years in prison for theft, forgery and conspiracy to commit insurance fraud. An account is provided in his autobiography *Death of an Idealist* (London: WH Allen 1975) and *My Trial* (London: Star Books 1976).

Sages, Spooks and Scions

Archibald Belaney (1888-1938), exposed in Lovat Dickson's *Wilderness Man: The Strange Story of Grey Owl* (1974) and

Armand Ruffo's less persuasive *Grey Owl: the mystery of Archie Belaney* (Toronto: Coteau 1996), successfully posed as Ojiibwa sage Grey Owl and produced three bestsellers about life as a member of the First Nations.

Contemporary Buffalo Child Long Lance (1890-1932), star of the 1930 film *The Silent Enemy* and author of the 1928 fake autobiography *Long Lance*, claimed to be a crack aviator, a war hero (appointed to West Point and awarded the Croix de Guerre) and sparring partner of Jack Dempsey.

Sadly he was not a "full-blooded Blackfeet Indian" who had been raised in a tipee and hunted buffalo from horseback. His name was not Buffalo Child Long Lance; he was African-American rather than a member of the US or Canadian First Nations and his father was a janitor rather than a chief. His career is discussed in *Chief Buffalo Child Long Lance: The Glorious Impostor* (Red Deer: Red Deer Press 1999) by Donald Smith.

More recently high profile historian Ward Churchill has featured in claims that he was not an American Indian, with the American Indian Movement Grand Governing Council for example saying he has fraudulently represented himself as an Indian, and a member of the American Indian Movement and has been masquerading as an Indian for years behind his dark glasses and beaded headband.

Belaney's peer Karl May (1842-1912)-who had earlier been imprisoned for impersonating German secret service agents and policemen-gained fame for 'wild west' genre novellas, presented as autobiographical although he didn't venture west to the English channel. Adoption of a false persona didn't inhibit sales, which were above 50 million copies after 1912.

He was rivalled by Lev Nussimbaum (1905-1942), aka Essad Bey, whose stranger than fiction life was explored by Tom Reiss in *The Orientalist: Solving the Mystery of a Strange & Dangerous Life* (New York: Random 2005).

'Louis de Rougemont' (1847-1921), aka Louis Grin, gained fame for journalism about his travels-which apparently did not extend much beyond the Reading Room of the British Museum. He was exposed after enthusing over the marvellous "flight of the wombat", implausible given that wombats are burrowing creatures with the aerodynamic qualities of a bag of cement. He was more successful than Jean Christoph de Lancourt de Brenil, supposed companion of Jack London, master of 25 languages, war hero, equestrian, aviator and long distance walker. Rougement biographies include Ron Howard's *The Fabulist: The Incredible Story of Louis de Rougemont* (Sydney: Random House 2006).

Across the Atlantic Joseph 'Yellow Kid' Weil (1877-1975) successfully posed as a major investor from Chicago, borrowing executive offices in several banks. His victims were then invited to the bank to meet that institution's CEO, duly being impressed by the surroundings and handing over large amounts of cash. Weil's ghosted memoir *Con Man: A Master Swindler's Own Story* (New York: Broadway 2004) features an afterword by Saul Bellow.

Competitor 'Count' Victor Lustig (1890-1947), described in *The Man Who Sold the Eiffel Tower* (Garden City: Doubleday 1961) by Floyd Miller, forged French government stationery and invited six scrap metal dealers to a confidential meeting at the Hotel Crillon, where he introduced himself as the Deputy Director-General of the Ministry of Posts & Telegraphs and sought bids for the Eiffel Tower. One dealer provided several hundred thousand francs payment in advance, along with the customary bribe. Lustig was caught when he sought extra sweeteners.

The 'Eiffel Tower' exploit has attracted more attention than scams in the 1890s that saw fraudsters extract several hundred thousand dollars from US millionaires by selling Trajan's Column, the Arch of Constantine, the Colosseum. Tower of London and the Parthenon. Swiss hotel pageboy Gottfried Kopp for example reinvented himself as Austrian aristocrat Godfrey von Kopp to 'sell' the Arch of Constantine to US restaurant magnate John R Thompson for US$0.5 million. The US millionaire paid a US$100,000 deposit before sailing back to New York. The Arch never arrived. Kopp went on to 'sell' Trajan's Column to Charles Yerkes for US$250,000.

Stanley Clifford Weyman (1890-1960) impersonated public officials, including the US Secretary of State, the US consul to Morocco, a military attaché from Serbia, a US Navy lieutenant, the US consul general for Romania and a company doctor in Peru, where he threw lavish parties until his credit ran out. Contemporary Serge Stavisky (1886-1934), like Madame Therese, decided that it was simpler to start his own bank, claiming authorisation from the French government and a wealth that was in fact based on ponzi-style marketing of bonds. His career is examined in *Stavisky: A Confidence Man in the Republic of Virtue* (Ithaca: Cornell Uni Press 2002) by Paul Jankowski.

Cassie Chadwick (1857-1907) pretended to be the illegitimate daughter of steel tycoon Andrew Carnegie, something that resulted in banks competing to lend her money-a total of US$10 million over eight years. Her scam was reinforced when she forged securities in Garnegie's name. She takes centre stage in John Crosbie's *The Incredible Mrs. Chadwick: The Most Notorious Woman of Her Age* (New York: McGraw-Hill 1975).

Ferdinand Demara (1921-1982)-who described his motivation as "rascality, pure rascality"-variously assumed the identity of real or fictitious civil engineers, police, psychologists, lawyers, monks (Benedictine and Cistercian), scientists and teachers. His career as an identity thief peaked when he stole the ID of Canadian navy surgeon Joseph Cyr during the Korean War, supposedly successfully undertaking surgery.

Andre Gide's 1914 *Les Caves du Vatican* reworks the 1892 scam, described by Jean de Pauly in 1895, in which a gang of conmen persuaded gullible Catholic traditionalists that Pope Leo VIII was being held captive in the Vatican cellars: Freemasons and Jesuits had diabolically replaced him with an impostor. The victims dutifully supplied hundreds of thousands of francs for a secret crusade to rescue God's vicar.

Some contemporary scammers such as Christopher Rocancourt, David Hampton, Robert Hendy-Freegard, Omid Amidi-Mazaheri, Jean-Claude Romand and Abraham Abdullah are featured in the following page of this profile.

For insights into more contemporary scamming see Frank Abagnale's *Catch Me if You Can* (New York: Broadway Books 2000) with Stan Redding and *The Art of the Steal* (New York: Broadway 2001).

Contemporary Conmen and Compulsives

This page considers contemporary conmen and women, along with some identity fraudsters who might be characterised as compulsives or merely desperate.

Media coverage of contemporary identity crime has often centred on exploitation of the 'rich & famous' and on the bizarre, for example imposters in dental and medical practice or purported survivors of disasters such as 9/11.

Most identity crime is more mundane. It is likely to happen to you, or someone you know, rather than something that only affects public figures. In aggregate the economic value of thefts from non-celebrities is greater than looting the stars. Arguably the day to day impact of identity crime on ordinary people is greater: they are not cushioned by wealth and have few of the comforts available to the rich in dealing with a sense of violation and ongoing disempowerment after an account has been drained or a credit profile tarnished.

It is clear from looking at some high profile con jobs that some scammers are there for the money. Some presumably are gratified by a sense of power as they deceive their victims. Some may enjoy the excitement of living on the edge.

Other identity criminals appear to have put on a new profile like a new set of clothes or a suit of armour. What we have characterised as compulsives on occasion appear to actually believe the lies that they told the people around them-including their closest friends and families-so that the lie becomes the person, the assumed identity more real, more meaningful than the one they shed while taking a bath.

Both groups of criminals demonstrate that questions of 'social engineering', exploitation of trust and willingness to be deceived are central to much identity crime.

Noted Imposters

Christopher Rocancourt, active around 2000, swindled the US rich and famous by variously pretending to a Rockefeller heir, a movie producer, a global financier, the son of Sophia Loren or the nephew of Dino De Laurentis. He had earlier posed as 'Prince Galitzine Christo' and dabbled in diamond smuggling, passport forgery and armed robbery. The *New York*

Times, with just a dash of hyperbole, claimed that "Women threw themselves at his feet; men threw cash".

David Hampton (1964-2003) immortalised in John Guare's 1990 *Six Degrees of Separation*, gained attention during the 1980s in relieving wealthy Manhattanites of their money by convincing them he was Sidney Poitier's son.

US waiter Abraham Abdullah was imprisoned in 2001 after fraudulently gaining over US$20 million by pretending to represent celebrities such as Steven Spielberg, Oprah Winfrey, Martha Stewart, Ross Perot and Warren Buffett. He began by googling those figures, using that information in forged Merrill Lynch and Goldman Sachs correspondence that persuaded credit reporting services such as Equifax and Experion to supply detailed reports. Those reports were then used to dupe banks and brokers into transferring money to accounts controlled by Abdullah.

Knowing that the institutions would want to verify the transfers, Abdullah typically included telephone numbers where he could be reached. The institutions according gained some reassurance through voicemail answered in the victim's name. At his arrest he had 800 fraudulent credit cards and a mere 20,000 blank credit cards.

His precursor was the more inventive US impostor Frederick Emerson Peters (1885-1959). Peters wrote bad cheques masquerading as famous people, often succeeding because the victims framed the cheques as mementos rather than passing them to a bank. He initially posed as Theodore Roosevelt II, later becoming antique expert 'RA Coleman' of the American Peace Society', 'JJ Morton' of the Widener Library, Franklin Delano Roosevelt, Booth Tarkington and Gifford Pinchot II. At Peters' death he was found to have five cheques on his pockets-each for different identities.

Assuming the persona of someone famous-however improbably-is not restricted to the US. Novelist Grahame Greene discovered during the 1980s that an imposter was busy in Asia, wining, dining, romancing and giving interviews. Alan Conway (1934-1998)-depicted in the 2006 film *Color Me Kubrick*-wined and dined his way through Europe and the US in the guise of Stanley Kubrick.

US serial ID thief Carlos Lomax was sentenced to 37 months in prison after pleading guilty to opening 14 credit accounts with Pittsburgh retailers stores using the identity of star Will Smith. At the time he was on probation after running up US$81,000 on an American Express card as sports journalist Steve Smith. As Will Smith he had pocketed over US$190,000.

UK authorities claimed in 2004 that Robert Hendy-Freegard posed as an MI5 officer, convincing people into spending years in hiding while stealing over £650,000 of their savings. It is alleged that he persuaded students and other victims that they were on an IRA hit list through their association with him, leading them to go undercover for years in 'safe houses' and travel on spy missions that featured waiting for hours at railway stations for non-existent people.

A year later Omid Amidi-Mazaheri was jailed for two years after stealing the identity of a dentist, which allowed him to become rich through shoddy treatment (drilling cavities without local anaesthetic, providing fillings that crumbled within days, dropping equipment down a patient's throat, failure to observe HIV protocols).

Sheldon Zelitt, former head of Canadian high tech company VisuaLabs, variously claimed to be a physicist, to have served in Vietnam, dismantled a MiG fighter plane, developed a spy satellite, and worked for the CIA and the Mossad. After that supposed invention of 3-D television seems to have been a mere bagatelle, albeit one that pushed VisuaLabs' share price. Things unravelled at the company's annual meeting in 2001, when he tried to pass off a Sony device as his new invention. Canadian authorities retrieved him after he fled to the Czech Republic.

Charles Albert Stopford fled the US in 1983 after attempting to blow up his boss with a pipe bomb. He assumed the name Christopher Edward Buckingham after stealing the identity of a baby who died in 1963. He thereafter purported to be the Earl of Buckingham, a UK title extinct for over 300 years, flaunting notepaper with the Buckingham coat of arms and telling his German landlady that he needed a large apartment to accommodate furniture from his English castle. The fake Earl was arrested at Dover in 2005 when an automated check of the the UK births & deaths database revealed his passport to be false; he was jailed for that offence amid speculation that he was a renegade CIA officer or even a mafia hitman. In prison he continued to insist that he was an aristocrat.

Charles Lee Crutcher, aka Charles Decrevecoeur, claimed to be Lord Peter de Vere Beauclerk before being jailed in 1994. Two years later Keith Andrews was on trial for fraud after some 20 years of persuading people that he was Marc Philip Justin Onslow Berkeley St Leger Curzon, the 10th Viscount of Doneraile, son of Joy Chantal Helene de Burgoyne of Paris and husband of Marie-Louise, daughter of the Duc de Brissac.

Delusions of blue blood were also apparent in the fake 2003 wedding of supposed Japanese Prince Satohito Arisugawa, in reality Yasuyuki Kitano-conman and son of a greengrocer. He made a career through product endorsements and as a recipient of wedding gifts from dazzled commoners, with the 2003 event bringing in a tidy 13 million yen.

Ottone Eugeno (aka Ottone Eugeno Camelio Bresselhau) claimed to be Austrian baron Otto Von Bressensdorf, principal of US investment bank Lyons Capital Inc. Together with his associates the supposed banker defrauded clients by convincing them to pay thousands of dollars in "advance fees". The US government drily commented that "In reality, however, Lyons rarely helped clients at all" (PDF) and questioned whether he was entitled to the title or the medals worn at business meetings. Lyons had provided fraudulent financial statements to Dunn & Bradstreet, which in turn produced a commercial credit rating used by potential clients in deciding whether to engage Lyons. Italian businessman Rosario Poidimani was arrested over involvement in a scam centred on the claim that he was the king of Portugal (the last king having expired in 1932). Poidimani allegedly sold imaginary aristocratic titles and fraudulent diplomatic passports, underpinned by imaginary offshore bank accounts and an elaborate throne room. His associates claimed to be working towards creation of a sovereign kingdom (variously in the Ukraine or on a Croatian islet) that would eventually become a EU member.

Compulsives

Perhaps more sadly, Emmanuel Carrère's *The Adversary: A True Story of Monstrous Deception* (London Picador 2001) profiles Jean-Claude Romand, who murdered his family when he could no longer maintain the fiction-as he had assiduously done for most of his adult life-that he was a senior World Health Organization bureaucrat.

Serial imposter Frédéric Bourdin recurrently posed as a teenager. In 2005, at age 31, he was exposed after spending a month at a French school in the guise of a 15 year old-supposedly a Spanish orphan named Francisco Hernandez-Fernandez-with forged identity papers. The headmistress explained he "appeared a bit older than his friends-two or three years at most".

Bourdin had previously served a six-year prison term in the US after posing as a long-lost son (living with the supposed parents for three months before his deception was exposed by a journalist and confirmed by a DNA test) and claiming in 2004 to be a boy of 14 who disappeared near Grenoble in 1996 at the age of six.

He was deported from Spain after he claimed to be Ruben Sanchez Espinosa, whose mother supposedly died in the Madrid train bombings of March 2004. He also posed as a tiger tamer, a rich British holidaymaker, a businessman and a college lecturer.

32 year old Brian MacKinnon duped teachers and pupils at Glasgow's Bearsden Academy into believing that he was 17 year old Canadian Brandon Lee. He had studied at Bearsden 13 years earlier. After matriculating from Bearsden he started a medical degree at the University of Dundee, being discovered when his passport was found during a holiday in Tenerife.

22 year old US sex offender Joshua Gardner less successfully posed in 2005 as 17 year old Caspian James Crichton-Stuart IV, supposed fifth Duke of Cleveland.

29 year old convicted sex offender Neil Rodreick attended an Arizona public school for four months in the guise of Casey Price, supposedly a seventh grader, and Oklahoma schools in 2005 as a supposed 12 year old. Rodreick was arrested in 2007.

German carpenter Gerhard Vilsmeier spent 25 years in the guise of a Roman Catholic priest. During the mid-1980s he was accepted in the Tyrolean parish of Schwarz as missionary priest 'Axel Kolbe'. Detection forced embarrassed religious authorities to redo the weddings and christenings at which Vilsmeier had officiated. He moved to Berlin, claiming to be a doctor of ecclesiastical law and a Bavarian priest on sabbatical.

He was detected after six months of service, with the church belatedly requesting to see his documentation.

Unabashed by a £1,400 from a Berlin court for false use of a title, he spent the closing months of 2005 in Austria as a priest, having persuaded the presumably pious folk of Neukirchen an der Enknach that he was an organist from a nearby parish and then a priest without a parish. A diocesan spokesperson explained "the man was extremely well-versed in all things theological".

We trust that there would be a somewhat more searching examination of fraudsters who appear to be extremely well versed in all things legal or medical.

Musician Massimiliano Muzzi more benignly toured the world in the guise of the Pope's organist, with his promoters claiming that he was a virtuoso who performed at private masses in the papal chapel and at organ at St Peter's Basilica.

Australian scammer Barry Faulkner came to police attention in 1968 when he posed as a doctor at Royal Brisbane Hospital, conducting bogus examinations on pregnant women.

He subsequently purported to be a US Air Force colonel, a US Marine Corps officer, Mike Nesmith of the Monkees, a CIA agent, a gynaecologist, an Olympic official and pilots for Virgin Blue, Ansett, Canadian Airlines, the Royal Flying Doctor Service and Lauda Air.

UK serial bride Emma Golightly was jailed in 2007 despite claims she suffered from a split personality. As an unemployed 19 year old she convinced a succession of men that she was a multimillionaire businesswoman with a terminal condition.

Despite a history of bounced cheques she persuaded her suitors-found through dating sites and lonelyhearts ads in newspapers-to shower her with treats, including the usual designer shoes and luxury cars, while she stole over £250,000 from their credit cards. The £12,000 reception after one bigamous wedding fizzled because she had not paid for a marriage registrar.

Survivor Fraud

For some observers a more disturbing phenomenon is that of people who falsely claim to be survivors of the Holocaust or disasters such as the 9/11 Twin Towers terrorist incidents, sometimes apparently truly believing their own claims and without a primary motivation of financial reward.

Such betrayal of good faith and appropriation of the respect for another's genuine suffering and endurance is apparent in literary frauds such as Wilkomirski and Doessekker-discussed elsewhere on this site-and the tawdriness of fakes such as Khouri, Darville/Demidenko, Fonseca/De Wael and JT LeRoy. Personal validation and/or profit by being the focus of community solicitude is not new: fraudulent 'survivors' appeared after the *Titanic* sinking, the Crusades and other events that grabbed public attention.

In 2007 questions were asked about Twin Towers personality Tania Head, prominent as a founder of the 9/11 Survivors' Network (WTCSN). Sceptics reported that, contrary to her claims, Merrill Lynch had no record of employing a Tania Head as a member of a mergers team in the south tower (all of whom, including her supposed fiancee, perished on 9/11 except her). Claims of a Harvard undergraduate degree and Stanford graduate degree appear inconsistent with statements by those universities that they could not find records of a student by her name.

Stolen honour

Elsewhere on this site we have discussed degree mills: entities that will sell you a degree from a fake university (or even a fake degree from a real university). They attract people who want to pad a resume or merely reinforce a wobbly ego and who are prepared to pay for an instant degree ("You can get a degree in any major that you desire in just 7 days!").

Some people, alas, have bought heroism-or esteem and financial rewards sometimes associated with military honours-by fraudulently claiming to have been awarded military decorations or otherwise recognised for combat service.

Pamla Sterner's 2005 *The Stolen Valor Act of 2005: Medal of Honor Legislative Changes* (PDF) for example notes the case of a US conman who had himself photographed wearing a USN Rear Admiral's uniform with a Medal of Honor ribbon and unsuccessfully tried to use a false NSA identity card when confronted by FBI investigators. Other incidents have included the Illinois judge who resigned after admitting that the Medal of Honor displayed in his chamber was a fake and that he was not entitled to the award.

In 2005 Australia's Charles Sturt University fired James Montgomery, who-as noted by ANZMI-had claimed to have been awarded the Victoria Cross (somewhat rarer than a Nobel Prize) and to have variously served as a US Marine, a US Navy SEAL, an Australian SAS Captain, a SAS Major, a Commando and a RAN Reserve Captain. A year later 'Colonel' Michael Nicholson appeared in a Sydney court after allegedly representing himself at an Anzac Day ceremony as a returned soldier, replete with numerous medals. He allegedly used fake ID to enter the Randwick Barracks, where he demanded free tailoring of official uniforms, and celebrated in the officers' mess at HMAS Watson.

Central Local Court magistrate Carney commented that uniforms defined a person's "role and task in society" and bestowed a degree of importance and authority. Nicholson had "acquired that authority through furtive means". He pleaded guilty to seven charges, including falsely representing to be a returned soldier, wearing service decorations when unentitled, possessing a prohibited weapon, trespass and obtaining financial advantage by deception.

He was given a six-month suspended sentence and fined $850. 'Major' Reg Newton, junior vice-president of the 8th Division Association in Australia, claimed a Military Cross and bar, service as a secret agent during the Cold War (setting up escape lines in East Germany in 1951, "awarded MC for heavy action Laos", almost killed in Mongolia and wounded in Korea) and decoration by King George VI. Alas, in 2006 evidence emerged that he was never a major, had never won a Military Cross and indeed never served overseas. He reportedly told acquaintances there are no records because his work was "top secret".

UK fantasist Alan McIlwraith claimed to be Captain Sir Alan McIlwraith, CBE, DSO, MC, MiD-war hero, officer in the

Parachute Regiment, top of his class at Sandhurst and a terrorism expert who served in Northern Ireland, the Balkans, Sierra Leone and Afghanistan. Unabashed, he created his own Wikipedia entry.

There are few hard statistics on the extent of such offences and much of the literature is deeply politicised.

Works on appropriation in the US include the revisionist *Stolen Valor: How the Vietnam Generation Was Robbed of Its Heroes and Its History* (Dallas: Verity Press 1998) by B G Burkett & Glenna Whitley and equally fervent *Fake Warriors: Identifying, Exposing, & Punishing Those Who Falsify Their Military Service* (Philadelphia: Xlibris 2003) by Henry & Erika Holzer

We are engulfed in a national scandal. Unknown to most Americans, there is a virtual epidemic of impostors in this country-countless thousands of men (and a few women) who, since the Vietnam War, have been either inventing a non-existent military service, or inflating their war records. Veterans' benefits amounting to hundreds of millions of dollars are being stolen. Military decorations are being falsely claimed, and often worn, by men never authorized to receive them-the kind earned the hard way by genuine war heroes.

Critics have noted that UK film star Trevor Howard (1916-1988) gained the respect of his peers through tales of military exploits that included parachuting into Nazi-occupied Norway and taking part in the Allied invasion of Sicily (recognised through award of the Military Cross). Following his death UK files revealed that Howard had been invalided out of the army in 1943, judged as "mentally unstable" with a "psychopathic personality".

PAPER AND PLASTIC

This discussion 7considers contemporary identity theft/fraud involving paper and plastic money.

Woody Guthrie's 1939 *Pretty Boy Floyd* reminded the listener that

I've seen lots of funny men;
Some will rob you with a six-gun,
And some with a fountain pen.

Contemporary identity crime is an extension of the offences discussed in the preceding page of this profile, rather than an unprecedented new development.

As in the past it encompasses a range of misbehaviour, from direct financial theft through to people-smuggling, sullying someone's reputation on a non-financial basis or improperly claiming expertise. It has largely been addressed through traditional law, explored later in this profile, and through action by regulators, financial institutions and individuals.

Some of that action would be familiar to a person living in the 1650s. Other action, including biometric verification services, is a distinctly modern response to uncertainties about identity and authorisation. It forms the basis for responses to much online identity crime and, more broadly, for questions about identity in electronic networks where perceptions of risk allow substantial anonymity/pseudonymity.

Responses have been complicated by mythologising about the extent and shape of identity crime. Some pundits and journalists for example have indicated that it is uniquely modern or unprecedented, that it is "the crime of the century" and that it primarily involves gangs of skilled criminals, often depicted as lurking behind a computer screen somewhere offshore.

Politicians and government officials have similarly succumbed to the temptation to simplify, on occasion referring to a wave of welfare fraud-unsubstantiated by statistics-or identity abuse by terrorists that can supposedly be comprehensively addressed through mechanisms such as an Australia Card. Solution vendors have hyped particular tools. Consumer advocates have noted concerns about responses by some data custodians or merely the irresponsibility of some large organisations.

The US Federal Trade Commission notes that the basket of offences characterised as 'identity theft' is the top consumer fraud in that country, a comment consistent with experience in Australia and New Zealand.

The FTC indicates that as of 2004 only 11% of known identity theft cases occurred online (of which around half involved spyware and the rest phishing or hackers). Much involved traditional misuse of paper.

Around 30% of its 'identity fraud crimes' involved loss of a wallet, chequebook or credit card. Under 5% was a result of information being removed from personal garbage; over 10% occurred when personal information was misused by a family member, friend or acquaintance. 32% of identity theft victims (in cases where the perpetrator's identity was known) found a family member or relative was responsible; 18% had been victimized by a friend, neighbor or in-home employee.

Complete strangers outside the workplace accounted for only 24% of identity thefts, with a colleague perpetrating only 4% of identity thefts. Much identity theft involved insiders within data custodians: staff/contractors at organisations with access to personal information were responsible for 13% of identity theft.

The UK Cabinet Office, consistent with studies by the Australian National Audit Office, concluded that the incidence of identity offences in pension and other social services was a fraction of 1% of recipients and was not growing significantly.

Building Blocks

The following methods have been noted by law enforcement agencies –

- retrieving documents containing personal information (eg bank and credit card statements) from rubbish-'dumpster diving'
- intercepting credit cards, debit cards and documents such as passport applications in post offices, letter boxes or courier service premises and bags
- stealing wallets, coats and other items that contain cards and identification papers.

Elsewhere we have highlighted theft, sale or forgery of breeder documents such as birth certificates and passports. In May 2007 UK police revealed that at least 200 of 850 blank birth certificates stolen from Erewash in Derbyshire during 2005 had been used to create fake identities and claim student loans. Adeleke Adebayo created 17 separate identities and signed himself up for courses at universities across the UK, collecting the loans but not going to class. At London Metropolitan University he was enrolled in five degree courses using five bogus identities.

PAYMENT SYSTEMS

Electronic 'skimming' of credit cards and ATM cards updates misuse of the carbons, with illicit capture of information from the magnetic stripe on the back of a card. At its simplest it involves unauthorised swiping of a card when a consumer makes a payment, for example in a restaurant when a waiter takes the card away to pay the bill. At its most exotic it has involved scams where criminals collect information (including PINs) via a fake ATM in a public place or where there is covert surveillance of a PIN when the consumer confirms an authorised swipe.

Arguably there has been more media attention and consumer angst about 'shoulder surfing', with thieves observing people at automatic teller machines while keying in identifiers or listening while an individual provides a credit card number to someone by mobile telephone. That information generally is insufficient for an effective fraud but provides a building block for identity theft.

'Mail non-receipt fraud' occurs when a criminal intercepts a new or replacement card from a retailer or financial institution, for example inside a post office or by removing the envelope from letterboxes. That has led most card issuers to send out 'inactive' cards, which are not authorised until the account holder confirms that person's identify and card number.

One writer in the London *Times*, discussing exposure of 45 million credit cards in the TJX incident, claimed that cardersmarket.com, cardingworld.cc, scandinaviancarding.com and darkmarket.ws act as "an eBay for hackers", allowing criminals to buy and sell stolen card details.

Who are the Criminals?

As the preceding paragraphs suggest, there is no single discrete type of identity criminal: theft is not restricted to a cyberliterate Russian mafiya or people over 21.

Some criminals wear suits and are active in boardrooms and executive suites at the big end of town, having engaged in resume fraud. Others are your neighbour's children (misusing mum's credit card) or the students in your classroom (editing an identity document to gain a cheap fare or evade age-based restrictions regarding entertainment venues and purchases).

Some are itinerants who steal individual credit cards from bags and letterboxes (easier than stealing your VCR or turning your car into spare parts). Others operate on an industrial scale, illicitly accessing databases or trading in details obtained from those databases. As with much retail crime, some offences involve insiders-whether behind the till or in the computer suite.

In 2002 for example a group of US high school students bought US$36,000 worth of goods online after stealing credit card data from a Chase Bankcard office where they had worked as interns. One 16 year old student was arrested after altering addresses and phone numbers on credit card accounts to direct online purchases to abandoned houses in his neighborhood, where he collected the packages. The theft was detected when customers complained about being billed for the goods.

Dido Mayue-Belezika led a gang of around 220 people who stole around £20m from people in the UK. Mayue-Belezika for example intercepted every chequebook he encountered as a postman, indulging in gangsta bling such as £1,400 for a pair of shoes that featured his initials engraved on the soles. In a separate UK case during 2006 Ali Dahir indicated that a gang used over 3,000 stolen cards, extracted from letterboxes and postal sorting rooms, to buy luxury goods worth £870,000.

Australian Cases

There has been no comprehensive dissection of reported Australian identity crime. The following paragraphs offer blurry snapshots of particular incidents, illustrating the range of offences and perpretrators.

NSW police received a bag during 2004, apparently found in a Sydney street. It reportedly contained disks featuring templates for manufacture of bogus Medicare cards, drivers' licences, utility bills, bank statements and birth and marriage certificates, ie 'breeder documents' for creation of an identity and for establishment of bank accounts. The bag also contained fake certificates from the Civil Aviation Authority regarding authorisation to fly light aircraft. Follow-up action saw the arrest of two men for 234 forgery-related offences. One of the perpetrators spent $35,000 on a ski boat unwisely named 'Crime Pays'.

In the mid-1990s a Victorian used desktop publishing skills to concoct 41 birth certificates and student identification cards, gaining the requisite 100 points for a mere 42 bank accounts, registration of a business name, sales tax refunds and equipment purchases.

Another criminal obtained the birth certificates of four babies who had died in the 1970s, using their identity to obtain $20,857 in unemployment benefits. On arrest he was in possession of fake proof of identity documents such as rental leases, mobile phone accounts, motor vehicle learner's permits and student cards. A contemporary used up to 50 false identities in a $7 million property fraud in NSW, Victoria and the ACT, obtaining home loans from financial institutions.

Not to be outdone, a bank manager and assistant created accounts in fictitious names and in the names of relatives, circumventing proof of identity protocols to snaffle $1.5 million in unauthorised loans. The scam was discovered in 2001 when an account went into default and the bank could not find the fictitious customer.

A solicitor similarly relied on old-fashioned methods of making money, relying on fake birth certificates and drivers' licences to disguise money looted from the accounts of his clients. During 1997 an adventurous 24 year old gained 45 credit cards in different names (after applying for 61). She had charmingly appropriated some names from school acquaintances. This resulted in the destruction of credit of many, one of whom also suffered the additional indignity of being named by the applicant as her co-offender and mentor in the frauds.

More bizarrely, a murdererer entered Australia using the passport of a female friend's brother, subsequently exploiting the passport of another brother before being convicted with that person's murder.

A group of car thieves operated on a more industrial scale, using personal details of owners of cars with the same make and model as vehicles stolen by the gang. The information was used to obtain duplicate registration certificates, number plates and labels to 're-birth' those vehicles prior to sale to unsuspecting purchasers interstate. One victim discovered that the thieves had amended his name by deed poll to facilitate further offences; other victims experienced difficulty in proving lack of involvement in the scam.

Other People's Money: The Rise And Fall Of Britain's Most Audacious Credit Card Fraudster (London: Pan Macmillan 2007) by Neil Forsyth with Elliot Castro.

RESUMES

This page considers fake CVs and résumé massaging.

Concerns regarding certification and 'resume fraud' reflect the credentialism that is an integral feature of 'anonymist' information economies, ones where:

- most potential employees are not personally known by prospective employers or vouched for by an employer's personal contacts
- job markets may be highly competitive and where reruitment applications may be decided on the basis of the applicant's possession of academic or other qualifications
- an individual faces the temptation of polishing a curriculum vitae by adding a degree that wasn't obtained, adding non-existant expertise and professional affiliations or exaggerating a current salary
- there are perceptions that everyone is 'massaging' their CVs
- the paper, rather than the clothes, are what maketh the man.

The significance of tweaking a CV or inventing an employment history and qualifications varies. The shape of offences also varies.

Some instances simply involve 'enhancement' of a legitimate curriculum vitae, putting a positive spin on a job description. Others involve omitting or inventing information for a job application, presumably with the hope that the qualifications won't be checked or omissions identified. Other individuals have comprehensively manufactured qualifications and employment histories. Some people conveniently forget about past employers who would make poor referees or occupations that do not fit perceptions of the prospective employer's job profile. Some applicants want to get past a filter to a job interview (eg withstand sorting in an online recruitment site) or get a promotion.

Others, as corporate security services recurrently note, do not intend to stay. Instead they intend to work in an organisation just long enough to illicitly access data or install malware. Ricardo Garotte for example stole £4 million from two UK banks after using false references to obtain temporary posts.

Statistics

It is common to encounter claims that "approximately 75% of all CVs have some form of embellishment and 25% contain outright lies". We have thus sighted suggestions that suggestions that up to 500,000 false tertiary degrees are in 'use' in the USA (eg were cited for employment purposes), including 10,000 false medical degrees. One perspective is provided in a 1996 study (PDF) by Michael Finn & Joe Baker.

Other claims suggest that 30% of employees were hired with 'massaged' credentials, although most massaging appears to relate to being economical with the truth rather than fundamental misrepresentation.

Estimates of the prevalence and seriousness of resume fraud vary widely, with higher figures (up to 80% incidence) coming from commercial resume verification services. The February 2003 issue of *Assessment Council News* (PDF) notes a range from 11% to 67%.

UK verification service Control Risks estimated in 2003 that "about one in four CVs contains lies". Local pre-employment screening service Australian Background claimed in 2005 that 21% of 1,000 candidates in the industrial, banking, public sector and finance industries had engaged in CV fraud. Of that 21% some 60% had reportedly omitted to mention criminal convictions such as fraud, drug possession and embezzlement.

The UK Chartered Institute of Personnel & Developments claimed in its 2005 Annual Recruitment, Retention and Turnover survey that one in four companies rescinded a job offer during 2004 because of CV fraud, with 23% of employers sacking staff after discovering discrepancies in information provided during the selection process.

Demographics are problematical. One verfication service claims that 64% of people are "willing to invent information to put on their CVs to try to land a job", with men being supposedly more likely to lie than women. It is claimed that office workers "have the highest propensity to lie", followed by students, manual workers, skilled trades and retail workers but arguably that ranking reflects the nature of recruitment in US markets.

The predominant inaccuracy appears to be exaggeration of the applicant's current salary in a bid to increase remuneration by the prospective employer. Other popular exaggerations include qualifications, length of service in a previous job, level of experience and-for emloyers who consider such attributes are meaningful predictors of performance-hobbies and community involvement.

Incidents

Most incidents of resume tweaking or outright invention are not reported. Media coverage does, however, give some sense of the chutzpah, desperation or merely ineptitude of some public figures. Exposure by colleagues or journalists has encompassed government officials, business figures, military and educational administrators and academics.

In the US, UK and Australia misstatements in CVs have embarrassed the great and ungood.

Veritas CFO Ken Lonchar for example resigned after falsely claiming that he had a Stanford MBA. Bausch & Lomb CEO Ronald Zarrella forfeited a US$1.1 million bonus because his resume featured a non-existent MBA from New York University. Televangelist Pat Robertson merely claimed war service in Korea. David Edmondson, CEO of RadioShack and former Baptist minister, claimed that he had received degrees in theology and psychology. Patrick Imbardelli resigned a £300,000 pa job as head of InterContinental Hotels' Asia Pacific operations days before joining the parent company's board, after it was revealed that he had falsely claimed a bachelor of business degree from the University of Victoria and a BSc and MBA from Cornell University. His demise was prompted by a whistleblower.

Brian Valery duped major New York law firm Anderson Kill & Olick. He was hired as a paralegal in 1996 and in 2004 informed his superiors that he had passed the bar exam after gaining a law degree through Fordham University's evening program. Anderson Kill promoted him to an associate and adding his name to its stationery. He was arrested in Connecticut in 2007 after applying to join that state's Bar, with a potential sentence of five years imprisonment for perjury and practicing law without being a lawyer.

Chris Tyler, CEO of Telstra subsidiary Solution 6, was revealed in 2000 to have had been been convicted of marijuana possession (more than 22.7 kilograms, for which he received a 10-year suspended sentence), involved with a North American company, Lessonware, that had collapsed and with a series of blunders as head of New Zealand Telecom's internet operations. Telstra did not know about Lessonware or the drug conviction. Queried why he had not told the boards of Solution 6 and Telstra about his past, Tyler commented that he was "never asked".

Telstra had previously been embarrassed by the revelation in 1993 that Bruno Sorrentino, head of its IT arm and research laboratories (and former ANZ Bank chief information officer), had not attended London's Imperial College, let alone completed a claimed PhD in physics.

In the UK Alison Ryan, appointed to a £125,000-a-year job as PR supremo for Manchester United, claimed to have a first class degree from Cambridge University and a distinction in her professional examination. In reality, she had gained a second class and had later been disbarred by the Bar Council after being charged with nine counts of professional misconduct.

MIT dean of admissions Marilee Jones resigned in 2007 after nearly three decades, saying "I misrepresented my academic degrees when I first applied to M.I.T. 28 years ago and did not have the courage to correct my résumé when I applied for my current job or at any time since". On various occasions she had claimed to have degrees from Albany Medical College, Union College and Rensselaer Polytechnic Institute but alas had no degrees from those places or anywhere else.

The Australian National Safety Council's John Friedrich (aka Friedrich Hohenberger), is believed to have used a false passport, invented qualifications and impressive career achievements. That creativity was presumably useful in a fraud that saw around $300 million go missing-followed by Friedrich's disappearance in 1989 and suicide in 1991.

In the UK Neil Taylor was chosen unanimously for the £115,000-a-year job as head of the Shrewsbury & Telford Hospitals NHS Trust after claiming to have a first-class degree from the University of Nottingham. Alas, he had massaged his CV.

When asked to provide his certificates for a routine salary review in 2004 he supplied a homemade diploma with "a crude copy of the Nottingham University logo", claiming that the paper was for a BA in business administration and economics. Why stop there? He also claimed to be a graduate of the non-existent Institute of Personnel Management at Nottingham and to have a postgraduate diploma in Forensic Medicine. Taylor had previously worked, apparently quite effectively, as chief executive at the Royal Orthopaedic Hospital in Birmingham for four years and another four as head of the Royal Shrewsbury Hospital. In sentencing him to 12 months in custody the judge commented "lies come back to haunt you".

Notre Dame football coach George O'Leary was forced to resign five days after being hired in 2001, admitting he lied about academic credentials that included a 'masters degree' from New York University. James Gulliver's multi-billion dollar takeover of Distillers in 1985 was hobbled after competitors revealed that the high profile entrepreneur had not gained an MBA from Harvard.

Denis Smith, former chief executive of the WA city of Joondalup, was found to have lied about postgraduate qualifications he claimed to have obtained from UTS and RMIT.

Michael Brown, head of the Federal Emergency Management Agency (FEMA), was revealed to have been merely a student at Central State University rather than "Outstanding Political Science Professor". Other parts of his resume were similarly inventive.

Jeffrey Archer, whose defamation action is highlighted elsewhere on this site, recurrently buffed his profile. He claimed that he was born in Somerset, rather than in the more prosaic central London's City Road area, and painted his father as an upstanding war hero although dad was a bigamist who fled to New York in 1914 to avoid arrest for fraud. One Archer CV listed a year at Sandhurst military college and an army physical training instruction course, which as the *Guardian* sniffed was "a surprise to Sandhurst and the regiment".

In 2002 John Davy was sentenced to eight months imprisonment in New Zealand for CV fraud. He had been controversially appointed as $NZ140,000-a-year inaugural head of the Maori Television Service. That appointment reflected supposed strong financial and management skills; Davy had no television experience, knew little of Maori culture and was unfamiliar with the language. He had claimed an MBA from the Ashland School of Business at Denver State University, an accounting certificate, experience as a member of the British Columbia Securities Commission and authorship of two books.

Unfortunately the Commission had not heard of him and the 'University' was discovered to be an online diploma mill. Davy claimed that he had been 'undercover', with his academic and financial history being wiped as part of a witness protection program. In reality he had been twice declared bankrupt and had worked as an accountant in Whistler, rather than as a regulator.

In the same year Brigadier-General Ernest Zwane, head of the South African National Defence Force's legal department, was arrested after claims that his CV was decorated with an illicit BA degree from the University of Fort Hare and a B Proc and LLB from Vista University.

Jeffrey Papows, author of *Enterprise.com: Market Leadership in the Information Age* (New York: Perseus 1999), resigned as president of IBM's Lotus unit in 2000 after being savaged by the *Wall Street Journal* in 1999 over what appeared to be some tall tales. IBM initially dismissed criticism as nothing but "rumors strung together by commentary".

The Register Unkindly Commented

So he's not an orphan, his parents are alive and well. He wasn't a Marine Corps captain, he was a lieutenant. He didn't save a buddy by throwing a live grenade out of a trench. He didn't burst an eardrum when ejecting from a Phantom F4, which didn't crash, not killing his co-pilot. He's not a tae kwon do black belt, and he doesn't have a PhD from Pepperdine University.

Rather than dashing exploits as an aviator, the US Marine Corps indicated that Lt Papows was an air traffic control operative.

In NSW Glen Oakley rose from a mortician's assistant to become Director-General of the state Department of Business & Regional Development, partly on the strength of his academic background. Unfortunately his degrees, including a BSc (Hons) and Grad Dip in Education from the University of Newcastle, MBA from UNSW and a PhD, were all fake.

'Linda Astor' persuaded the NZ Medical Council, Royal College of Psychiatrists and Nelson Marlborough District Health Board that she had psychiatric qualifications and extensive experience. That gained her a job as Clinical Director of Mental Health at Nelson. The US institution cited on her CV did not exist and it appears that she invented her referee Dr Zbignew Poddubuick.

Astor fled New Zealand amid claims of negligence, being arrested in the US during 2001 for shoplifting and deported to Poland. By 2004, as Dr Linda Hoffman, she was a senior psychiatrist, with 20 staff and for hundreds of patients. Her adventures in New Zealand had vanished from her CV.

Less spectacular incidents have involved the Mittyesque story of the 'airline pilot' whose qualifications related to bus driving, dental and medical assistants practicing as dentists and doctors, 'accountants' who at best had bookkeeping certificates and 'lawyers' whose skills were derived from watching US television dramas.

In 2006 George Deutsch, who had gained notoriety for requiring NASA staff to add the word "theory" at every mention of the Big Bang, resigned amid confirmation by officials at Texas A&M University that he had not graduated from that institution, contrary to the claim on his NASA résumé.

World Intellectual Property Organization (WIPO) Director General Kamil Idris is alleged to have repeatedly signed official documents showing his birth date to be nine years earlier than it is. *Intellectual Property Watch*, correctly or otherwise, noted suggestions that Idris may have moved up the ranks at WIPO based on the error. In 2007 high profile South Korean curator Shin Jeong-ah, youngest professor at Seoul's prestigious Dongguk University, was revealed to have improperly claimed a doctorate from Yale and a master's degree from Kansas University. Following gossip about her qualifications Kansas issued a statement indicating that although Shin had attended classes between 1992 and 1996 she had not graduated. Officials at the Gwanju Biennale released a 2005 fax, purportedly from Yale, indicating that Shin entered Yale's art history department in 1996 and graduated in 2005 with a doctoral degree in art.

Shin told journalists "I certainly did receive a degree from Yale, which is proven by the document Dongguk received from Yale in 2005. I will make a statement and take legal action as soon as I return to Seoul." Yale subsequently stated that Shin did not graduate with a doctorate in 2005 and indeed had never been registered with the university. Shin's dissertation at Dongguk University on Apollinaire was revealed as "almost identical" as a 1981 work by Ekaterini Samaltanou-Tsiakma.

Later in 2007 prominent Buddhist monk the Venerable Jigwang was revealed to have falsely claimed a Seoul National University degree. Kim Ock-rang resigned from her professorship at Dankook University after admitting she had purchased her degree from a Californian diploma mill in California. Radio presenter Lee Ji-young was fired by Korea Broadcasting System after discovery of fictitious degrees.

In 2007 US and French media were embarrassed by news that terrorism expert Alexis Debat had faked his academic credentials and entire interviews with international figures. Debat was a consultant to ABC television, a senior fellow on terrorism at the Nixon Centre, a contributor to the *National Interest* and *Politique International*. He falsely claimed a PhD at the Sorbonne; he had more brazenly concocted interviews with Kofi Annan, Michael Bloomberg, Bill Gates, Alan Greenspan and Barack Obama.

A few months later UK broadcaster Channel 4 was embarrassed after revelation that its heavily promoted 'celebrity nanny', star of the *Bringing Up Baby* series and self-styled "Cruella de Vil of the baby world", did not possess claimed diplomas in child daycare and pre-school practice, lacked claimed qualifications in maternity practice and paediatrics ("This person never enrolled on any of our courses and as such has never been trained by us") and did not have a degree in Business Studies from York University. York indicated that it had no records of her and indeed did not offer a business studies degree.

Gene Morrison faced legal action in the UK in 2007 after acting as a professional expert witness in litigation and offering a "first-class objective and professional" service to the legal and insurance professions since 1977. Morrison claimed a BSc and PhD, alas purchased from 'Rochville University' for US$1,398.

Celebrity chef Robert Irvine, star of *Dinner: Impossible*, acknowledged in 2008 that he had fabricated parts of his resume, including that he had a knighthood, was a friend of the Prince of Wales, owned a castle in Scotland, and had cooked for the British Royal Family and US presidents. Irvine said "I was wrong to exaggerate in statements related to my experiences in the White House and the Royal Family". *Resume: Implausible*?

Responses

Perceptions of systemic dishonesty have fuelled-and been fuelled by-what is often referred to as the verification industry: identity reference services, recruitment agencies and pre-screening services.

Identity reference services, discussed in more detail elsewhere on this site, involve a convergence of traditional human resource management, consumer credit reporting and private investigation services. They vary considerably in price, sophistication and methodology.

Some seek to verify information provided in resumes by consulting referees, putative employers and entities that have awarded credentials.

That consultation might be limited to a quick web search (eg to determine whether an educational institution or professional body does indeed exist). It might be more effective, involving contact with an institution to determine whether an individual both attended a university and gained the degree referred to on a CV. Intensive checking might involve contact via switchboards rather than relying on a nominated direct number that in fact is used by an associate or family member of an applicant. Particular industries have emphasised standard searches of credit reference databases (eg to determine whether the person has gone bankrupt or has a history of financial problems) and criminal records, including public offender registers.

Many employers-or their agents-will ask to see the certification associated with a resume, for example a formal unit by unit transcript of academic achievement or the individual's diploma. Such scrutiny may be ineffective, as few people have a background in forensics and an applicant may have acquired a forged document. Others of course simply buy a degree from a diploma mill.

There is no comprehensive publicly accessible official national register of graduates from Australian tertiary institutions. (The extent of non-government databases, compiled by commercial services from lists published by individual institutions, is unknown.)

It is clear from the incidents noted above that some checking is ineffective. The past five years has seen a move away from traditional supplementary mechanisms such as the polygraph (or erratic indicators of honesty such as whether the applicant blinks, rubs her nose or has big ears) to what are claimed to be 'smart' services such as software that supposedly detects "suspicious statements" in CVs.

Such vetting software is claimed to identify "text patterns and numbers that can change when a lie or exaggeration" is made in a resume. One of the more ambitious software applications supposedly analyses the language used in describing past jobs to see whether that accurately reflects the job description. Given the opacity-or merely brevity-of many job descriptions our skeptics are dubious about such tools, particularly if an applicant has adopted the language of someone else's CV to describe a job that he/she actually performed or has instead used a commercial resume-writing service.

Making Sense

What should you do if you are writing, or reading, a CV? There is little agreement.

One pundit comments that 'editing' is inevitable:

Your CV needs to flirt, not to reveal all. It should make you sound so attractive that they want to find out more about you.

Another characterised a fake academic qualification as like carrying a ticking timebomb with no idea of when it could go off. It could happen when you claim the qualification for the first time, or it might take years before it explodes in your face-taking your riches and your reputation with it.

Consumers should thus avoid the temptation to buy a real certificate from a fake university or a fake certificate that pretends to be from a real university. There is general acceptance that it is unwise to put anything on a CV that will be difficult to explain away at an interview or to falsely claim attributes that can be readily tested (eg foreign language skills or a year of birth). Expunged criminal records may or may not need to be referred to, depending on the nature of the job.

Human resource specialists and identity verification services, apart from touting their expertise and databases, offer tips for potential employers such as-

- check basic facts in resumes and supporting documentation to ensure information such as qualifications and date of birth are consistent
- verify academic and professional qualifications with the institutions that issued that certification, rather than relying on course transcripts or paper diplomas supplied by a candidate
- go online to determine whether institutions indeed exist
- make intelligent use of application forms rather than relying wholly on a CV, for example to facilitate comparison of different applicants and reduce opportunities for eliding gaps in employment and training
- check with referees, bearing in mind that some former employers/colleagues may be influenced by friendship, fear of defamation action, embarrassment or merely desperation to unload an unwanted person

Studies

Much of the literature on resume massaging is distinctly anecdotal or reflects the interests of particular stakeholders

such as commercial 'pre-screening' services. One point of entry to the professional literature is *Deception in Selection* (New York: Wiley 1998) by Liz Walley & Mike Smith.

The discussion of job search sites and services elsewhere on this site features pointers to works such as the 2003 paper *In With the New, Out With the Old: Has the Technological Revolution Eliminated the Traditional Job Search Process?* by Van Rooy, Alonso & Fairchild, Mark Granovetter's landmark *Getting a job: a study of contacts and careers* (Cambridge: Harvard Uni Press 1974) and *The Strength of Weak Ties: A Network Theory Revisited* (PDF), and *Gurus, Hired Guns, & Warm Bodies: Itinerant Experts in a Knowledge Economy* (Princeton: Princeton Uni Press 2004) by Stephen Barley & Gideon Kunda.

Coverage of corporate embarrassments often appears as part of broader studies of corporate failure. One example is Martin Thomas' *The Fraud* (Richmond: Pagemasters 1991), about CEO John Friedrich's fabrications in the lead up to a $244 million fraud. It is complemented by *Codename Iago: the Story of John Friedrich, Former Chief Executive of the Victorian NSCA* (Melbourne: Heinemann 1991) by Friedrich & Richard Flanagan.

Not For Novelty Purposes Only: Fake Degrees, Phony Transcripts & Verification Services (PDF) discusses fake degrees-and fake universities-in the US and Canada. For Australia see the range of cogent papers by scholar George Brown discussing malpractice and remedies. The much-cited 500,000 fake US degrees figure appears in the 1985 *Fraudulent Credentials* report by the US House of Representatives Subcommittee on Health & Long-term Care, updated in *Degree Mills, The Billion Dollar Industry That Has Sold Over A Million Fake Diplomas* (Amherst: Prometheus 2005) by John Bear & Allen Ezell.

Other pointers are provided in the exploration of diploma mills elsewhere on this site.

DIGITAL

Accounts of identity theft in recent mass media and in film or literature have centred on the exploits of 'hackers'-variously lauded or reviled-who are depicted as cleverly subverting corporate firewalls or other data protection defences to gain unauthorised access to credit card details, personnel records and other information.

Reality is more complicated, with electronic identity fraud taking a range of forms.

The impact of those forms is not necessarily quantifiable as a financial loss; it can involve intangible damage to reputation, time spent dealing with disinformation and exclusion from particular fora or services because a stolen name has been used improperly.

Overall we can consider electronic networks as :

- an enabler for identity theft, with the thief for example gaining information online for action offline
- the basis for theft or other injury online.

Gary Marx's 1999 paper *What's in a Name? Some Reflections on the Sociology of Anonymity* notes that identity and anonymity are features of social relationships rather than something that is integral to a person. His insights encapsulate research on anonymity and authenticity highlighted elsewhere on this site, such as the 2002 paper by Jack Edwards & Greg Scott on *Traps, Pitfalls, Swindles, Lies, Doubts & Suspicions in Human-Computer Interaction: A Counter-Case for the Study of Good Etiquette* (PDF)

Data Mining

A downside to the notion of the net as a universally-accessible global library and archive is that it potentially provides the malign with a rich source of personal information for identity theft. That information can be as basic as an email address. It can be as powerful as a detailed curriculum vitae (replete with phone numbers and residential address) or an official register.

Web publication of official registers of births, deaths and marriages has thus been welcomed by genealogists (and commercial vetting services) as a way of bringing people together or authenticating claims. Property registers similarly offer a transparency that is praised by some social theorists and real estate agents or insurers.

Electronic access to such data, outside the bounds of a government office, does however enable data mining by identity thieves. Why scour past newspapers for obituary notices when information can be sourced from an electronic register?

Email and other Addresses

Some people have first encountered identity theft through appropriation of their email address or instant messaging service name, with a spammer for example using a name that appears on the web (on a personal or corporate site or in a web newsgroup archive) as a false identity in messages to people across the globe.

That theft is of concern because most of the online population has yet to recognise that email addresses are readily forged and thus assume that the owner of a stolen address has either authorised the message or has failed to maintain effective anti-virus protection and thereby allowed a spammer to propagate messages from a 'zombie' machine.

Appropriation of an address or online name is also of concern because it may result in blockage of legitimate communications from the owner of that name, in some instances forcing the unfortunate owner to acquire a new name. Some observers have criticised vigilante online spam filters for simply blocking names without proper investigation.

Name appropriation is not restricted to email addresses. Contacts in China have lamented that their online names in messaging services such as QQ and their avatars in gaming or other social networking spaces have been stolen, typically through surveillance while using a cybercafe. That theft poisons their online identity-the owner typically abandons the name/avatar-and can imperil online relationships.

Advance Fee Scams and other Frauds

Traditional advance fee scams and other frauds have migrated onto the net, with organisations and individuals across the world receiving email that solicits their assistance in transfer of supposed illicit funds (typically from the estates of deposed dictators) or announces that the recipient has won a lottery.

Such messages involve two kinds of identity fraud. The '419' or 'Nigerian' advanced fee scam-discussed in detail elsewhere on this site-both invites the recipient to supply contact/ financial details and uses the identity of a real or fictitious person/organisation, such as Suha Arafat, Adnan Khashoggi, Laurent Kabila or UNICEF. Lottery scams typically invite the potential victim to supply information.

As with the provision of details in the 419 scam, responding signifies that the address is 'live' and the victim is willing. It also offer opportunities for ID theft and for sale of the address to spammers.

Joe Jobs

One of the more obscure forms of online identity theft is an update of traditional political, personal or corporate smears, which saw an opponent disseminate a letter or statement supposedly authored by an entity to be discredited.

Such communications in paper formats included fictitious acknowledgements of sexual or financial impropriety (eg US presidential candidates 'confessing' to children out of wedlock or across the colour barrier), endorsement of unpopular causes such as the Communist Party or fake attacks on popular causes. They have been characterised as 'identity pollution' or as 'joe jobs'.

In the online environment 'joe jobs' as part of the digital intifada or US 'culture wars' have included email messages that purport to come from figures such as Noam Chomsky, Hillary Clinton and Arial Sharon or from entities such as the Israeli government, Procter & Gamble, the ACLU or World Bank. In 2005 a fake media release outing Scottish Executive minister Malcolm Chisholm (supposedly announcing that he wanted to end "speculation" about his sexuality and that he was "gay and in love") was emailed to the media.

In 2003 a Sydney employee lost her job after a former boyfriend harassed her by sending 419 scam-style email (messages which informed recipients that they were the owner of an unclaimed bank account or beneficiary of a deceased estate) with her work number as the contact.

Telephone joe jobs have featured in US robocalls (use of databases to call all/specified numbers with a recorded message from a political candidate or advocate), apparently in efforts to misrespresent the supposed caller or merely to damage that person's reputation by annoy the recipient after receiving ten or more messages per day.

The intention of such forgeries is generally to gain media attention (eg encourage journalists to report a "widely circulated rumour"), erode a reputation, reinforce negative perceptions of the subject and provoke email responses (eg counter messages that flood the real inbox or result in blacklisting of messages from the owner of the name).

Phishing and Pharming

Phishing involves attempts to fraudulently acquire sensitive information such as passwords and credit card details by masquerading in an email or instant message as a legitimate organisation (eg a bank) or individual (eg a system administrator) with a genuine need for that information. The message is generally underpinned by direction to a fake corporate site that invites the victim to enter the details-a process known as pharming-which can then be used by the thief to access the victim's account.

Phishing thus involves

- appropriation of the organisation or individual's identity and
- the victim providing information for the theft of the victim's identity

Like offline pretexting is a form of social engineering, which as noted earlier in this profile is easier and often more effective than dynamiting bank vaults or drilling through electronic firewalls. Why be a safecracker when the victim, if offered a plausible story, will hand you the keys to the safe? Phishing typically is not directed only at customers of a particular institution and instead has the distribution characteristics of much spam. We have for example received requests to 'confirm' accounts in Australian and overseas financial institutions with which we have never had a relationship; the US Honeypot project notes that in 2004 around 54% of phishing emails in one survey purported to come from CitiBank.

Spam filter vendor Brightmail estimated that there were 3 billion phishing emails worldwide during April 2004.

Christopher Abad's 2005 *The economy of phishing: A survey of the operations of the phishing market* paper and the 2006 *Why Phishing Works* (PDF) by Rachna Dhamija & Marti Hearst offer other statistics.

Responses to phishing have varied. It has been claimed that phishing cost US$1.2 billion in "damage" to US financial institutions in 2003 and that, more problematically, an estimated 10% or 19% of the adult US online population were credulous enough to click on a link in a phishing message despite warnings by government agencies and businesses that organisations do not ask people to confirm/update their details online. A supposed 3% reported actually entering sensitive personal or financial details.

The Australian Securities & Investments Commission reported in June 2005 that the number of complaints about phishing had doubled over the preceding year. The extent to which consumers are becoming more savvy is unclear.

Spyware

Some spyware-discussed in more detail elsewhere on this site-can be used for identity theft, in particular unauthorised collection and transmission from a personal computer of the user's personal information, such as bank account and credit card numbers.

It comprises 'malware' that is not knowingly installed by a user and that covertly supplies information to another party. That malware may get onto the machine when the user interacts with a service such as Kazaa, downloads a game or accesses other content.

A 2004 study by the National Cyber-Security Alliance claimed that 80% of surveyed users had some form of spyware, with 89% of infected users being unaware and an unsurprising 95% indicating that they had not given permission for installation. The extent to which spyware is being used for identity theft is uncertain.

Cracking

Film, fiction and much technology journalism have promoted the image of the intrepid/malign hacker bathed in a suitably unearthly blue light while breaking silently into a strongly secured corporate or database. In practice unauthorised access to personnel files and financial data is more prosaic. It generally takes three forms.

The first-arguably the least common in terms of serious impact-is an offender breaking through inadequate security protection on a corporate database or accessing an unprotected personal computer.

The extent of such access is contentious: some analysts argue that most breaches are undetected and that much unauthorised access to corporate facilities goes unreported because managers are loath to erode confidence in their activity/organisation or encourage further attacks.

Breaches of major corporate facilities-and belated admission that there may have been unauthorised access to over 40 million files in some instances-have led critics to call for mandatory standards for data protection, with substantial penalties by corporate regulators and compensation to individuals whose data may have been exposed.

Other analysts, including government auditors such as Australia's ANAO, note that loss of laptops-including devices with extensive unencrypted sensitive data collections-is an ongoing problem for organisations in the defence, financial services and health sectors.

A second form of access involves misbehaviour by an organisation's staff or contractors, rather than outsiders.

Within the Australian federal government, for example, one contractor in the Department of Finance & Administration used a colleague's name and passwords to remove $8.7 million, subsequently using the identities of other colleagues in an unsuccessful effort to obscure the audit trail. A more humble employee in Centrelink stole the identities of pensioners, generating benefit cards that were then used to withdraw cash from automatic teller machines.

Some thieves have simply bought paper and electronic versions of databases from employees, with AOL for example experiencing a major security breach after one staffer sold several million files.

A third-and perhaps most surprising-form of access is through corporate loss of records in transit.

2005 for example saw admission by major US financial institutions that they had recurrently misplaced computer tapes during shipment across the country; those tapes were not encrypted and contained millions of files. It is unclear whether the records were stolen or simply ended up in a dumpster as unrecognised trash. However it is alarming to think that major organisations are so cavalier about customer data and that regulators have been so slow in detecting and preventing such losses.

Call Centres

Offshoring of data processing and the emergence of large-scale call centres has raised concerns about theft of consumer bank account, credit card and other information

Media coverage has centred on incidents in India, highlighted in the note on data losses, but in practice it is clear that some abuses are occurring in the UK, US and other locations. Theft of information handled by data centres reflects poor management, employee turnover, the scale of data and opportunity, and poor remuneration of call centre employees.

In 2004 for example a NatWest callcentre worker in the UK supplied a gang with the bank details of comedian Ricky Gervais. The thieves were subsequently caught using Gervais' account to buy £200,000 of gold bullion. An employee of US payment intermediary iBill is believed to have been involved in release of 17 million customer records; an employee of major US payment processor Fidelity National Information Services improperly sold 2.3 million consumer records to an unidentified data broker.

10

Identity Crime Statistics

INTRODUCTION

Figures on the extent, severity and composition of identity crime are problematical. Different estimates and forecasts abound; interpretation of particular statistics varies widely, as does assessment of the effectiveness of some responses.

As one client commented to us, it is thus possible to go statistics shopping for figures that appear to support/disprove a particular argument or-as discussed in the following page of this profile-to substantiate a headline or two.

(2007) by Chris Hoofnagle's 2007 'Identity Theft: Making the Known Unknowns Known' in 21 *Harvard Journal of Law and Technology* commented.

There is widespread agreement that identity theft causes financial damage to consumers, lending institutions, retail establishments, and the economy as a whole. Surprisingly, there is little good public information available about the scope of the crime and the actual damages it inflicts. The publicly available data on identity theft come mainly from survey research. Methodologically, these survey polls of the public suffer from being both under and over-inclusive in measuring the problem. As a result, low estimates attribute tens of billions of dollars in costs to the economy and consumers, the highest estimates place losses in the hundreds of billions.

To identify proper interventions and appropriately allocate resources we need comprehensive, hard data on the scope and effect of identity theft. One way to provide concrete data is to require lending institutions to publicly report figures on identity theft. Such public reporting will help identify the relative need for intervention and the likely efficacy of interventions. These disclosures are necessary to provide a sound baseline for investment by businesses and action by regulators. They are also warranted because the public pays the price of identity theft directly when they are the victim, and indirectly through higher fees, interest rates, and because the losses are tax subsidized.

Identity Fraud in Australia, a 2003 report by the Securities Industry Research Centre of Asia-Pacific (SIRCA) for financial intelligence agency AUSTRAC, claimed that identity fraud cost the Australian community $1.1 billion in 2001-02 (with an estimation error of $130 million), with over half of that amount concerned with 'response' activity. The 2003 Australian Institute of Criminology (AIC) and PricewaterhouseCoopers *Serious Fraud in Australia & New Zealand* study (PDF) estimated overall fraud at around $5.8 billion.

A 2002 US Federal Trade Commission survey calculated the cost of identity crime to business and financial institutions at around $US48 billion, with consumers losing $US5 billion. That survey was based on responses from 4,000 people and has been enshrined in media coverage of ID theft. As the following page notes, however, the 48 billion figure has been disputed and direct losses are likely to be much lower.

Between January and December 2004 the FTC's Consumer Sentinel complaint database received over 635,000 consumer fraud and identity theft complaints, with US consumers reporting losses of over US$547 million. 39% of those complaints concerned identity theft.

The UK Cabinet Office reported estimates that in the private sector around 1-2% of transaction value is lost through fraud, with about 3-5% of all UK fraud involving an identity crime.

It commented that,

It is not easy to gauge the amount of identity fraud. But the minimum cost to the economy is in excess of £1.3bn per annum. This compares with the estimated total economic cost of all fraud of at least £13.8bn per annum. This figure is certainly an underestimate, as it only includes those figures that are available, and does not include areas such as Local Government, health services or education where it is known that identity fraud exists, but there is not sufficient data available to estimate the cost

Incidences are uncertain. It has been claimed that 37% of online credit card transactions in the United States involve stolen or forged cards, a figure that appears to be substantially too high (and does not equate to 37% of payments or losses). However it is clear that major lists of numbers are available online (whether for free or for sale) on an illicit basis.

SCOPING THE PROBLEM

Australian Federal Attorney General's Department 2001 *Scoping Identity Fraud* study commented that

There is widespread agreement by all organisations that identity fraud already represents a significant problem, that is likely to grow further. The lack of statistics on the incidence and cost of identity-related fraud makes the total cost to the community impossible to accurately quantify. Without reliable estimates of the overall cost it becomes more difficult to convince decision-makers that urgent attention is required

The Federal House of Representatives Standing Committee on Economics, Finance & Public Administration (EFPA) in its *Numbers on the Run* report (PDF) on the ANAO examination of tax file number management commented that anecdotes and estimates suggested that the instance and cost of identity fraud was increasing. However it was "concerned at the lack of figures available on the extent and cost of identity fraud".

Uncertainty is attributable to-

- definitional disagreements, highlighted in the 2004 *Standardisation of definitions of identity crime terms* (PDF) from the Australasian Centre for Policing Research and the 2007 *Identity Fraud Trends and Patterns: Building a Data-Based Foundation for Proactive Enforcement* study (PDF) by Gary Gordon, Donald Rebovich, Kyung-Seok Choo and Judith Gordon of the Utica College Center for Identity Management & Information Protection
- the unavailability or muddiness of data, highlighted in Russell Smith's 1998 *Measuring the Extent of Fraud in Australia* paper (PDF)

- different assessments of the extent to which identity crime is underreported
- disagreements about the extent to which data losses result in identity theft
- disagreement about the nature of costs (or merely who carries those costs)

The attribution of costs is explored in the following page of this profile.

EXTENT AND SEVERITY IN AUSTRALIA

The extent and severity of identity theft/fraud in Australia-and the balance between online and offline fraud-is unclear.

The EFPA Committee noted above commented that

- an estimated 25% of reported frauds to the Australian Federal Police involve assumption of false identities (perhaps not surprising, as reporting to the AFP regarding fraud is biased towards welfare/health services fraud rather than corporate crime.
- 'identity kits' (described as "a set of fabricated documents for a false identity") are "increasing in availability, particularly due to the ability of modern technology to generate forged documents of very high quality" and that forged or altered documents of various types are for sale.
- 13% of a sample of birth certificates examined by Westpac bank and the NSW Registry of Births, Deaths & Marriages were found to be defective
- during 1999 Centrelink detected "about $12 million worth of fraud from identity"

The federal Attorney-General reported in 2005 that the Australian Bankers Association estimated that identity fraud cost the banking industry a mere $25 million per year.

The AusCERT 2005 Australian Computer Crime & Security Survey claimed 9% of respondents reported incidents of online ID theft against their staff, customers or clients, with 5% reporting financial loss as a result of this activity. Between April 2004 and April 2005 AusCERT handled around 700 incidents of online identity theft targeting customers of ISPs and financial and e-commerce institutions in Australia and overseas, with ID theft trojans accounting for around 20% of those incidents.

In 2007 the federal Office of the Privacy Commissioner drew on a telephone survey of a "representative sample" of 1500 Australians in inferring that around 2 million Australians "have had their personal details stolen and used fraudulently by a third party". The OFPC reported that only 17% of Australians trusted "online businesses" to handle their personal information responsibly, compared with 37% for "regular retailers", 73% for government agencies and 91% for health service providers. Nine per cent of the sample claimed to have been a victim of "ID theft"; 17% claimed to know someone who had been a victim. In May of that year Galaxy Research found that 87% of Australians were "concerned about identity theft": 79% were most concerned about financial loss, 67% about "a sense of feeling personally violated", 55% potential "embarrassment if transactions are declined" and 53 "worry about having a poor credit rating".

An August 2007 Newspoll (1,202 people) found Australians were "more concerned about the misuse of their personal information than national security in relation to war or terrorism", although it is unclear whether that concern was reflected in action to manage their personal data.

Bibliography

Arrow, Kenneth J.: *Social Choice and Individual Values,* New York, Wiley, 1951.

Campbell, J.Y., Lo, A.W.: *The Econometrics of Financial Markets,* Princeton University Press, 1996.

Chaudhuri, Pramit: *The Indian Economy: Poverty and Development,* New York, St. Martin's Press, 1979.

Dhingra, C.: *The Indian Economy: Resources, Planning, Development, and Problems,* Delhi, Sultan Chand, 1983.

Greer, Douglas F.: *Industrial Organization and Public Policy,* MacMillan Publishing Company, 1992.

Ishwar, C.: *The Indian Economy: Resources, Planning, Development, and Problems,* Delhi, Sultan Chand, 1983.

Little, I.M.D.: *India: Macroeconomics and Political Economy, 1964-1991,* Washington, World Bank, 1994.

Mongia, J.N.: *India's Economic Development Strategies, 1951-2000 A.D..* New Delhi, Allied, 1986.

Pranab, K.: *The Political Economy of Development in India,* Delhi, Oxford University Press, 1984.

Sargent, Thomas J.: *Dynamic Macroeconomic Theory,* Harvard University Press, 1987.

Tirole, Jean: *The Theory of Industrial Organization,* MIT Press, 1988.

Williamson, Jeffrey G.: *American Inequality: A Macroeconomic History,* New York, Academic Press, 1980.

Xavier Sala-i-Martin: *Economic Growth.* McGraw-Hill, 1995.

Index

G

I

J

L

M

O

P

R

S

T